Richard Wright

BOOKS & WRITERS

Richard Wright

BOOKS & WRITERS

by Michel Fabre

University Press of Mississippi
JACKSON AND LONDON

Copyright © 1990 by the University Press of
Mississippi
All rights reserved
Manufactured in the United States of America

93 92 91 90   4 3 2 1

The paper in this book meets the guidelines for permanence and durability of the Committee on Production
Guidelines for Book Longevity of the Council on Library Resources.∞

Library of Congress Cataloging-in-Publication Data

Fabre, Michel.
    Richard Wright : books and writers / Michel Fabre.
        p.   cm.
    Includes bibliographical references.
    ISBN 0-87805-403-0 (alk. paper)
    1. Wright, Richard, 1908–1960—Books and reading. 2. Wright,
Richard, 1908–1960—Library—Catalogs. I. Title.
PS3545.R815Z65128   1990
813'.52—dc20   89-37020
                                                            CIP

British Library Cataloguing-in-Publication data available

Contents

Introduction

If a writer's library and readings represent an invaluable guide to an understanding of the development of ideology and style, this is even truer in the case of a largely self-taught writer such as Richard Wright. In addition, in Wright's education, what Harold Bloom has defined as "the anxiety of influence" was largely balanced and partly offset by the truly liberating effect of the influences he welcomed.

Black Boy still forcibly reminds us that a Negro youngster was barred from borrowing books for his own use from the Memphis Public Library in 1925 and that Wright himself had to forge notes in order to request volumes supposedly for the use of one of his fellow employees.

That books always were "living things" and "companions" to Wright is evidenced by his many enthusiastic references to authors and books in his own writings. Probably in the early forties, he even drafted a brief outline for a comical sketch, called "The Battle of the Books," which shows that dead and living authors were in his mind the avatars of an ongoing intellectual exchange or fight:

The Battle of the Books

Idea for scenes:

Huge books with authors standing beside them, beckoning for readers to come in; we see Shakespeare, Dante, Machiavelli, etc., beckoning to Hemingway. And a young girl dances out to the books; she is invited into each one as each author sings a song. Then a soldier sets up an Army book and starts singing the Marine song, or the Infantry song, or the Navy song. The girl runs to him.
Dostoievsky does a Russian dance beside *Crime and Punishment.*

Shakespeare simmers and acts like a homo.

Hemingway roars and beats his chest.
Hitler growls beside *Mein Kampf*

The authors get together and Shakespeare makes a speech from a soapbox, calling upon the scribblers to unite, "Scribblers of the world, unite." They gather together and sing:

> Arise, ye writers of starvation,
> Ye wretched of the ink
> For we see an American lass
> Dancing and dressed in pink—

They rush the American soldier who blows a bugle and out comes a company of US Marines who rounds up the company of scribblers. The Captain asks each: "Do you like women?" And all except Hitler answer: "Yes! Up comes Sherlock Holmes and strips, from the girl dancer her dress and there stands an American soldier. "Tricked him, good and clean, eh!" Dostoievsky comes forward and says: "Confess, you murderer!" Hitler runs into *Mein Kampf* and the scribblers and the soldiers charge the book, tearing away the cover which reveals a bevy of storm troopers.

I first thought about completing a study of Richard Wright's reading in 1965, when, in the course of my research on his work, Ellen Wright allowed me to go through the books that she had gathered from his shelves in his rue Régis apartment, and installed in the rue de Turenne apartment where she lived at the time. Mrs. Wright helped me to eliminate the volumes that were connected with her position as a literary agent, which her husband could not have read, and to establish which books belonged to him before their marriage. Indeed, in 1940, she had marked his own holdings "Wright" in black ink. In 1965, Wright's library was intact with the exception of a score of volumes at most.

In 1968, when I had access to Wright's archives, kept in the attic and closets in the rue Jacob apartment to which Mrs. Wright had moved, I came across more printed material, not only the volumes in which his works had been printed, reprinted or excerpted, but also newspapers, magazines, and pamphlets, which helped me complete the list of what can be truly called his holdings. I referred extensively to Wright's use of, and acquaintance with, other authors in *The Unfinished Quest of Richard Wright* (William Morrow, 1973) and in essays that have been collected under the title *The World of Richard Wright* (University Press of Mississippi, 1985). Because the detailed information I had provided in 1972 to a few American doctoral students was about to be published without being completely accurate, I felt compelled to write "Richard Wright's First Hundred Books," which the *CLA Journal* accepted for publication on short notice the following year. It represents, in a nutshell, what I am attempting here on a larger scale—to provide accurate information for the study of intertextuality in the works of Richard Wright.

Since then, a number of scholars have published discussions, generally convincing and illuminating, of the literary influences that have been brought to bear on Wright's own writing. I am not listing those systematically in this volume, but they can easily be traced through Keneth Kinnamon's exhaustive *A Richard Wright Bibliography: Fifty Years of Criticism and Commentary, 1933–1982.* For a while, I was tempted to provide a full-length study of intertextuality in Wright, but I am convinced that this will best be achieved by the converging essays of a multitude of scholars. I am therefore merely attempting to provide some facts that will serve as a basis and as safeguards for such attempts.

To return to Wright's library. It clearly was gathered in several stages.

Before 1940, his wife wrote his name in black ink on the first page of all his books with the exception of his Bible, his two-volume set of Proust's *Remembrance of Time Past,* and a score of Communist pamphlets printed by International Publishers. Due to Wright's sometimes extreme poverty in Chicago, most of those books were bought secondhand. Some were presented by friends. Some he borrowed and never returned (especially those from Abe Aaron, a Post Office friend and writer who introduced him to several novelists and to Marxist thinkers). Among books actually purchased, Wright bought a few at the time they were published, either because they were inexpensive Communist Party publications and "required" reading, or because he was eager to read them quickly, like Proust's, Faulkner's, Saroyan's or Wolfe's novels. Yet, during those years, the fact that Wright bought a book new or secondhand is no clear indication of the degree of his avidity to read it or of his interest.

From 1940 to 1946, Wright lived in New York City and was sufficiently well off to satisfy his desire to own books from which he could learn more about society. In the early 1940s, he acquired much contemporary American literature and a variety of studies about Afro-Americans, mostly sociological. In 1945 he bought a larger number of psychological studies along with his *Webster's Dictionary,* the *Encyclopaedia Britannica,* and the *Encyclopaedia of Social Sciences.* He also continued to buy extensively in psychology, psychiatry, criminology, and the social sciences.

In 1947, Wright settled in Paris, where he lived until his death in

1960. His main interest became philosophy, mostly Existentialist, and he acquired scores of volumes in that field. He ordered some of them in the United States, but bought them mostly in England (hence the indication of prices in pounds and shillings) or in Paris. There, the few bookshops where he could order or buy English books were Galignani, on rue de Rivoli, which deals only in new books, but has sales once a year; Ricour and Chevillet (or Royvaux et Chevillet), where he bought many new and used books at bargain prices from 1947 to 1949 when they closed; the English Bookshop, run by his friend Gaite Froget on rue de Seine, where Wright often placed orders; Joseph Gibert, a Latin Quarter bookstore with a section of foreign books, mostly classics and European editions like Tauschnitz and "Albatross," not to be sold in the United States or United Kingdom; and Brentano's, on rue de l'Opéra, operating like Galignani. Finally, from the mid-fifties on, Wright patronized the Mistral Bookshop. It was later renamed Shakespeare and Company, after the death of Sylvia Beach and the closing of her store. Wright occasionally gave readings there. Its proprietor, George Whitman, was more than a bookseller; he provided the English-speaking community with a kind of bohemian "cultural center" where one could consult or borrow from the thousands of new and used volumes on his shelves. Wright himself often went there to look up a book before ordering it from London if he found it necessary. He seldom went to the American Library on the Champs-Elysées. As for French public libraries, they had hardly any books in the English language.

In this listing of books Wright owned, prices are given when available. For French booksellers, they appear in "old" francs, since the "new" franc system began only in January 1960. They reflect the rate of inflation over two decades, rising from a 200/600 F range for new books in 1947 to a 1000/3000 F range at the time of Wright's death. Imported books were far more expensive, but secondhand books in English were often inexpensive. This may explain why Wright bought many English-language "classics" while in Paris, although his interest in them may not have been paramount. In addition, searching for original editions in the bookstalls along the banks of the Seine was a kind of sport, with occasional finds such as an inscribed copy of James Weldon Johnson's *God's Trombones,* Claude McKay's *Banjo,* and Solomon Northup's *Twelve Years a Slave.* In such cases, Wright might take advantage of a bargain, without necessarily reading the book.

In some instances, it is difficult to ascertain whether Wright read the books he owned. He probably did in the case of gifts from close friends, like Chester Himes or Melvin B. Tolson; he probably did not in the case of admirers and travel acquaintances who, by the inscriptions shown, presented him with their works. Inscriptions in these books, which I have noted in all cases, help determine Wright's intimacy with the signer and his possible interest in the book. In addition, in the case of French or European editions where the pages have to be cut before reading, it was easy to indicate when a book was not read. I should add that Wright's French was not adequate to read the books in French he received from such acquaintances as Gide and Sartre.

In a final stage of making up this list, I have gone beyond Wright's actual holdings and the contents of his library. I have made use of indications in his published or unpublished writings, and in other people's testimonies, to add significant numbers of authors and titles to the initial inventory. This includes especially Afro-American writers, with many of whom Wright was personally acquainted, or whose works he read in anthologies like *The Negro Caravan* or in libraries, but did not own because they had become unavailable in bookstores, as was the case of Jean Toomer's *Cane*. Significantly, in his lecture and essay on "The Literature of the Negro in the United States," Wright mentioned and quoted many a black writer whose works he never owned, but who represented for him a stage in or variation upon the prevailing literary trends. Likewise, in his pre-1940 essays dealing with writing from the Left in an "ethnic" perspective, he referred to many authors who were not represented in his library but who exerted some influence on his literary perspectives. Providing such indications was essential, and I have accordingly added explanatory comments. These comments are based on my research in the Wright papers— journals, diaries, letters, interviews—at Yale University. They give an assessment of the importance of a writer or a book to Richard Wright by providing (1) their degree of acquaintance, (2) mentions of the writer's works in Wright's work, and (3) quotations of Wright's comments on them in not readily available texts, such as unpublished essays, correspondence, blurbs, interviews.

I have not, however, attempted to do this on an exhaustive basis, because this would entail a long, bibliographical essay on intertextuality in Wright. Rather, I see this volume and the evidence in it as an encouragement for the research student, the scholar, or the interested general reader to launch into more research—on literary filiation, on influences, on intertextuality, and mostly on Wright's aesthetics. If a man's library is no indication of the books a man has actually read, it is a reliable enough indication of those he might have read and of when he could, or could not, have read them. Only when based on such historical, factual basis can sophisticated deduction and inference be said to carry a certain amount of historical truth. Such factual grounding is necessary at a time when intertextual criticism has become such a fashion that it occasionally runs the risk of leading to unfounded literary connections.

Concerning biographical information, I have found it convenient to refer the reader to my *Unfinished Quest of Richard Wright* (William Morrow, 1973), which is simply indicated by "Fabre," followed by the page number. Concerning certain points of influence and intertextuality, I also refer to my collection of essays, *The World of Richard Wright,* abbreviated as *World,* followed by page numbers. For quotations from not readily available texts, reference is made, as a rule, to Charles T. Davis and Michel Fabre, *Richard Wright: a Primary Bibliography* (G. K. Hall, 1982), abbreviated as *Biblio.,* followed by page and item number. The mention "See" followed by a writer's name in block letters allows cross-referencing. A typical entry thus reads:

> NAME and first name of author
> *Title of book*
> Publisher, place and date of publication
> Date acquired, bought second-hand, bookseller's stamp or sticker, price paid, autograph mention
> Inscription
> Mentions and/or quotations of the author or book in works by or interviews with Richard Wright, in chronological order
> References to Fabre, *World* and/or *Biblio.*

The first appendix includes Wright's unpublished and published book reviews, introductions, blurbs, and comments on specific books and writers which do not appear in the annotations following each author. The order is alphabetical by authors. Appendix B includes: (1) A bibliography on "The Negro in Illinois" Wright compiled in 1936 for the Chicago W.P.A. It was found in the files of the George Cleveland Hall Branch of the Chicago Public Library and was first published in *New Letters* in 1972. (2) Lists of books and authors which Wright made on several occasions and which were found in his files. They confirm the importance of certain titles, and allow us to add a few references. (3) Wright's summary of the major points he found interesting in Egri's *How to Write a Play,* which sheds light on his way of structuring not only drama but fiction.

I am deeply grateful to Ellen Wright for allowing me to quote from the published and unpublished work of Richard Wright. (All published material, after the first printing, has been copyrighted in the name of the Estate of Richard Wright.) My thanks also to: Keneth Kinammon and John Reilly for their many helpful suggestions; Seetha Srinivasan of the University Press of Mississippi for her help and guidance; Gail Graves and the staff of the Reference Division of the University of Mississippi Library for their generous cooperation and support of the research for this project; the Center for the Study of Southern Culture for making available its resources; and finally to Sue Hart without whose expert work this book could not have been published.

Richard Wright

B O O K S & W R I T E R S

A

ABRAHAM, Gerald. *Nietzsche*. London: Duckworth, 1933.
  Bought in Paris, 200F.
ABRAHAM, Karl. *Selected Papers on Psycho-analysis*. London: Hogarth Press and the Institute of Psycho-analysis, 1927.
ABRAHAMS, Peter. *The Path of Thunder*. New York: Harper, 1948.
  Inscribed: "Dear Dick, / Here it is, / you had so much to do with its appearance / and we are so very grateful / for all you have done. As ever. / Peter. / Feb. 4, 1948. London."
  Wright read the novel in manuscript form and recommended it to Harper's. A March 27, 1947, memorandum by Edward C. Aswell reads:

"Richard Wright says of Peter Abrahams' *Quiet Valley* [later *The Path of Thunder*]:
  'Because of their racial and social experience, there are some writers whose passion on earth is to affirm our common humanity. Peter Abrahams' novel, *Quiet Valley*, is the muted cry of men, divided by race, color and creed, who are striving to fulfill their deepest and noblest impulses. His novel begins as innocently as a spring morning in the country, but rises to heights of bitter passion, and implicit in every poetic word he writes is a belief in life and humanity. Abrahams is a new voice, a new passion, a new style, telling the old but ever-new story of man's hope and suffering. That the characters are the whites, the coloreds, and the natives of South Africa will make his story familiar to Americans who have lived three hundred years with the same racial reality. To read Abrahams is to be haunted by the feeling that he is writing about our own problems. His art is powerful enough to bridge the gap of oceans and cultures, and make you feel and think.' "

Part of this was used as a blurb on the dust-jacket of the novel. Wright later noted:

"Bought a history of the circus and will send it to George Davis as a gift. Talked long with Odette [Lieutier] about publishing a list of books from America. . . . I mentioned Fritz von Unruh's *The End Is Not Yet* and Peter

Abrahams' *The Path of Thunder,* both of which are available." (*Ibid.,* August 17, 1947)

————. *Tell Freedom.* London: Faber, 1954.

"I read a section of Peter Abrahams' autobiography. It is very good and will no doubt make a great impression as it is published in the United States." (Unpublished journal, August 2nd, 1947)

"Last night, finished reading Peter Abrahams' manuscript. Good stuff; was sorry when it ended abruptly (I have only a section of it with me). I hope I can see Pete and tell him how swell I think his book is." (*Ibid.,* August 4, 1947)

————. *Wild Conquest.* New York: Harper & Brothers, 1950.

See WORLD, pp. 195–97.

ABRAHAMSEN, David. *The Mind and Death of a Genius.* New York: Columbia University Press, 1946.

ACTON, John Emerich Edward Dalberg-Acton, 1st baron. *Lectures on Modern History.* Edited by John Nevis Figgis and Reginald Vere Laurence. London: Macmillan, 1952.

ADAMS, Walter A. See WARNER, W. Lloyd.

ADLOFF, Richard. See THOMPSON, Virginia McLean.

ADOLF FRIEDRICH, Duke of Mecklenburg-Schwerin. *From the Congo to the Niger and the Nile: An Account of the German Central African Expedition of 1910–1911.* 2 vols. With 514 Illustrations from Photographs and Drawings and a Map. London: Duckworth & Co., 1913.

Bought after 1940.

AGEE, James. *A Death in the Family.* London: Peter Owen, 1958.

———— and EVANS, Walker. *Let Us Now Praise Famous Men.* Boston: Houghton Mifflin, 1941.

AGYEMAN, Nana Yaw Twum Duah. *West Africa on the March, An Intimate Survey of Problems and Potentialities.* New York: William-Frederick Press, 1952.

AIKEN, Conrad, ed. *Modern American Poetry.* New York: Modern Library, 1927.

ALEXANDER, Franz G. *Our Age of Unreason: A Study of the Irrational Forces in Social Life.* New York: Lippincott, 1942.

ALEXANDER, Martha. See STEIN, Leopold.

ALEXANDER, W. W. See JOHNSON, Charles S.

ALGER, Horatio.

Wright wrote a review of Alger's *Struggling Upwards and Other Works* (1890) reprinted in a 1945 edition. ". . . the old-fashioned,

morally uplifting tales . . . were a part of the dream of my youth."
("Alger Revisited, or My Stars! Did We Read That Stuff?," *P.M.
Magazine*, Sept. 16, 1945, p. 8.) See APPENDIX, pp. 181–82.

ALGREN, Nelson. *The Man with the Golden Arm*. New York:
Pocket Books, 1951.

　　Wright was a close acquaintance of Algren from 1933 to the
early 1940s. He used the first, discarded title of what became
Somebody in Boots (1934) as a title for his own novel *Native Son*,
and wrote an introduction for *Never Come Morning* (New York:
Harper, 1942). He still listed Algren among his favorite writers at
the end of his life.

"In each individual writer this transitional happening took various forms.
In Rebecca Pitts it was philosophical; in Meridel Le Seuer it was the emotional relationship of women to our society; in Nelson Algren it was the
plight of the lumpen proletariat; with the worker writer, however, it was
different——his work was primarily protest, such as Conroy's *Disinherited*." ("Writing from the Left," *Biblio.*, p. 170, U 74, Wright Misc. 812,
p. 7.)

"I have two [writers] in mind which, I think, hold more than they promise.
They have the real stuff. First is Nelson Algren whose novel *Never Come
Morning* is as hard-hitting a realistic piece of writing as you will ever read.
Lawrence Lipton's *Brother, the Laugh is Bitter* is another excellent novel
about Chicago. The latter deals with Jewish life and Algren's novel with
Polish life." ("Readers and Writers," a radio interview by Edwin Seaver,
December 23, 1941.)

"If Nelson Algren can give forth a series of novels like this I think he will
establish himself quite as securely as Faulkner has. Algren's ability to get
into the maze-like minds of these twisted people and make them think and
talk and reveal themselves is something that holds me spellbound."
(Wright to Edward Aswell, Sept. 24, 1941.)

"I have not read the Beat Generation novelists. As to the great novelists I
like to read again and again, they are Sherwood Anderson, Mark Twain,
James T. Farrell, Nelson Algren, Thomas Hardy, Maupassant, Proust,
Dostoievsky." (Interview by Annie Brièrre, *France-USA*, Sept.-Oct.,
1960, 2.)

　　See APPENDIX, pp. 183–84.

ALLEN, Chalinder. *The Tyranny of Time*. New York: Philosophical
Library, 1947.

ALLEN, Clifford. *The Sexual Perversions and Abnormalities: A*

Study in the Psychology of Paraphilia. 2d ed. London: Oxford University Press, H. Milford, 1949.

Galignani, Paris, sticker.

ALLEN, Frederick Lewis. *Paul Revere Reynolds: A Biographical Sketch.* New York: Privately printed, 1944.

Sent by Paul R. Reynolds, Jr., after the death of his father (Wright's literary agent).

ALLEN, George Leonard.

Four lines from the black poet's "Pilate in Modern America" are quoted by Wright in "The Literature of the Negro in the United States," which is printed in *White Man, Listen!*. They are seen as an attempt to evoke compassion in white America by stressing the biblical theme. See *White Man, Listen!*, pp. 140–41.

ALLEN, James S. *The Negro Question in the United States.* New York: International Publishers, 1936.

ALLEN, Samuel W.

Allen gave Wright a copy of his first volume of verse *Elfenbeinzähne* [*Ivory Tusks*] published in 1956 under the pseudonym Paul Vesey.

ANDERSON, Sherwood. *Beyond Desire.* New York: Liveright, 1932.

Bought secondhand after 1940.

———. *Dark Laughter.* New York: Pocket Book, 1952.

USIS Library, Paris.

———. *Many Marriages.* New York: B. W. Huebsch, 1923.

———. *Winesburg, Ohio.* New York: Modern Library, n.d.

Wright read *Dark Laughter* (1925), *Tar* (1926), and *Winesburg, Ohio* in Memphis and/or Chicago.

"I read Mencken, Dreiser, Anderson while doing menial work in Chicago." (New York *World Telegram*, Feb. 15, 1938)

"Anderson pictured the lonely soul of the crushed petit bourgeois." ("Personalism" (1935–37?), *Biblio.*, p. 167, U 62.)

See BLACK BOY, p. 218.

APTHEKER, Herbert. *The Negro in the American Revolution.* New York: International Publishers, 1940.

———. *The Negro in the Civil War.* New York: International Publishers, 1938.

———. *Negro Slave Revolts in the United States, 1526–1850.* New York: International Publishers, 1939.

On Aptheker's criticism of "the Wright-Cayton-Myrdal School," see Fabre, 293–94.

ARAGON, Louis. *The Red Front.* Translated by E. E. Cummings. Chapel Hill, N.C.: Contempo Publishers, 1933.

Gift from Abe Aaron: "To Richard Wright /—than which there can be / no more appropriate gift on this day / Roosevelt agrees to run against Wilkie, /what for? / With lotta love from / Minna and Ab"

Wright imitated *The Red Front* in his poem "Transcontinental (For Louis Aragon, in praise of *Red Front*)," (*International Literature,* Jan., 1936, p. 52–57 in *World*, pp. 240–46.)

ARENDT, Hannah. *The Burden of Our Time.* London: Secker and Warburg, 1951.

Bought secondhand.

Wright met Hannah Arendt at Dorothy Norman's in early 1946 to talk about existentialism.

Wright alluded to Hannah Arendt's *The Burden of Our Time* and Gunnar Myrdal's *An International Economy* as "this new literature which is destined to modify the attitude of white men toward themselves."

ARGOSY ALL STORY/WEEKLY. According to *Black Boy*, Wright read the magazine while in Memphis in 1923–25, including the serialized text of *Riders of the Purple Sage* by Zane Grey.

ARMS, George W. and Locke, Louis, eds. *Symposium.* New York: Rinehart, 1954.

Reprints an excerpt from *Black Boy*.

ARMSTRONG, Lucille. *Dances of Spain.* 2 vols. London: Parrish, 1950.

ARNOLD, Thurman W. *The Folklore of Capitalism.* New Haven: Yale University Press, 1937.

Bought after 1940.

"Thurman Arnold, in his *The Folklore of Capitalism,* says in effect that the more idealistic men wax in defending an institution, the more one should suspect that the institution has become separated from the needs of reality and is serving narrow, anti-social ends . . ." ("Psychiatry Comes to Harlem," *Free World*, Sept., 1946, p. 50.)

ARTZIBASHEV, Mikhail P. *Sanine.* Translated by Percy Pinkerton. New York: Modern Library, 1931.

Bought before 1940.

ARVIN, Newton.

"Newton Arvin, writer and critic, in a brilliant paper depicted the cultural reserves of America and called upon writers to draw upon this heritage of liberty and revolt in their struggle against reaction." ("The Barometer Points to Storm," *Biblio.*, p. 164, U 45, Wright Misc. 271, p. 3)

ASHTON-WOLFE, Harry. *The Underworld: A Series of Reminiscences and Adventures in Many Lands.* London: Hurst & Blackett, 1926.
   Bought secondhand.

ASWELL, Mary L. *The World Within: Fiction Illuminating Neuroses of Our Time.* New York: McGraw-Hill, 1947.

ATHAS, Daphne. *The Fourth World: A Novel.* London: Secker and Warburg, 1957.
   Inscribed: "For Richard Wright, while we are sitting in Hyde Park."

ATKINSON, Benjamin P. See BROWN, Leonard S.

ATTAWAY, William. *Blood on the Forge, A Novel.* Garden City, N.Y.: Doubleday, Doran & Co., 1941.
   Inscribed: "To the Wrights / Bill Attaway." Wright met Attaway in 1936.

   "*Blood on the Forge* deals with one of the major themes I have in mind . . . the impact of industrialization on the folk temperament. I think it brings out new material and explores new fields." ("Readers and Writers," Dec. 23, 1941.)

AUDEN, W. H. *Collected Poetry.* New York: Random House, 1945.
   Bought on April 17, 1945.

AURELIUS ANTONINUS, Marcus, emperor of Rome, 121–180. *Meditations of the Emperor Marcus Aurelius Antoninus.* Translated by George Long. New York: Hurst & Co. [1900?]
   Bought before 1940.

AUSTEN, Jane. *The Complete Novels.* New York: Modern Library, 1933.
   Bought secondhand for $1.25 after 1940.

B

BACON, Francis, viscount St. Albans. *Essays.* London: J. M. Dent; New York: E. P. Dutton, 1946.

    Bought after 1940.

BÄCHLIN, Peter. See SCHMIDT, Georg.

BAKER, Carlos. See THORP, Willard.

BAKER, Frank.

    Wright wrote a report of *Mr. Allenby Loses the Way* (New York: Coward-McCann, 1945) for the Book-of-the-Month Club on April 16, 1945. He found the novel dull.

    See *Biblio.*, p. 173, U 88.

BALCHIN, Nigel. *The Borgia Testament.* Boston: Houghton-Mifflin, 1949.

BALDWIN, James. *Go Tell It on the Mountain.* New York: Knopf, 1953.

"I must tell you that there existed between Chester Himes and me on the one hand, and Baldwin on the other, a certain tension stemming from our view of race relations. To us, the work of Baldwin seemed to carry a certain burden of apology for being a Negro and we always felt that between his sensitive sentences there were the echoes of a kind of unmanly weeping. Now Chester Himes and I are of a different stamp. Himes is a naturalist and I'm something, no matter how crudely, of a psychologist." ("The Position of the Negro Artist and Intellectual in the United States," *Biblio.*, p. 168, U 63, Wright Misc. 622, O. 27 [1960])

"James Baldwin, in *Notes of a Native Son,* describes an incident that happens in Paris. I describe a version of the same incident (in "Island of Hallucinations"). This is not plagiarism. My recounting Baldwin's incident is to criticize what he said, put it in a normal, human light . . ." (To Paul R. Reynolds, Jr., Feb. 16, 1959.)

BALZAC, Honoré de. *Seraphita: Louis Lambert.* Philadelphia: 1900

    Bought secondhand before 1940.

"Negro got religious in White South. Religious level of South very low, and Negro took his from whites. / He made something else again out of it, something he needed. / But Negro religious expression in forms acceptable to intellectual Western whites has not come. Not Saint Augustine, not Balzac's *Seraphita*." (Notes on card for a lecture on the Negro in America, 1945–46?)

B A R B U S S E, Henri.

"Eliot, Stein, Joyce, Proust, Hemingway and Anderson; Gorki, Barbusse, Nexo and Jack London no less than the folklore of the Negro himself should form the heritage of the Negro writer." ("Blueprint for Negro Writing," *New Challenge*, 2 (Fall 1937), 60.)

Wright met Barbusse at the Chicago John Reed Club in 1933 and read *Under Fire* at that time.

B A R D O L P H, Richard. *The Negro Vanguard*. New York: Rinehart, 1959.

B A R K E R, George. *Janus*. London: Faber & Faber, 1938.
    Bought afer 1940.

B A R N E S, Djuna. *Nightwood*. New York: New Classics, 1937.
    Bought after 1940.

B A R N E S, Margaret C. *My Lady of Cleves, A Novel*. Philadelphia: MacCrae-Smith, 1946.

B A R R E T T, William. *What Is Existentialism?* [New York: Partisan Review, 1947]

B A R T L E T T, John. *Complete Concordance, or Verbal Index to Words, Phrases, and Passages in the Dramatic Works of Shakespeare; with a Supplementary Concordance to the Poems*. New York: St. Martin's; London & Toronto: Macmillan, 1953.

B A R T Z, Karl. *The Downfall of the German Secret Service*. With an Introduction by Ian Colvin. Translated from the German by Edward Fitzgerald. London: W. Kimber, 1956.
    Bought in Paris, 350F

B A U D E L A I R E, Charles. *Selected Poems*. With Translations by Geoffrey Wagner and an Introduction by Enid Starkie. London: Falcon Press, 1946.

B A X T E R, Richard. *Guilty Women*. London: Quality Press, 1941.
    Bought secondhand in Paris for 100F.

B E A C H, Joseph Warren. *American Fiction, 1920–1940*. New York: Macmillan, 1941.
    Ricour, Paris, sticker.

—————. *The Twentieth Century Novel.* New York: Appleton, 1932.
New York Public Library copy.

BEAUVOIR, Simone de. *L'Amerique au jour le jour.* Paris: Gallimard, 1948.

The Wrights are frequently mentioned. On Wright's friendship with her, see Fabre, 320–22; *World,* 169–71, 253–56.

—————. *The Second Sex.* Translated and Edited by H. M. Parshley. New York: Knopf, 1953.

Inscribed: "To Dick and Ellen,/with my best. Simone de Beauvoir."

BEDDIE, James Stuart. See SONTAG, Raymond James.

BEECHER, John. *"And I Will Be Heard."* New York: Twice a Year Press, 1940.

On cover: Two Talks to the American People.

BELDEN, Jane. *Still Time to Die* (1944).

Wright mentions reading the book in his January 1945 diary.

BELFRAGE, Cedric. *Abide with Me, A Novel.* London: Secker & Warburg, 1950.

Mentioned in "Suggestions for the launching of American Pages," *Biblio.* p. 177. U 100, Wright Misc. 238, p. 6: "Portraits of black and white Southern preachers of the folk variety (à la *South of God*). Descriptions of cults."

—————. *South of God.* New York: Modern Age Books, 1941.

BELLAMY, Edward. *Looking Backward, 2000–1887.*

With an Introduction by Paul Bellamy and Decorations by George Salter. Cleveland and New York: World Pub. Co., 1945.

BELLOW, Saul. *The Victim.* New York: Vanguard Press, 1947.

BENNETT, Arnold. *Mr. Prohack.* New York: George H. Doran Co., 1922.

Bought secondhand for 5¢ before 1940.

—————. *Old Wives Tales.* New York: Harper, 1950.

Mistral Bookshop, Paris, 1950s.

In *Black Power,* p. 7, the English landscape is compared to descriptions by Arnold Bennett, D. H. Lawrence, and George Moore.

BENTLEY, Eric. *The Cult of the Superman: A Study of the Idea of Heroism in Carlyle and Nietzsche, with Notes on Hero-worshippers of Modern Times.* With an Appreciation by C. S. Lewis. New York: R. Hale, 1947.

Bought in Paris for 600F.

BERDIAEV, Nikolai A. *The Destiny of Man.* 2d ed. Translated from the Russian by Natalie Duddington. London: G. Bles, The Centenary Press, 1945.

———. *Freedom and the Spirit.* 3d ed. Translated by Oliver Fielding Clark. London: G. Bles, 1944.

———. *Slavery and Freedom.* New York: C. Scribner's Sons, 1944.

BERGLER, Edmund. *Counterfeit-sex: Homosexuality, Impotence, Frigidity.* 2d ed. New York: Grune, 1958.

> Bought in England for £2.

———. *The Writer and Psychoanalysis.* 2d. ed. New York: R. Brunner, 1954.

> Bought in Paris, 2000F.

BERGSON, Henri. *Creative Evolution.* In the Authorized Translation by Arthur Mitchell with a Foreword by Irwin Edman. New York: Modern Library, 1944.

> Bought on March 21, 1945.

BERNSOHN, Al and Bernsohn, DeVera. *Developing, Printing, and Englarging.* Chicago, New York: Ziff-Davis, 1939.

> Inscribed: "To my pal Dick Wright . . . Agnes Shey."

BERNSOHN, DeVera. See BERNSOHN, Al.

BHAGAVAD-GITA. *The Bhagavadgītā.* With an Introductory Essay, Sanskrit Text, English Translation, and Notes by S. Radhakrishnan. London: G. Unwin & Allen, 1953.

BIBLE. *The Holy Bible, Containing the Old and New Testaments. . . .* Philadelphia: Published by The Bible Association of Friends in America, 1831.

———. *The Bible Designed to Be Read as Living Literature. The Old and the New Testaments in the King James Version, 1936.* This Edition Arranged and Edited by Ernest Sutherland Bates. New York: Simon and Schuster, 1936.

> Bought around 1936.

———. *The Holy Bible, Self-pronouncing Containing the Old and New Testaments, Translated Out of the Original Tongues and with the Former Translations Diligently Compared and Revised by His Majesty's Special Command, Appointed to Be Read in Churches.* Authorized King James Version. Cleveland: World Publishing Co., 1950?

> Wright bought a Bible on June 9, 1945, in Quebec City.

"A few years under the care of his religious grandmother left Richard Wright steeped in the language of the Bible——he says that he has never known a Negro who didn't read the Bible." (May Cameron, "Author! Author!," *New York Post,* March 16, 1938.)

"How could our spiritual mentors refuse to endorse a dish as fundamentally American as strawberry short-cake a la carte and fried spring chicken? And if dissenters should arise, quote them that symbolic and prophetic gem taken from *Revelation* 19:18 ' . . . *you may eat of the flesh of the kings, and the flesh of captains, and the flesh of mighty men, and the flesh of horses, and of them that sit on them, and the flesh of all men, both small and great. . . .* '" ("Repeating a Modest Proposal," *Biblio.,* p. 168, U 65, Wright Misc. 645, p. 4.)

See *Black Boy,* 119, 132–36, etc.; *Twelve Million Black Voices,* 65, 68, 72; *Native Son,* and as epigraph; Job quoted in *Black Power,* 83; Paul quoted in *The Outsider,* 223, 264; also as epigraph to that novel (Job) and to Part III (Paul). Quoted as epigraph to *Savage Holiday* (Job 1:19); to Part I (Exodus 20: 9–10); to Part III (Paul, I Corinthians 11–25).

BIERCE, Ambrose. *The Devil's Dictionary.* Cleveland: World, 1941.

BIRDOFF, Harry. *The World's Greatest Hit: Uncle Tom's Cabin.* New York: S. F. Vanni, 1947.

Wright was instrumental in finding a publisher for the book.

BIRMINGHAM, George A. [James Owen Hannay]. *Famous Murders.* London: Chatto, 1935.

Bought secondhand in Paris, 250F.

BLACKHAM, Harold J. *Six Existentialist Thinkers.* London: Routledge & K. Paul, 1952.

BLACKMORE, Richard D. *Lorna Doone: A Romance of Exmoor.* Edited with an Introduction and Notes by Albert L. Barbour. New York: Macmillan, 1921.

Bought secondhand before 1940 for 10¢.

BLAIR, Walter, et al., eds. *The Literature of the United States: An Anthology and a History.* Rev. Single Vol. Ed. Glenview, Ill.: Scott, Foresman, 1957.

Includes the essay "The Ethics of Living Jim Crow."

BLAKE, William. *Poetry and Prose.* Edited by Geoffrey Keynes. London: Nonesuch Press, 1948.

Quoted in epigraph to "Obsession":

Cruelty has a Human Heart
And Jealousy a Human Face
Terror the Human Form Divine
And Secrecy the Human Dress

Quoted as epigraph to *White Man, Listen!:*

In every cry of every Man,
In every Infant's cry of fear,
In every voice, in every ban,
The mind forg'd manacles I hear

"Mysticism . . . is a personal vision. The drawback of such visions is that they are mostly held together by arbitrary elements selected by the artist, and not agreed upon and approved by the society. Sometimes such visions carry great validity, such as the visions of Blake." (Notes for a lecture in Bandung, 1955.)

BLANCH, Lesley. *The Wilder Shores of Love.* London: Murray, 1954.
    Bought secondhand.

BLAND, Alden. *Behold a Cry.* New York: Scribner's, 1947.
    Wright was a friend of Bland in Chicago in the thirties.

BLAUSTEIN, Albert J. See BLAUSTEIN, Phyllis.

BLAUSTEIN, Phyllis and BLAUSTEIN, Albert J., eds. *Doctor's Choice: Sixteen Stories about Doctors and Medicine Selected by Famous Physicians.* With an Introduction by Walter C. Alvarez. New York: Wilfred Funk, 1957.
    "What You Don't Know Won't Hurt You" is reprinted.

BLOCH, Herbert A. *Disorganization, Personal and Social.* New York: Knopf, 1952.
    Galignani, Paris, $5.00.

BLOCH, Jean Richard. "*—& Co.*" (1929) is mentioned:

"The basic unit of personalist creation will be the image, that is, an emotional perception of reality . . . This image can be as simple as the picture of rain; it can be as complex as a character of Dostoevsky. The symbol can be as simple as that used by Japanese writers in their short stories; it can be as complex as that used by Bloch in his *& Co.*" ("Personalism," *Biblio.,* p. 167, U 62, Wright Misc. 515, p. 4.)

BLYTH, Reginald H. *Haïku.* 4 vols. Tokyo: Hokuseido, 1949–52.
    Bought by Ellen Wright in London in 1959 at the request of Wright, who was using a set borrowed from Sinclair Beiles.

BOBBIO, Norberto. *The Philosophy of Decadentism: A Study in Existentialism.* Translated by David Moore. Oxford: Blackwell, 1948.
    6/sh.

BOBROVSKAYA, C. *Lenin and Krupskaya.* New York: Workers Library Publishers, 1940.

BOCCACCIO, Giovanni. *The Decameron*. Translated by John Payne. New York: Modern Library. 1931?
Bought before 1940.

BODKIN, Maud. *Archetypal Patterns in Poetry: The Psychological Studies of Imagination*. London: Oxford University Press, H. Milford, 1951.

BOER, Hans Alfred de. *The Bridge Is Love: Jottings from a Traveller's Notebook*. Foreword by Dr. Martin Niemöller. London: Marshall, Morgan and Scott, 1958.

BONTEMPS, Arna. *Black Thunder*. New York: Macmillan, 1940.
Inscribed: "To Dick Wright,/one of the tallest minds——Arna Bontemps, 14 Feb. 1940."

———. *Chariot in the Sky: A Story of the Jubilee Singers*. Philadelphia: Winston, 1951.

———. *Golden Slippers: An Anthology of Negro Poetry for Young Readers*. With Drawings by Henrietta Bruce Sharon. New York: Harper & Row, 1941.
Inscribed: "To Dick and Ellen/(to say nothing of the next generation)/with warm regards. 4 Nov. 1941. Chicago."

Wright reviewed *Black Thunder* in "A Tale of Folk Courage," *Partisan Review & Anvil*, 3 (April 1936), 31. He met Bontemps in 1935 and they were friends until 1960. See APPENDIX, pp. 184–85.

In "The Literature of the Negro in the United States," Wright quotes "Nocturne at Bethesda":

The golden days are gone. Why do we wait
So long upon the marble steps, blood
Falling from our open wounds? and why
Do our black faces search the sky?
It is characterized by "a mood of poignant despair."
(*White Man, Listen!*, p. 141)

See also HUGHES, Langston.

BORNEMAN, Ernest.
In October, 1945, Wright wrote an introduction [unpublished] to Borneman's volume, *A Critic Looks at Jazz* (1946).

BORROW, George H. *The Bible in Spain*. Everyman's Library, no. 151. London: J. M. Dent; New York: E. P. Dutton, 1947.

———. *Lavengro*. Everyman's Library, Fiction no. 119. London: J. M. Dent & Sons, Ltd., New York: E. P. Dutton & Co., 1933.
Bought used.

———. *The Zincali: An Account of the Gypsies of Spain.* London: J. Murray, 1923.
   Bought used at Foyle's, London.
BOTKIN, Benjamin A., ed. *Lay My Burden Down: A Folk History of Slavery.* Chicago: University of Chicago Press, 1945.
———. *A Treasury of American Folklore: Stories, Ballads, and Traditions of the People.* With a Foreword by Carl Sandburg. New York: Crown, 1944.

> "B. A. Botkin, of the University of Oklahoma, presented a thesis of unusual interest dealing with aspects of regional culture. The sessions were enlivened by a sharp debate between Botkin and John Gould Fletcher, Imagist poet and spokesman for the anti-Negro, anti-Jew and anti-Catholic attitude of the South as advocated by such Southerners as Herbert Agar." ("The Barometer Points to Storm," *Biblio.*, p. 164, U 45, Wright Misc. 237, p. 3.)

BOUCHER, Paul E. *Fundamentals of Photography, with Laboratory Experiments.* 2d ed. New York: Van Nostrand, 1947.
   Bought used in Paris, 1000F.
BOURRET, F. M. *The Gold Coast: A Survey of the Gold Coast and British Togoland, 1919–1951.* 2d ed. London: Oxford University Press, 1952.
BOWEN, Elenore Smith. *Return to Laughter.* New York: Harper, 1954.
BOWERS, Claude G. *My Mission to Spain: Watching the Rehearsal of World War II.* London: Victor Gollancz, 1954.
   Galignani, Paris, sticker.
   The Galignani receipt for this title is dated June 10, 1955, 1.325FF.
BOYON, Jacques. *Naissance c'un Etat africain: Le Ghana; la Gold Coast de las colonisation a l'independence.* Pref. de Georges Balandier. Cahiers de la Fondation nationale des sciences politiques, 93. Paris: A. Colin, 1958.
   Inscribed: "To Richard Wright,/with my thanks for help and advice./ Jacques Boyon."
BRADBROOK, M. C. *Joseph Conrad, Józef Teodor Konrad Nałęcz Korzeniowski: Poland's English Genius.* Cambridge [Eng.]: The University Press, 1941.
   Bought in Paris, 200F.
BRADFORD, Roark. *This Side of Jordan.* With Drawings by Erick Berry. New York, London: Harper & Brothers, 1929.

BRADLEY, A. C. *Shakespearean Tragedy: Lectures on Hamlet, Othello, King Lear, Macbeth.* London: Macmillan and Co.; New York: St. Martin's Press, 1956.

Bought used after April 1959.

BRANDES, Georg M. C. *William Shakespeare.* London: Heinemann, 1902.

Bought on October 20, 1945.

BRANDON, Samuel G. F. *Time and Mankind: An Historical and Philosophical Study of Mankind's Attitude to the Phenomena of Change.* London: Hutchinson, 1951.

Bought in Paris, 500F.

BRASOL, Boris Leo. *The Mighty Three: Poushkin, Gogol, Dostoievsky, A Critical Trilogy.* Introduction by Clarence A. Manning. London: W. F. Payson, 1934.

BRAWLEY, Benjamin G.

As part of his research for a 1945 lecture at Columbia University, Wright read *The Negro Genius* (1937).

BRETON, André.

Wright associated with Breton in 1948 for the congress of the Rassemblement démocratique révolutionnaire. He alluded to surrealist writing as early as 1946.

BREUER, Josef and FREUD, Sigmund. *Studies in Hysteria.* Boston: Beacon, 1950.

BRIFFAULT, Robert. *The Mothers: A Study of the Origins of Sentiments and Institutions.* 3 vols. London: Allen & Unwin; New York: Macmillan, 1927–1952.

Many passages underlined; quoted as epigraph to *Black Power.*

BROD, Max. *Franz Kafka: A Biography.* Translated from the German by G. Humphreys-Roberts. New York: Shocken Books, 1947.

BROGAN, D. W. *The American Problem.* London: H. Hamilton, 1944.

BRONTE, Charlotte. *Shirley.* With an Introduction by Mrs. Humphry Ward. London: Jan Murray, 1929.

Bought used before 1940, 20¢.

BRONTE, Emily. *Wuthering Heights.* New York: Modern Library, n.d.

Bought on August 10, 1945.

BROOKS, Gwendolyn. *Annie Allen.* Harper & Brothers, 1949.

(Galley proofs).

———. *A Street in Bronzeville.* New York and London: Harper & Brothers, 1945.

Includes Wright's blurb on dust jacket. On July 18, 1944, Gwendolyn Brooks submitted *A Street in Bronzeville* to Harper & Brothers. Senior editor Edward C. Aswell sent the manuscript to Wright for an evaluation. He responded enthusiastically to the work and its accurate portrayal of Negro life although he judged the manuscript too slight for a volume. He took exception to only one poem, "The Mother," because of its subject matter, abortion.

Wright felt that the poet's strength lay in ballads and blues and the glimpses of lost people in an urban black society.

"He reads aloud, and he loves it, 'The Ballad of Pearl May Lee', which he had *Présence Africaine* publish." (Fernanda Pivano, "A Parigi con Wright," *Avanti*, May 19, 1948.)

Brooks is mentioned in *White Man, Listen!,* along with Baldwin and Ellison, p. 142, 147; See APPENDIX, pp. 185–86; and *Biblio.,* p. 73, 1949–12, for *Annie Allen*.

B R O O K S, Richard.
Wright wrote a review of *The Brick Foxhole* (1945). ("A Non-Combat Soldier Strips Words for Action," *P.M. Magazine*, June 24, 1945, p. 16.)

See APPENDIX, pp. 187–89; *Biblio.,* p. 51, 1945–13.

B R O O K S, Van Wyck. *America's Coming-of-Age* (1915).
Quoted as epigraph to *Lawd Today,* Part I. (Walker, 1963).

B R O W N, Frank London. *Trumbull Park, A Novel.* Chicago: Regnery, 1959.

B R O W N, Leonard S.; WAITE, Harlow O.; and ATKINSON, Benjamin P., eds. *Literature for Our Time: An Anthology for College Freshmen.* New York: H. Holt, 1947.
Includes "How Bigger Was Born."

B R O W N, Sterling. *The Negro in American Fiction.* Bronze Booklet, no. 6. Washington, D.C.: The Associates in Negro Folk Education, 1937.
Wright read *Southern Road* (1932) in the late 1930s.
Fifteen lines of Brown's poem, "Old Lem," are quoted in "The Literature of the Negro in the United States" as an expression of possible Negro resistance if the odds were more equal. See *White Man, Listen!,* p. 144.

———; DAVIS, Arthur P.; and LEE, Ulysses, eds. *The Negro Caravan: Writings of American Negroes.* New York: Dryden Press, 1941.
Includes Wright's essay "The Ethics of Living Jim Crow."

B U B E R, Martin. *I and Thou.* London: Clark, 1955.
Bought in London, 5 sh.

BUCKMASTER, Henrietta. *Let My People Go: The Story of the Underground Railroad and the Growth of the Abolition Movement.* 4th ed. New York: Harper, 1941.

Wright's comment on the history of the Underground Railroad is quoted on the dust jacket:

". . . it is not only a magnificent picture of the struggle of the negro for freedom, not only the best story of the Underground Railroad and the Abolition Movement I've yet read, but it is also a provocative and impassioned depiction of the revolutionary impulses of a nation. In an hour of national peril (the author) resurrects and holds aloft a glorious era in our history, an era in which the hunger for freedom transcended the laws of the land and the rights of property, in which the desire for human dignity and human right became an active and creative force. I have read this book with the feeling that we Americans have lost something, have forgotten something, that we will never be ourselves again until we have recaptured and made our own the fire that once burned in the hearts of Garrison, Douglass, Stowe, Lovejoy, Emerson, Longfellow, Phillips, John Brown, and others."

See *Biblio.*, 1941–17, p. 35.

BUKHARIN, Nikolas I., defendant. *Report of Court Proceedings in the Case of the Anti-Soviet "Bloc of Rights and Trotskyites," Heard Before the Military Collegium of the Supreme Court of the U.S.S.R., Moscow, March 2–13, 1938.* Moscow: The People's Commissariat of Justice of the U.S.S.R., 1938.

Bought before 1940.

See also ZHDANOV, A.

BULLOCK, Alan. *Hitler: A Study in Tyranny.* London: Odham, 1954.

BUNYAN, John. *The Pilgrim's Progress.* New York: Manhattan Press, 19—?

Bought before 1940.

BURDICK, Eugene. See LEDERER, William J.

BURKE, Kenneth. *A Grammar of Motives.* New York: Prentice-Hall, 1945.

———. *Permanence and Change: An Anatomy of Purpose.* New York: New Republic, Inc., 1937.

Bought before 1940.

"Kenneth Burke, in *Permanence and Change*, sought to frame a definition of Marxist aesthetics in terms of a poetry of action; from Burke's point of view, Communism becomes a poetic conception of life, of man unfolding their personalities through action." ("Writing from the Left," *Biblio.*, p. 170, U 74, Wright Misc. 812, p. 8.)

———. *The Philosophy of Literary Form: Studies in Symbolic Action.* Baton Rouge: Louisiana University Press, 1941.
Wright copied Burke's paragraph on *Native Son*.

BURLEY, Dan. *Dan Burley's Original Handbook of Harlem Jive.* New York: [no publisher], 1944.

"Dan Burley's *Book of Harlem Jive* . . . I think, ought to amuse you no end . . . It is badly written. But it does reveal a lot about the ways of current Negro speech in America." (To Gertrude Stein, June 23, 1945.)

BURNETT, Whit, ed. *America's 93 Greatest Living Authors Present "This Is My Best": Over 150 Self-chosen and Complete Masterpieces, Together with Their Reasons for Their Selections.* Philadelphia: Blackiston, 1945.
Includes Wright's "How Bigger Was Born."

———. *105 Greatest Living Authors Present the World's Best Stories, Humor, Drama, Biography, History, Essays, Poetry.* New York: Dial Press, 1950.
Includes "Introduction to *American Hunger.*" See *Biblio.*, p. 77, 1950–17.

Burnett had conceived the project of a collection of stories on Negroes, to be called *The Violent Conflict,* and Wright wrote a preface to it when Burnett was in Neuilly in August 1955. The choices were "Pantaloon in Black" by William Faulkner; Chapter 8 of *The Street* by Ann Petry; "Keela, the Outcast Indian Maiden" by Eudora Welty; "Battle Royal" from *The Invisible Man* by Ralph Ellison. However, it was not until 1971 that a collection by Burnett appeared called *Black Hands on a White Face.* It only partly duplicated the earlier collection.
See *Biblio.*, p. 175, U 96.

BURNHAM, James. *The Coming Defeat of Communism.* New York: John Day, 1950.
Bought at Pigmalion, Buenos-Aires.

———. *Containment or Liberation? An Inquiry into the Aims of United States Foreign Policy.* New York: John Day, 1953.
Galignani, Paris, sticker.

———. *The Machiavellians, Defenders of Freedom.* New York: John Day, 1943.

————. *The Managerial Revolution: What Is Happening in the World.* New York: John Day, 1941.

————. *The Struggle for the World.* London: Jonathan Cape, 1947.

BURNS, Alan C., Sir. *Colonial Civil Servant.* London: Allen & Unwin, 1949.

BURNS, Cecil Delisle. *The Horizon of Experience: A Story of Modern Minds.* London: Allen & Unwin, 1935.

> Bought in Paris, 400F.

BURNS, Robert. *The Songs of Robert Burns.* With a Prefatory Notice, Biographical and Critical by Joseph Skipsey. London, New York: W. Scott, Ltd., 1885?

> At head of title: Canterbury Poets.
> Bought before 1940.
> Only the first quarter of the pages have been cut.

BURRIS-MEYER, Elizabeth. *Decorating Livable Homes.* New York: Prentice-Hall, 1945.

BURROWS, Trigant. *The Social Basis of Consciousness* (1927).

> "Wright got the idea for 'Down By the Riverside' while reading the book at the Chicago Public Library; 'A passage in the book told of a woman standing on the edge of a lake in Switzerland. The woman saw a man on the lake in a canoe. The canoe capsized and this woman plunged in to save the man. The author pointed out that this showed that social consciousness, the desire to save and serve others, is more powerful than one's own sense of self-preservation. That was the spark that set going a whole train of thought—the Mississippi River, the excitement and the fear that accompany flood waters. I decided to use a flood to show the relationship between the two races in the South in a time of general tragedy.'" (*Writers Club Bulletin*, Columbia University, vol. 1, 1938, 15.)

BUSIA, Kofi A. *The Position of the Chief in the Modern Political System of Ashanti: A Study of the Influence of Contemporary Social Changes on Ashanti Political Institutions.* London, New York: Published for the International African Institute, by the Oxford University Press, 1951.

> Bought in Ghana.
> Passages underlined.

————. *Report on a Social Survey of Sekondi-Takoradi.* London: Crown Agents for the Colonies on Behalf of the Government of the Gold Coast, 1950.

BUTCHER, Margaret Just. *The Negro in American Culture: Based on Materials Left by Alaine Locke.* New York: Mentor Books, 1957.

Mistral, Paris, stamp.

BUTLER, Samuel. *The Way of All Flesh.* London: Jonathan Cape, 1922.

Mistral, Paris, stamp.

———. *The Way of All Flesh.* Wood Blocks by Howard Simon. Cleveland: World Pub., 1935.

BYRON, George Gordon, 6th baron.

Wright probably read *Childe Harold* and *Don Juan* in the 1930s. His poem "Everywhere Burning Waters Rise" (*Left Front,* No. 4, May-June 1934, p. 97) has a line "Sweep on, o red stream of molten lava," which is reminiscent of Byron's apostrophe to the ocean. See *World,* p. 272.

"With some measure of justification based on historical fact, the general public regards writers as strange creatures. The lives of writers today and in the past seem to support this attitude. Recalling at random a few well-known figures, the attitudes at first glance seem correct. Byron's life was one of long torment, envied by nobody, perhaps, except adolescents. Dean Swift, one of the great lights of English letters, died insane. Coming closer to home, who would envy the life of Edgar Allen Poe with all of its straining and isolation? And a few years ago Hart Crane leaped into the ocean, ending a life which from the vantage point of even our own today seems hideous." ("The American Writer in a Democratic Society," WPA Radio Division, Station WQXB, June 24, 1938.)

C

CALDWELL, Erskine. *God's Little Acre*. With a New Introduction by the Author. New York: Modern Library Edition, 1934.

Bought before 1940.

Handwritten notation: "Dick Wright"

Wright saw the performance of the stage adaptation of *Tobacco Road* by John Kirkland in June 1935. He reviewed *Trouble in July* in "Lynching Bee," *New Republic,* 102 (March 11, 1940), 351 and was enthusiastic about *Kneel to the Rising Sun* (Washington *Star,* Nov. 11, 1945).

He spoke about Caldwell, Dos Passos, Hemingway and Faulkner on June 28, 1946, at a party given by the Société des Gens de Lettres in Paris.

He mentioned Caldwell, along with Dreiser, Lewis and Faulkner, in an interview by Peter Schmidt (Nov. 18, 1946, Zurich).

In Chicago "he spent all his spare time reading Conrad, Dreiser, Sandburg, Stein, Caldwell, Hemingway, yes, even Saroyan." (*The Kaputschkan,* August, 1940.)

See APPENDIX, pp. 189–90.

CALMER, Alan. See HICKS, Granville.

CALVERTON, Victor F., ed. *Anthology of American Negro Literature*. New York: Modern Library, 1929.

CAMPBELL, Alexander. *The Heart of Africa*. New York: Knopf, 1954.

CAMPBELL, Oscar J.; VAN GUNDY, Justine; and SHRODES, Caroline. *Patterns for Living*. 4th ed. New York: Macmillan, 1955.

Reprints "American Hunger."

CAMPBELL, Robert. . . . *L'Existentialisme*. Paris: Foucher, 1948.

At head of title: Expliquez moi . . .

CAMUS, Albert. *Caligula and Cross Purposes (Le malentendu)*. Translated by Stuart Gilbert. London: H. Hamilton, 1947.

————. "The Human Crisis."
Offprint from *Twice a Year*, 14–15 (Fall-Winter 1946).
————. *The Plague*. Translated from the French by Stuart Gilbert.
London: H. Hamilton, 1948.
————. *The Rebel*. With a Foreword by Sir Herbert Read. Translated
from the French by Anthony Bower. London: H. Hamilton, 1953.
Bought at Galignani's, Paris.
————. *The Stranger*. Translated from the French by Stuart Gilbert.
New York: A. A. Knopf, 1946.

"It [*The Stranger*] is a neat job but devoid of passion. He makes his point
with dispatch and his prose is solid and good. In America a book like this
would not attract much attention, for it would be said that he lacks feeling. He does however draw his character very well. What is of course
really interesting in this book is the use of fiction to express a philosophical
point of view. This he does with ease. I now want to read his other stuff.
There is still something about this Camus that bothers me. Maybe it is
because he is the artist and Sartre and de Beauvoir are not primarily." (Unpublished journal, Sept. 6, 1947; *Biblio.*, p. 180, U 120)

On Wright's relationship with Camus, see Fabre, 320–27.
See *World*, 158–75.

C A N A D A. Royal Commission to Investigate Disclosures of Secret
and Confidential Information to Unauthorized Persons. *The Re-
port of the Royal Commission Appointed under Order in Council
P.C. 411 of February 5, 1946, to Investigate the Facts Relating to
and the Circumstances Surrounding the Communication, by Public
Officials and Other Persons in Positions of Trust, of Secret and
Confidential Information to Agents of a Foreign Power.* June 27,
1946. Honourable Mr. Justice Robert Taschereau, Honourable
Mr. Justice R. L. Kellock, Commissioners. Ottawa: E. Cloutier,
Printer to the King, 1946.

C A N N O N, Alexander. *The Invisible Influence: A Story of the Mystic
Orient with Great Truths Which Can Never Die.* London, New
York: Rider, 1948.
Bought in Paris, 500F.
————. *Powers That Be: (The Mayfair Lectures).* New York: Dutton,
1948.
————. *The Power Within: The Re-examination of Certain Psycholog-
ical and Philosophical Concepts in the Light of Recent Investiga-
tions and Discoveries.* London: Rider, 1950.

C A N T W E L L, Robert.

"Sherwood Anderson's *Marching Men* showed the romantic beginnings of class consciousness, while William Rollins' *The Shadow Before* and Robert Cantwell's *The Land of Plenty* showed characters struggling for a sharply defined and definite social goal." ("Writing from the Left," *Biblio.*, p. 170, U74, Wright Misc. 812, p. 1.)

C A P O T E, Truman. *Other Voices, Other Rooms.* New York: New American Library, 1948.

Wright became acquainted with Capote in Brooklyn in the early 1940s and inscribed his own books "To little Truman."

C A R E Y, Arthur A. *Memoirs of a Murder Man.* Garden City, N.Y.: Doubleday, Doran & Co., 1930.

Bought secondhand.

C A R L S O N, Esther.

Wright heard Esther Carlson read at the Greenwich Village Writers' Club in 1945. "She read the story ('The Radiant Wood') and I had goose pimples on me . . . It was a story of symbolized incest, of a little girl who followed her father when he ran away from home. She did not know what the meaning of the story was." (Unpublished journal, February 15, 1945)

C A R L Y L E, Thomas. *The French Revolution.* London: T. Nelson, 1902?

Galignani, Paris, sticker.

———. *Past and Present.* [Exmoor ed.] New York: Home Book Co., 190–.

Bought used before 1940, 5¢.

———. *Sartor Resartus: The Life and Opinions of Herr Teufelsdröckh.* Vol. 1 of his *Works.* London: Chapman & Hall, n.d.

Bought before 1940.

C A R R, Edward H. *The Soviet Impact on the Western World.* London: Macmillan, 1946.

Inscribed: "To Richard Wright,/in the highest esteem and affection,/a thought-provoking book. /George Padmore, /3 Jan. 1947."

C A R R I C K, Edward [pseud.]. *Designing for Films.* New ed. How To Do It Series, no. 27. London, New York: Studio Publications, 1949.

C A R R O L L, Lewis [Charles Dodgson].

"I'm reading Lowe's book on *The Road to Xanadu.* It is a good study on the creative process. Just finished [Kenneth] Fearing's *Dead Reckonings.* A little disappointed. Bought Malraux's *Man's Hope,* but have not read it yet. And, for the first time in my life, I read the book which everybody, I suppose, has read: *Alice in Wonderland!!!"* (To Margaret Walker, [?], 1938.)

C A R T E R, Hodding. *The Winds of Fear.* New York: Farrar & Rinehart, 1944.

Wright wrote a blurb for the novel, partly printed on the dust jacket:

"A vividly and brutally honest book . . . A manly and courageous one . . . In its pages is the story of how one southern white boy came back from the war and helped to make his country the ideal for which he had fought and bled!"

See APPENDIX, pp. 191–92; *Biblio.,* p. 47, 1944–9.

C A R T M E L L, Van H. See CERF, Bennett.

C A R Y, Joyce. *An American Visitor.* London: Michael Joseph, 1952.

——. *A Fearful Joy.* London: Michael Joseph, 1952.

——. *Mister Johnson, A Novel.* New York: Harper, 1951.

Bought in Paris, 250F.

——. *Prisoner of Grace.* London: Michael Johnson, 1952.

C A S S I R E R, Ernst. *Language and Myth.* Translated by Susanne K. Langer. New York and London: Harper & Bros., 1946.

C A S T R O, Americo. *The Structure of Spanish History.* Translated by Edmund L. King. Princeton: Princeton University Press, 1954.

Wright ordered the book when he wrote *Pagan Spain* in 1955.

C A U D W E L L, Christopher [Christopher St. John Sprigg]. *Further Studies in a Dying Culture.* Edited with a Preface by Edgell Richword. London: Bodley Head, 1949.

——. *Illusion and Reality: A Study of the Sources of Poetry.* New York: Macmillan & Co., 1937.

——. *Studies in a Dying Culture.* With an Introduction by John Strachey. London: John Lane, 1938.

C A Y T O N, Horace R.

"The majority of concepts and interpretations upon which I have relied most heavily in the assembling and writing of this text came from *The Negro Family in the United States* by E. Franklin Frazier; *Rum, Romance and Rebellion* by Charles W. Taussig; *Sharecroppers All* by Arthur Raper and Ira de A. Reid; *History of the American Negro People, 1619–1918* by Elizabeth Lawson; "Urbanism as a Way of Life" (from the *American Journal of Sociology,* volume xliv, number 1, July 1938) by Louis Wirth; and

Black Workers and the New Unions by Horace R. Cayton and George S. Mitchell. I take this opportunity to extend my thanks and appreciation to Mr. Horace R. Cayton . . . for his making available his immense files of materials on urban life among Negroes, and, above all, for the advice and guidance which made sections of this book possible." ("Foreword" to *Twelve Million Black Voices,* Viking Press, New York, 1941, p. 6.)

On Wright's relationship with Cayton, see Fabre, 232–33, 248–50, 293–94, and Horace Cayton, *Old Long Road* (New York: Trident Press, 1965.)

See also DRAKE, St. Clair.

CÉLINE, Louis-Ferdinand [pseud.]. *Death on the Installment Plan.* Translated from the French by John H. P. Marks. Norfolk, Conn.: New Directions, 1938.

Copy taken from the Brooklyn Public Library in November, 1940.

———. *Guignol's Band.* Translated from the French by Bernard Frechtman and Jack T. Nile. London: Vision Press, 1954.

———. *Journey to the End of the Night.* Translated from the French by John H. P. Marks. Boston: Little, Brown, 1934.

Bought in London, 6sh.

A CENTURY OF DETECTIVE STORIES. With an Introduction by G. K. Chesterton. London: Hutchinson, 1935.

Bought used after 1940.

CERF, Bennett, ed. *Modern American Short Stories, With an Introduction and Critical and Biographical Notes.* Cleveland, New York: World Pub. Co., 1945.

Includes "Almos' A Man."

——— and CARTMELL, Van H., eds. *Sixteen Famous American Plays.* New York: Garden City Pub. Co., 1946.

CÉSAIRE, Aimé.

Although Wright met Césaire a few times there is no indication that he read any of his works except perhaps "Lettre à Maurice Thorez" and his contributions to *Présence Africaine.*

CHAMBERLAIN, Basil H. *Things Japanese, Being Notes on Various Subjects Connected with Japan for the Use of Travellers and Others.* 5th ed. rev. London: J. Murray, 1905.

Bought in Paris, 200F.

CHAMBERS, Whittaker. *Witness.* New York: Random House, 1952.

Galignani, Paris, sticker.

CHAUCER, Geoffrey. *Complete Poetical Works. Now First Put Into Modern English by John S. P. Tatlock and Percy MacKaye.* Illustrated by Warwick Goble. New York: Macmillan, 1936.

———. *The Poetical Works of Geoffrey Chaucer.* A New Text, with Illustrative Notes by Thomas Wright. New York: Thomas Y. Crowell, 1880.

CHEKHOV, Anton. *Plays: The Sea Gull; The Cherry Orchard; On the High Road; The Wedding; The Proposal; The Anniversary; The Bear; The Three Sisters.* Woodcuts by Howard Simon. New York: Three Sirens Press, 1935.

Bought before 1940.

"I take an author, study his works carefully, go into his life with the same thoroughness, follow the way the facts of his life are related to the fiction he created. I have done this with Dostoievsky, Chekhov, Conrad, Turgeniev." (Interview by Marcia Minor, *Daily Worker,* Dec. 13, 1938.)

CHERNE, Leo M. *The Rest of Your Life.* Garden City, N.Y.: Doubleday, Doran & Co., 1944.

Inscribed: "To Richard Wright,/ one of the pioneers of / a new insight and wider freedom, / and greater dignity for all men. / Leo Cherne."

CHESTERTON, G. K. *The Innocence of Father Brown.* Harmondsworth, England: Penguin, 1958.

———. *The Man Who Was Thursday, A Nightmare.* Harmondsworth, England: Penguin, 1958.

"I'd say that most revolutionary movements in the Western world are government sponsored; they are launched by agent provocateurs to organize the discontented so that the Government can keep an eye on them. If you fail to grasp the meaning of what I'm saying, I can only recommend that you read a classic in this field, G. K. Chesterton's *The Man Who Was Thursday.*" ("The Position of the Negro Artist and Intellectual in American Society," *Biblio.,* p. 160, U 63. Wright Misc. 622, p. 24 [1960]).

In the spring, 1960, M. de Sablonière told Richard Wright she would write a booklet on his nonfiction with many quotations, just to bring more people to his work and asked him what had influenced him. Then he said, after thinking: "Chesterton: *The Man Who Was Thursday.*" She understood intellectually that the man who was Thursday and who suffered so much "must have been a kind of identification for Richard," but he "did not feel it emotionally." (De Sablonière to M. Fabre, April 15, 1962.)

CHESTOV, Leon. See SHESTOV, Lev.

CIANO, Galeazzo, comte. *The Ciano Diaries, 1939–1943.* Edited by Hugh Gibson. New York: Doubleday, 1946.

CLARKE, Arthur C. *The Making of a Moon.* London: Frederic Muller, 1957.

CLAUDEL, Paul. *Poetic Art.* Translated by Renee Spodheim. New York: Philosophical Library, 1948.

COCTEAU, Jean.

In June 1951, Wright and Cocteau inaugurated the Cercle International du Théatre et du Cinéma in Paris. In March they signed a telegram in support of the People's Congress Against Imperialism in Rome. There is no precise data on Wright's reading of Cocteau, however.

COHEN, Octavus Roy.

"Most American writers have refused to treat the Negro as a human being, but caricature and type him. . . . It is the Florian Slappeys that I protest against most. Mr. Octavus Roy Cohen is a widely read writer in the popular magazines and he sticks to the oldest and most dishonest trick of the writing trade when he types Negroes——and does the most damage. The Uncle Remus stories of Joel Chandler Harris fall somewhere in the folklore class, but even there I stamp my foot down when possible." (Interview by Coit Henley, "Richard Wright Stresses Realism in Dealing with Fictional Negro Types," Washington *Star,* November 11, 1945.)

COMFORT, Alexander. *Art and Social Responsibility: Lectures on the Ideology of Romanticism.* London: Falcon Press, 1946.

COMMUNIST PARTY OF THE UNITED STATES OF AMERICA. *Race Hatred on Trial.* [New York: Workers Library Publishers, 1931?]

Acquired after 1940.

CONNOLLY, Cyril. *Enemies of Promise.* Boston: Little, Brown, 1939.

Bought after 1940.

———. *The Missing Diplomats.* London: Queen Anne Press, 1952.

Galignani, Paris, sticker.

CONRAD, Earl. *Harriet Tubman.* Washington, D.C.: Associated Publishers, 1943.

Inscribed: "To Dick Wright,/with best wishes /Earl Conrad"

See also PATTERSON, Haywood.

CONRAD, Joseph. *The Arrow of Gold, A Story Between Two Notes.*

With Decorations by William Kemp Starrett. Malay ed. Garden City, N.Y.: Doubleday, Doran, 1929.
Bought before 1940.
——. *Chance.* Garden City, N.Y.: Doubleday, 1923.
Bought before 1940, $1.50.
——. *Nostromo.* Garden City, N.Y. and Toronto: Doubleday, Page & Co., 1923.
Bought before 1940.
——. *A Personal Record, The Shadow Line: A Confession.* With Decorations by William Kemp Starrett. Malay ed. Garden City, N.Y.: Doubleday, Doran, 1928.
Bought before 1940.
——. *Typhoon and Other Stories.* Garden City, N.Y.: Doubleday, Doran & Co., 1929.
Bought before 1940.
——. *Victory.* Garden City, N.Y.: Garden City Pub. Co., 1921.
Bought between 1935 and 1940.
——. *Youth, and Two Other Stories.* New York: Grosset and Dunlap, 1903.
Bought before 1940.
According to a conversation with Ed Gourfain, Wright read *The Nigger of the Narcissus* in Chicago. "I only know that up until that moment [reading Stein's 'Melanctha'] I had been trying to write and I had been trying to write in the English of Joseph Conrad." ("Memories of My Grandmother," *Biblio.,* p. 166, U 58, Wright Misc. 473, p. 18.)

"Thus, though you will be enthralled by the art, suspense and document of these stories, you will also be able, if you have a mind or will to, to enjoy, as Joseph Conrad put it, 'that modicum of truth for which you forgot to ask. . . .'" ("Foreword" to *Lest We Forget, Biblio.,* p. 125, U 94, Wright Misc. 456 [1955].)

"There is more than a hint of awe in his voice when he speaks of Dostoievsky and Conrad." (In "Profile," by Joseph Gollomb, *Book of the Month Club News,* Feb. 1945, pp. 8–9)
    An allusion to "the kind of hotel that one read about in a Conrad novel," (*Black Power,* p. 80) points at Wright's having read *Heart of Darkness.*
    On Wright reading Conrad, see Fabre, 83–85.

CONROY, Jack.

Conroy published Wright's early revolutionary poems in his magazine *The Anvil* in 1933–34. On his friendship with Wright, see Fabre, 118–19.

Wright repeatedly alluded to Conroy's novel *The Disinherited* (1934) as a rare example of proletarian writing.

"Most of the fiction coming from the left was in the form of sketches; even Jack Conroy's *The Disinherited* was constructed mainly upon the sketch principle." ("Writing from the Left," *Biblio.*, p. 170, U 74, Wright Misc. 812, p. 6.)

"The literary activites and vast correspondance of Jack Conroy have touched the lives and work of many young writers in America. Such a statement made about any other writer would have but a nominal meaning; but when it is remembered that Jack Conroy is a proletarian writer, the fact assumes unique importance. In that immense cultural desert known as the Midwest, Jack Conroy has to date launched two magazines, *Anvil* and *New Anvil;* he has written two novels, *The Disinherited* and *A World to Win.* All of his work has been directed singularly towards one goal: the enlightenment of the American people of the realities of the lives and potentialities of American labor, and the encouragement of the young worker-writer. From that faith and labor, he has not swerved one iota." (Draft for a blurb for *New Anvil.*)

COOK, Mercer.

Wright discussed black nationalism and integration in depth with Mercer Cook at the September 1956 conference of black writers and artists in Paris. He had read some of Cook's articles in Afro-American magazines.

COOLEY, Donald G. *The New Way to Eat and Get Slim.* New York: W. Funk, 1946.

COOPER, Gordon. *Your Holiday in Spain and Portugal.* 2d ed. London: A. Redman, 1954.

COPLESTON, Frederick G. *Friedrich Nietzsche, Philosopher of Culture.* London: Burns, Oates & Washbourne, 1942.

CORROTHERS, James D.

In "The Literature of the Negro in the United States," Wright quotes "At the Closed Gates of Justice" in which black clergyman James D. Corrothers compares the plight of the Negro to that of Christ. Five lines are quoted in *White Man, Listen!*, p. 140.

CORY, Donald W. [pseud.]. *Homosexual in America: A Subjective*

Approach. Introduction by Albert Ellis. New York: Greenberg, 1951.

C O S G R O V E, Frances. *Scenes for Student Actors: Dramatic Selections from New Plays.* Edited with Notes by Frances Cosgrove. New York, Los Angeles: S. French; London: S. French, Ltd., 1942.
> Reprints an excerpt from *Native Son: A Play.*

C O U S I N S, Norman. *Modern Man Is Obsolete.* New York: Viking Press, 1945.
> Bought used.

C O W L E Y, Malcolm.

> "Malcolm Cowley, journalist and associate editor of the *New Republic* sketched a moving picture of what seven years of crisis have done to the American writer." ("The Barometer Points to Storm," *Biblio.*, p. 164, U 45, Wright Misc. 237, p. 3)

C O X, Oliver C. *Caste, Class and Race: A Study in Social Dynamics.* Introduction by Joseph S. Roucek. New York: Monthly Review Press, 1959.
> Inscribed: "To Richard,/with all good wishes—/Oliver."
———. *The Foundations of Capitalism.* Foreword by Harry Elmer Barnes. New York: Philosophical Library, 1959.
> Inscribed: "To Richard,/with all good wishes—/Oliver."

C R A N E, Hart. *The Collected Poems.* Edited with an Introduction by Waldo Frank. New York: Liveright, 1933.
> Bought on April 17, 1945.
> The last two stanzas of "To Brooklyn Bridge" are quoted as epigraph to *The Color Curtain.*
> The first two lines of "Legend," the first piece in *White Buildings* (1926), are quoted as epigraph to the "Dream" section of *The Long Dream.*

C R A N E, Stephen. *Men, Women and Boats.* Edited with an Introduction by Vincent Starret. New York: Modern Library, 1921?
> Bought before 1940, 25¢
———. *Twenty Stories.* Selected, with an Introduction by Carl Van Doren. Cleveland, New York: World Pub. Co., 1945.
> Mentioned in *Black Boy*, 262. Wright read *The Red Badge of Courage*, and very probably Crane's short stories in 1927–28.

> "Stephen Crane's *Maggie*, a girl of the streets, is simply a cold, materialistic picture of poverty, while Jack Conroy's *The Disinherited* is the picture

of men and women groping their way to a new concept of human dignity."
("Writing from the Left," *Biblio.*, p. 170, U 74)

See FABRE, 68, 84.

C R O S S M A N,   Richard, ed. *The God That Failed, by Arthur Koestler*
[*and others*]. New York: Harper, 1949.

Stephen Spender, Andre Gide, Louis Fischer, and Ignazio Silone
were contributors with Wright.

C U L L E N,   Countee. *On These I Stand: An Anthology of the Best
Poems of Countee Cullen.* Selected by Himself and Including Six
New Poems Never Before Published. New York, London: Harper
& Brothers, 1947.

Bought as a gift for Julia Wright: "To my darling little daughter,
/ for Xmas, this book of lyrics. / Love. / Daddy. / Dec. 25, 1950.
Paris."

On May 6, 1939, Wright participated with Countee Cullen,
Alain Locke, Langston Hughes, and Warren Cochrane in a debate
on Negro writing organized by the Harlem Cultural Congress at
the Black Community Art Center.

Countee Cullen's "Heritage" is quoted in "The Literature of the
Negro in the United States" as proof that, even "at the apex of
lyrical utterance, color and race form the core of meaning" for
him:

What is Africa to me:
Copper sun or scarlet sea,
Jungle star or jungle track,
Strong bronzed men, or regal black
Women from whose loins I sprang
When the birds of Eden sang?
(*White Man, Listen!*, p. 140)

Again a few lines from "Heritage" are quoted as epigraph to
Black Power. Two stanzas from "Heritage" are quoted in *Black
Power.* The first stanza is also quoted in *White Man, Listen!*, p.
161, and four lines, p. 166.

C U M M I N G S,   E. E. *Eimi.* New York: Covici, Friede, 1933.

Bought before 1940.

———. *The Enormous Room* (1922).

Was not in his library, but was bought by Wright around 1935.
He enjoyed its absurd, almost existentialist, tone.

See FABRE, 111.

CUMONT, Franz V. *The Mysteries of Mithra*. Translated from the 2d rev. French ed. by Thomas J. McCormack. New York: Dover Publications, 1956.
   Bought in Paris, 1100F.
———. *The Oriental Religions in Roman Paganism*. With an Introductory Essay by Grant Showerman. Authorized Translation. New York: Dover Publications, 1956.
   Bought in Paris, 960F.
CUNEY, Waring.
   The "bitter, fighting lyrics of Waring Cuney, who sums up what Jim Crowism in wartime means to Negroes" are quoted in "The Literature of the Negro in the United States" (6 lines). See *White Man, Listen!*, p. 134.
CURRY, S. S. *Imagination and Dramatic Instinct: Some Practical Steps for Their Development*. Boston: School of Expression, 1896.
   Bought used before 1940.
CURTI, Merle. See THORP, Willard.

D

DAHLBERG, Edward. *The Flea of Sodom.* Norfolk, Conn.: New Directions, 1950.

DAICHES, David. *The Novel and the Modern World.* Chicago: University of Chicago Press, 1939.

———. *Poetry and the Modern World: A Study of Poetry in England Between 1900 and 1939.* Chicago: University of Chicago Press, 1940.

DAILY WORKER.

Wright kept 224 clippings of the some 250 articles he wrote for the Communist daily from June 8 to December 28,1927. See *Biblio.*, pp. 17–19; 1937–1 to 224. Also June 22, 1938 (item 1938–12).

D'ANNUNZIO, Gabriele. *The Maidens of the Rocks.* Translated from the Italian by Annetta Halliday-Antona and Giuseppe Antona. New York: Modern Library, 1926.

Bought used before 1940, 60¢.

DANQUAH, Joseph B. *Akan Laws and Customs.*

This title is mentioned on a receipt dated 1953 from the University College Bookshop in the Gold Coast. The title appears on the spine of the book, which is actually entitled *Gold Coast: Akan Laws and Customs and the Akim Abuakwa Constitution* (1928).

DANTE ALIGHIERI. *The Divine Comedy.* Translated by H. F. Cary. Introduction by Edmund G. Gardner. Everyman's Library. Poetry & the Drama, no. 308. London: J. M. Dent; New York: E. P. Dutton, 1908?

DAUDET, Alphonse. *Tartarin of Tarascon & Tartarin on the Alps.* London: J. M. Dent & Sons; New York: E .P. Dutton, 1909.

Bought after 1940.

DAVIS, Allison and **DOLLARD**, John. *Children of Bondage. The Personality Development of Negro Youth in the Urban South.* Washington, D.C.: American Council on Education, 1940.

"A series of articles detailing a character study of a Negro man, or woman, white man or woman, Japanese man or woman, Mexican man or woman, or children of any minority group; these sketches would be so written as to weigh, probe, and reveal the manner of life lived, the frustrations, frictions, longings, etc. Men like Nelson Algren, James Farrell, Allison Davis, Robert Rice, would be ideal for getting material of this sort." ("Suggestions for the Launching of *American Pages*," Biblio., p. 177, U 100, Wright Misc. 238, p. 6.)

D A V I S, Arthur P. See BROWN, Sterling A.

D A V I S, Frank Marshall. *Through Sepia Eyes:* [Four poems]. Decorations by William Fleming. Chicago: Black Cat Press, 1938.

Inscribed: "To Richard Wright, / with sincere friendship. / Frank Marshall Davis, / October 22, 1938"

Davis belonged to the Chicago Southside Writers Club in the 1930s.

"For the first time since Phillis Wheatley, the Negro began to make a wholehearted commitment to a new world. . . . it was possible for him to write out of the shared hopes and aspirations of millions of people. Phillis Wheatley visited the headquarters of George Washington, the father of our republic, Langston Hughes visited the headquarters of Lenin, the father of the Soviet Republic!

In the work of poets like [Frank Marshall] Davis, [Melvin B.] Tolson, [Sterling] Brown, [Margaret] Walker, [Gwendolyn] Brooks and [Arna] Bontemps this new vision was reflected." (In "The Literature of the Negro in the United States," included in *White Man, Listen!*, p. 142.)

D A V I S, George. *The Opening of a Door, A Novel.* London: H. Hamilton, 1931.

Used, from the Sylvia Beach bookstore in Paris.

D A V I S, Joe Lee; FREDERICK, John T.; and MOTT, Frank Luther, eds. *American Literature: An Anthology and Critical Survey, Since 1900.* Chicago: Scribner, 1949.

Includes excerpt of *Black Boy.*

D E C A R A V A, Roy and HUGHES, Langston, eds. *The Sweet Flypaper of Life.* New York: Simon & Schuster, 1955.

Bought in Paris for 500F.

D E L C A S T I L L O, Michel. *The Disinherited.* Translated from the French by Humphrey Hare. New York: Knopf, 1960.

Wright reviewed the book in "The Voiceless Ones," *Saturday Review*, 43 (April 16, 1960), 53–54.

See APPENDIX, pp. 192–95.

DELPECH, Jacques. *Les protestants en Espagne.* [Sévres]: Editions "Pro Hispania," 1954.
A gift from the author.
DEMPSEY, Peter J. R. *The Psychology of Sartre.* Oxford: Blackwell, 1950.
Bought in Paris, 400F.
DENDRICKSON, George and THOMAS, Frederick. *The Truth about Dartmoor.* London: Gollancz, 1954.
DENNIS, Geoffrey P. *The End of the World.* London: Eyre & Spottiswoods, 1948.
Bought in Paris, 200F.
DESAN, Wilfrid. *The Tragic Finale: An Essay on the Philosophy of Jean-Paul Sartre.* Cambridge [Mass.]: Harvard University Press, 1954.
Bought in Paris, 300F.
DESCARTES, René. *Descartes' Philosophical Writings.* Selected and Translated by Norman Kemp Smith. London: Macmillan, 1952.
———. *A Discourse on Method.* London: J. M. Dent; New York: E. P. Dutton, 1949.
Bought in Paris, 400F.
———. *The Living Thoughts of Descartes.* Presented by Paul Valéry. London: Cassell, 1948.
DE TOLEDANO, Ralph and LASKY, Victor. *Seeds of Treason: The Strange Case of Alger Hiss.* London: Secker & Warburg, 1950.
Galignani, Paris, sticker.
DEUTSCH, Helen. *Psycho-analysis of the Neuroses.* Translated by W. D. Robson-Scott. The International Psycho-analytical Library, no. 23. London: The Hogarth Press for the Institute of Psychoanalysis, 1951.
Bought in Paris, 900F.
DEWEY, John. *How We Think.* New York: D. C. Heath, 1910.
Bought after 1940, 650F.
According to my interview with Ed Gourfain, Wright was interested in Dewey's *Art as Experience* around 1936.
DICKENS, Charles. *Bleak House.* New York: A. L. Burt Co. 189–?
Bought before 1940.
———. *The Personal History of David Copperfield.* New York: A. L. Burt Co., 189-?
Bought before 1940.

————. *Posthumous Papers of the Pickwick Club*. New York: A. L. Burt Co., 19—?
> Bought before 1940.

————. *Sketches by Boz*. Paris: Baudry's European Library, 1839.
> Bought for 30F.

————. *Tale of Two Cities*. London: Educational Library, n.d.
> Bought used after 1940.

DICKINSON, Emily.
> Wright was a special guest speaker at a seminar on Mark Twain, Emily Dickinson, Thomas Wolfe, and Ernest Hemingway at the Blérancourt Cultural Center, France, on May 2 to 4, 1958.

DILNOT, George. *The Real Detective*. London: G. Bles, 1933.
> Bought in Paris, 350F.

DJILAS, Milovan. *The New Class: An Analysis of the Communist System*. New York: Praeger, 1957.

DODSON, Owen. *Powerful Long Ladder*. New York: Farrar, Straus & Co., 1946.
> Wright gave the proofs of the book to Sylvia Beach in the summer of 1946.

DOLLARD, John. *Caste and Class in a Southern Town*. New Haven: Published for the Institute of Human Relations by Yale University Press; London: H. Milford, Oxford University Press, 1937.
> Bought after 1940.
>
> See also DAVIS, Allison.

DOLPH, Edward A. *"Sound Off": Soldier Songs from the Revolution to World War II*. Music Arranged by Philip Egner. Illustrations by Lawrence Schick. New York: Farrar & Rinehart, 1942.

DONNE, John.
> Wright bought a copy of his *Poems* on September 3, 1945.

DOOB, Leonard W. *The Plans of Men*. New Haven: Published for the Institute of Human Relations by Yale University Press; London: H. Milford, Oxford University Press, 1940.

DOS PASSOS, John. *Manhattan Transfer*. New York: Penguin, 1946.
> Bought after 1940.

————. *Three Soldiers*. New York: George H. Doran, 1921.
> Bought before 1940.

————. *U.S.A.* New York: Modern Library, 1937.
> Bought after 1940.
>
> Wright discussed *The Big Money* (1936) with Margaret Walker

before leaving Chicago. He confessed having some difficulty in finishing *U.S.A. Lawd Today* reflects the influence of Dos Passos' "newsreel" technique.

On January 28, 1945, Wright noted in his journal that he had attempted to read the whole of *U.S.A.* for the third time, but had been too bored to finish the book.

DOSTOEVSKY, Fyodor. *Crime and Punishment.* Translated from the Russian by Constance Garnett. New York: Modern Library, 1932.

Bought after 1943.

Dog-eared at beginning of Chap. 5 of Part 4.

———. *The House of the Dead: A Novel in Two Parts.* From the Russian by Constance Garnett. New York: Macmillan, 1919.

Bought before 1940.

Dog-eared, pages 75 and 97.

———. *The Idiot.* London: J. M. Dent & Sons; New York: E. P. Dutton & Co., Inc. 1934.

Bought in Paris, 200F.

———. *Injury and Insult.* Translated from the Russian by Frederick Whishaw. 3rd ed. London: Vizetelly & Co., 1887.

———. *The Possessed.* Translated from the Russian by Constance Garnett. With a Foreword by Avrahm Yarmolinsky and a Translation of the Hitherto Suppressed Chapter "At Tihon's." New York: Modern Library, 1936.

Bought before 1940.

———. *A Raw Youth: A Novel.* Introduction by Alfred Kazin. New York: The Dial Press, 1947.

———. *The Short Novels of Dostoevsky.* With an Introduction by Thomas Mann. New York: The Dial Press, 1945.

———. *The Short Stories of Dostoevsky.* Edited, with an Introduction by William Phillips. New York: The Dial Press, 1946.

Wright read *Poor Folk* in Memphis, and *Crime and Punishment* and *The Brothers Karamazov* in Chicago (*Book-of-the-Month Club News,* February 1940, p. 4). Dostoevsky is mentioned among the authors read by Cross in *The Outsider,* and discussed in Wright's review of Michel Del Castillo's *The Disinherited* (q.v.) in 1960. "The Man Who Lived Underground" (1944) is reminiscent of Dostoevsky's *Notes from Underground* and some scenes of *Native Son* of *Crime and Punishment,* while Houston in *The Outsider* derives from Porphyry.

"There is one thing it [the petty bourgeoisie] has in abundance——emotional consciousness, intense emotional consciousness. Its life can be linked to a man standing with his back to the wall, cowed, or a man holding above his head a great weight which he dares not turn loose, lest it should crush him. . . . His emotional intensity can be weighed in the works of Dostoevsky, Hemingway, etc." ("Personalism," *Biblio.*, p. 167, U 67, Wright Misc. 515 p. 2.)

"Was in Quebec——common origin / Negroes too came from simple culture / So in my reading books by European writers I got notions / Dostoevsky, *House of Dead* / Joyce, *Portrait of the Artist as Young Man* / Moore, *Confessions of a Young Man* / Lawrence, *Sons and Lovers*." (Notes for an essay or lecture, undated)

"In literature, some of my heroes are: Raskolnikov's in Dostoevsky's *Crime and Punishment;* the I of Proust's *A Remembrance of Things Past;* K. of Kafka's *The Trial;* Melanctha of Gertrude Stein's *Three Lives;* and Nietzsche himself in his own *Thus Spake Zarathustra.*

The books that have influenced me most would make a long list. I'll be selective. Foremost among all the writers who have influenced me in my attitude toward the psychological state of modern man is Dostoevsky. Proust's work has painted for me what I feel to be the end of the bourgeois class of Western Europe. Theodore Dreiser first revealed to me the nature of American life, and for that service, I place him at the pinnacle of American literature." (Interview in *L'Express,* October 18, 1955, p. 8)

"Ahead of all the writers who molded my philosophy concerning modern man comes Dostoevsky. . . . Raskolnikov is one of my heroes." (Interview in *L'Express,* November 8, 1960.)

DOUGLAS, Alfred, Lord. *Selected Poems.* London: M. Secker, 1926.

DOUGLAS, Kenneth. *A Critical Bibliography of Existentialism (the Paris School): Listing, with Brief Comments, Books and Articles in English and French by and about Jean-Paul Sartre, Simone de Beauvoir, Maurice Merleau-Ponty.* Yale French Studies Special Monograph, no. 1. New Haven: Yale French Studies, 1950.

DOUGLAS, Norman. *South Wind.* New York: Modern Library, n.d. Bought before 1940.

DRAKE, St. Clair and CAYTON, Horace. *Black Metropolis: A Study of Negro Life in a Northern City.* With an Introduction by Richard Wright. New York: Harcourt, Brace, 1945.

Wright's introduction to the book is on pp. xvi–xxiv. He wrote a second one to the new 1960 edition, but it was not used. (See *Bib-*

lio., p. 176, U 95.) He advised Simone de Beauvoir to read the book and was instrumental in having a section published in *Les Temps Modernes.* See *World*, p. 254.

D R E I S E R, Theodore. *The Best Short Stories of Theodore Dreiser.* With an Introduction by James T. Farrell. Cleveland: World Pub. Co., 1956.

——. *The Bulwark: A Novel.* New York: Doubleday & Co., 1946.

——. *The "Genius."* New York: Boni and Liveright, 1923. Bought used.

——. *Sister Carrie.* With a New Foreword by the Author. New York: Modern Library, n.d. Used Civic Association copy, Sept. 1942.

——. *The Titan.* New York: H. Liveright, 1925.

In early drafts of *Black Boy*, Wright mentions reading *The Financier* and *The Titan* when he was working at the optical company in Memphis. He also mentions that he read *Sister Carrie* and *Jennie Gerhardt* in Memphis and *The Titan, The Financier,* and *An American Tragedy* during his early Chicago years. See *Black Boy*, 254, 292.

Wright prepared notes in praise of Dreiser on invitation to a testimonial luncheon on March 1st, 1941, in New York City. See *Biblio.*, p. 182, U 134.

"Dreiser's *Sister Carrie* is a picture of a romantic working girl caught in the coils of a great city and carried to her end through her own folly; while the characters in the novels of Langston Hughes, Arna Bontemps, Meridel Le Sueur, Josephine Herbst are men and women who strive above all to act consciously, deliberately; they are haunted with the desire to make their lives meaningful." ("Writing from the Left," *Biblio.*, p. 170, U 74, Wright Misc. 812, p. 1)

"Dreiser tried to rationalize and justify the defeat of the individual in biological terms." ("Personalism" (1935–37), *Biblio.*, p. 167, U 62)

"Dreiser could get his sociology from a Spencer and get his notion of realism from a Zola, but Negro writers can't go to those sources for background. They are hemmed in by their educational system." ("Readers and Writers," an interview by Edwin Seaver, December 23, 1941)

"From Chicago have come Sandburg, [Sherwood] Anderson, Dreiser, [James] Farrell, [Meyer] Levin, Cohen, Algren, [Edgar] Lee Masters, Conroy; and even Sinclair Lewis lived there for a while. The imaginative expressions of these men have set the tone and pattern of literary thinking and feeling for a large part of the nation for almost two generations."

(Introduction to *Black Metropolis* by St. Clair Drake and Horace Cayton, p. xviii.)

"I admire Faulkner but don't know him personally. We write each other. For some time I have been the president of an association of American writers and have remained in touch with James T. Farrell, whom I know pretty well. . . . As to those I admire, there is Dreiser, whom I have known; there is Hemingway. But the influences during my youth have been European. I owe much to Dostoevsky, Turgenev, Flaubert. I also like the writings of Gertrude Stein very much." ("En Revista con Richard Wright," *Revista Branca,* Buenos Aires, 1950. Transl. M. Fabre)

"Among the great novelists whom I like to reread are Sherwood Anderson, Mark Twain, James T. Farrell, Nelson Algren, Thomas Hardy, Maupassant, Proust, Dostoevsky. But I'd give all of them for one book by Dreiser: he encompasses them all." (Interview by Annie Brièrre, *France-USA,* Sept.-Oct. 1960, p. 2. Transl. M. Fabre.)

See FABRE, 68–69, 85–86 and 265–66.

DREPPERD, Carl W. *Primer of American Antiques.* Garden City, N.Y.: Doubleday, Doran & Co., 1945.

DRUCKER, Peter F. *The End of Economic Man: A Study of the New Totalitarianism.* New York: John Day, 1939.

DU BOIS, W. E. B. *Black Folk, Then and Now: An Essay in the History and Sociology of the Negro Race.* New York: Holt, 1939.
    Bought after 1940.

———. *The Souls of Black Folk: Essays and Sketches.* New York: A. C. McClurg, 1907.
    Bought used Ricour, Paris.
    The Suppression of the African Slave Trade, 1638–1870 (1896) is quoted among the sources for "Portrait of Harlem" in *New York Panorama* (1938).
    Wright reviewed *Dusk of Dawn* for the Chicago *News,* (Dec. 4, 1940), 10.

"The Negro politician has never been portrayed in an authentic manner. . . . Dr. DuBois's *Dark Princess* . . . is only a romantic picture. The Negro doctor has never been pictured in a novel, Walter White's *Fire in the Flint* notwithstanding. There is no first rate story based on Negro college life." (Interview by Harry B. Weber, New Jersey *Herald-News,* April 5, 1941.)

"Dr. W. E. B. DuBois publicly said that he doubted if the things I described were true. He is a leader of the Negro people and he must feel that if what I wrote is true, then it reflects upon him as a leader who is trying to bring about better conditions. . . . The truth of the matter is that we Negroes have not yet really faced the real problem of our lives. We forget. Or we deny them, as Dr. Dubois did when he reviewed my book. But we cannot solve anything by forgetting or denying." (To Fred Hoskins, April 23, 1945)

"It is obvious that DuBois is a nineteenth-century idealist. The things that shock him about *Black Boy* would shock him about modern life. He wrote the review as if he was not acquainted with James Joyce and D. H. Lawrence. . . . A member of the talented tenth who has sought to deny the facts of race life because he did not want to be identified with a people so oppressed." ("Richard Wright Talks to the Afro-American," by Michael Carter, Baltimore *Afro-American,* March 24, 1945, p. 5)

"When the Western world started the discrimination on the colonies there was no voice to protest against it. But in America the New Negro idea began at the beginning of the 20th century. William E. B. DuBois has been one of the predecessors of the New Negro. The seed of escaping from the influence and the discrimination of the West came from the theories of Marx, and the enlightened period of the New Negro was supervised by the principles of Marxism." (Hans de Vaal, "Interview med Richard Wright, *Literair Pasport,* July-August, 1953, p. 162)

See APPENDIX, pp. 215–16.

DU BOIS, William. *Haiti* (1938), a play by this white dramatist, is mentioned in "Portrait of Harlem," *New York Panorama.*

DUDLEY, Dorothy. *Dreiser and the Land of the Free.* New York: Bachhurst Press, 1946.

Inscribed: "For Richard Wright, / from Dorothy Dudley, / Feb. 13, 1947– /Inscribed for you, / and it would give me pleasure / for you to have it / among your books / about our Dreiser. / D. D."

DUFRENNE, Mikel and RICOEUR, Paul. *Karl Jaspers et la Philosophie de l'Existence.* Preface by Karl Jaspers. Paris: Editions du Seuil, 1947.

DUHAMEL, Georges. *The Pasquier Chronicles.* Translated from the French by Beatrice de Holthoir. New York: H. Holt, 1938.

Bought used, $1.50.

DUMAS, Alexandre. *The Three Musketeers.* London: T. Nelson, 1907?

Bought used before 1940.

A page from *The Count of Monte Cristo* is quoted in "The Literature of the Negro in the United States" to show that Dumas was integrated into the culture of France and was a Frenchman. *White Man, Listen!,* p. 111.

DUNBAR, Paul Laurence. *Complete Poems.* With the Introduction to "Lyrics of Lowly Life" by W. D. Howells. New York: Dodd, Mead, 1922.
> Bought used in Paris, 180F.
> In "The Literature of the Negro in the United States," Wright quotes three instances of Dunbar's verse. The "sweet" lines of:

Ere sleep comes down to soothe the weary eyes
Which all the day with ceaseless care have sought
The magic gold from which the seeker flies. . . .
(9 lines in all)

> Then,

I know why the caged bird sings, ah me . . .
(7 lines in all)

> which are seen as reflecting a sense of the paradox in the popular poet's life. Finally, a section of "We Wear the Mask" (6 lines in all), an expression of what was in the black bard's heart. Dunbar is seen as a victim of the fatal conflict within him, out of which he managed "to wring a little unity." See *White Man, Listen!*, pp. 121–22.

DUNNE, John W. *An Experiment with Time.* London: A. & C. Black, 1927.
> Bought after 1940.

———. *Nothing Dies.* London: Faber, 1940.

———. *The Serial Universe.* London: Faber & Faber, 1934.
> Bought after 1940.

DURRELL, Lawrence. *Balthazar.* London: Faber, 1958.

———. *Clea.* London: Faber, 1960.

———. *Justine.* London: Faber, 1957.

———. *Mountolive.* London: Faber, 1958.

D'USSEAU, Arnaud and GOW, James.
> Wright wrote a review of their play, *Deep Are the Roots,* for *Life* magazine in September 1945, but it was never published.
> See APPENDIX, pp. 195–99; *Biblio.,* p. 173, U 86, Wright Misc. 665, P.7.

DUTT, Rajan Palme. *World Politics, 1918–1936.* New York: International Publishers, 1936.
> Bought after 1940.

E

E A S T M A N K O D A K C O M P A N Y. *How to Make Good Pictures.*
2 ed. Rochester, N.Y.
Bought before 1940.

E A S T M A N, Max.
Calder Willingham called Max Eastman's new book, *Reflections on the Failure of Socialism,* to Wright's attention in a letter on April 2, 1955.

E G R I, Lajos. *How to Write a Play. The Principles of Play Construction Applied to Creative Writing and to the Understanding of Human Motives.* With an Introduction by Gilbert Miller. New York: Simon & Schuster, 1942.
Wright did a meticulous summary of the volume, but noted in his journal for January 4, 1945: "I tried like all hell to write a play two years ago on these rules, but I didn't get anywhere."
See APPENDIX, p. 267.

E I N S T E I N, Albert. *Out of My Later Years.* London: Thames & Hudson, 1950.
Bought in Paris, 600F.

E I S E N S T E I N, Sergei. *The Film Sense.* Translated and Edited by Jay Leyda. New York: Harcourt, Brace & Co., 1942.

E L I A D E, Mircea. *The Myth of the Eternal Return.* Translated from the French by Willard R. Trask. London: Routledge & Kegan Paul, 1955.

E L I O T, T. S. *The Cultivation of Christmas Trees.* Illustrated by David Jones. New York: Farrar, Straus, Cudahy, 1956.

———. *Selected Essays.* London: Faber, 1932.
Bought in Paris, 350F.
Eliot's *The Waste Land* is quoted in epigraph to the third part of *Lawd Today.*
"... he just discovered T. S. Eliot at the Chicago John Reed Club." (*Book-of-the-Month Club News,* Feb. 1940, p. 4)

"I read Eliot, Pound, Joseph Wood Krutch, Huxley. I sort of got into the habit of reading about that time [the mid thirties]." (New York *Herald Tribune,* April 17, 1941.)

"This being forever excited about some new way to look at the world—— which is born of my rootlessness——will endure. I don't think I'll ever find it——
Because I do not hope to turn
Because I do not hope to turn again etc.
But what I must do is find a new language for the way I see life." (Unpublished journal, January 2, 1945)

A clipping from an interview by "Marietta" for the *Bulletin Board* (June 1950) quotes Wright as saying: "With the exception of T. S. Eliot and Rebecca West, no English writer impresses me."

"I looked at him [a white man whose main job in life is the hunting of communists] and said, paraphrasing Eliot:
This is the way the world ends
This is the way the world ends
This is the way the world ends
Not with a bang, not with a whimper, but with a giggle.
I could also paraphrase Shakespeare's *Macbeth* by saying in my conclusion:
Corruption and corruption and corruption
Eats into petty hearts from day to day
To the last jingle of the cash register
And all our illusions are leading fools
The way to moral death. . . . Our informers
Make life but a walking charade, a poor pretense
That struts and frets his hour of deception
And then slinks from our view; it is a tale
Told by betrayers, full of doublecrossing,
Signifying deceit.
("The Position of the Negro Artist and Intellectual in the United States," *Biblio.,* p. 168, U 63, Wright Misc. 622, p. 34.)

ELLISON, Ralph. *Invisible Man.* New York: Random House, 1952.
On February 11, 1945, Wright noted in his journal that Ralph Ellison kept his ideas for himself and had refused to lend him Reich's *Theory of the Orgone.*
"The Position of the Negro Artist and Intellectual in the United States," (*Biblio.,* p. 168, U 63, Wright Misc. 622, pp. 25–

26) alludes to Ellison's meeting the accusation that the novel was designed to please both whites and blacks.

E L W O O D, Muriel.
Wright did a reader's report for the Book-of-the-Month Club on her novel *Heritage of the River* (1945) in February 1945. See *Biblio.*, p. 171 U 80.

E M B R E E, Edwin R. *Brown Americans. The Story of a Tenth of the Nation.* New York: Viking, 1943.
Inscribed: "To Richard Wright, / with the warm admiration of / Edwin R. Embree / — Oct. 1943."

———. *13 Against the Odds.* New York: Viking Press, 1944.
"Richard Wright: Native Son" is one of the 13 essays included. See also JOHNSON, Charles S.

E M E R S O N, Ralph Waldo. *Essays: First Series.* New York: F. M. Lupton Co., 189–?
Bought before 1940 for 25¢.

———. *Essays. First Series and Second Series.* London: Nelson, 192–?
Bought used in Paris, 150F

———. *Emerson's Essays and Representative Men.* London & Glasgow: Collins' Clear-type Press, 19—?
Galignani, Paris, sticker.
"Emerson speculated and sang of the spiritual and moral perfection of the individual under what he hoped would be a truly democratic civilization." ("Personalism," *Biblio.*, p. 167, U 62.)

E M P S O N, William. *Seven Types of Ambiguity.*[2d ed. rev. and re-set] London: Chatto & Windus, 1947.

E N C O U N T E R.
Wright had a few issues of this magazine, mostly those in which his work appeared from 1954 to 1956.

E N C Y C L O P A E D I A   B R I T A N N I C A. 24 vols. Chicago, London: Encyclopaedia Britannica, 1945.

E N C Y C L O P A E D I A   O F   T H E   S O C I A L   S C I E N C E S. 15 vols. in 8. New York: Macmillan, 1944.

E N G E L S, Friedrich. *Herr Eugen Dühring's Revolution in Science (Anti-Dühring).* Translated by Emile Burns. Edited by C. P. Dutt. New York: International Publishers, 1939.
Bought in Paris, 550F.

———. *Socialism, Utopian and Scientific.* New York: International Publishers, 1935.
Bought after 1940.

―――. *Socialism, Utopian and Scientific.* Translated by Edward Av-
eling. With a Special Introduction by the Author. Chicago: C. H.
Kerr, 1910.
    This copy belonged to A. J. Aaron, Butler, Pa.
    See also MARX, Karl.
EPICETUS. *The Works of Epicetus. Consisting of His Discourses in
Four Books, the Enchiridion, and Fragments.* A Translation from
the Greek Based on That of Elizabeth Carter, by Thomas Went-
worth Higgins. Boston: Little, Brown, 1866.
ESTABROOKS, George H. *Hypnotism.* New York: E. P. Dutton,
1946.
    Bought used in Paris, 200F.
EVANS, Walker. See AGEE, James.

F

FADIMAN, Clifton, ed. *The American Treasury, 1455–1955.* New York: Harper, 1955.

FAGE, J. D. *An Introduction to the History of West Africa.* [2d ed.] Cambridge [Eng.]: University Press, 1959.

FALANGE ESPAÑOLA TRADICIONALISTA Y DE LAS JUNTAS OFENSIVAS NACIONAL-SINDICALISTAS. SECCIÓN FEMININA. *Formacion Político: Leccions para los Flechas.* Novena ed. Madrid: Seccion Feminina de F.E.T. y de las J.O.N.-S., 1954.
 Repeatedly quoted in *Pagan Spain.*

FARNHAM, Marynia. See LUNDBERG, Ferdinand.

FARRELL, James T. *Bernard Clare.* New York: Vanguard, 1946.
 Inscribed: "For Ellen, Julia and Dick Wright. / With best wishes /- Jim Farrell."

————. *Gas-house McGinty: A Novel.* Cleveland: World Pub. Co., 1944.

————. *Studs Lonigan: A Trilogy Containing Young Lonigan, The Young Manhood of Studs Lonigan, Judgment Day.* With a New Introduction by the Author. New York: Modern Library, 1938.

————. *Tommy Gallagher's Crusade.* New York: Vanguard Press, 1939.
 Bought in 1939.

————. *A World I Never Made.* New York: Vanguard, 1936.
 Bought used in Paris, 100F.
 On Farrell's influence on *Lawd Today* and advice about it, see Fabre, 135. Wright admired Farrell's stand at the American Writers Congress in 1937. He read *Studs Lonigan* before 1935.

FAST, Howard. *The American: A Middle Western Legend.* New York: Duell, Sloan & Pearce, 1946.

————. *Citizen Tom Paine.* New York: Duell, Sloan & Pearce, 1943.

————. *Freedom Road.* New York: Book Find Club, 1944.

49

———. *Literature and Reality.* New York: International Publishers, 1950.

———. *Spartacus: A Novel.* London: Bodley Head, 1952.

FAULKNER, William. *Go Down, Moses.* New York: Random House, 1942.

———. *Intruder in the Dust.* New York: Signet Books, 1949.

———. *Knight's Gambit.* New York: Random House, 1949. Bought in Buenos Aires.

———. *Light in August.* New York: H. Smith & R. Haas, 1932. Bought used after 1940, 25¢.

———. *The Portable Faulkner.* Edited by Malcolm Cowley. New York: Viking Press, 1946.

———. *Pylon.* The Albatross Modern Continental Library, v. 293. London, Paris: The Albatross, 1935. Bought used after 1940.

———. *Sanctuary.* Modern Masterpieces in English, no. 3. Paris: Crosby Continental Editions, 1932. Bought in Paris, 420F.

———. *Soldiers' Pay.* Garden City, N.Y.: Sundial Press, 1937. Bought before 1940.

———. *The Sound and the Fury & As I Lay Dying.* With a New Appendix as a Foreword by the Author. New York: Modern Library, 1946.

———. *The Wild Palms.* Stockholm: The Continental Book Co. AB, 1947.

Wright read a few Faulkner novels, including *Absalom, Absalom!* and *Sanctuary,* before 1940.

"He likes to read *Metamorphosis, Ulysses, Moby Dick, The Sound and the Fury.*" ("A Parigi Con Wright," interview by Fernanda Pivano, *Avanti,* May 19, 1948.)

"The achievement of Faulkner is all the more arresting as he is a southern white man, the product of a section of America which has withstood and nursed the stings of a Civil War defeat which it could never accept, and misinterpreted that defeat in the most infantile and emotional manner. . . . But the South could not remain isolated forever; wars and convulsions of social change were bound to engulf it, industrialization induced such impersonal social relations that controls loosened and allowed a certain degree of negative freedom, and it was in this transition period of confusion that the genius of Faulkner leaped and presented itself to a startled world." ("L'Homme du Sud," *France-Etats-Unis,* December 1950, p. 2). Carbon of English text in Wright Archive (*Biblio.,* p. 76, 1950 - 15.)

"Faulkner is close to realism when he writes about Negroes in the South, but he confesses he has never been able to get into the skin of a Negro." ("Interview," Oslo *Dagbladet,* Nov. 29, 1956) On Wright and Faulkner, see *World,* pp. 89–92.

See APPENDIX, pp. 199–200.

FEARING, Kenneth. *Afternoon of a Pawnbroker, and Other Poems.* New York: Harcourt, Brace & Co., 1943.

Bought on September 29, 1945.

———. *Collected Poems.* New York: Random House, 1940.

Inscribed: "Best regards to the Wrights / and a happy stay in the Village. / Kenneth Fearing"

———. *Dead Reckoning. A Book of Poetry.* New York: Random House, 1938.

Acquired after 1940.

———. *Poems.* Introduction by Edward Dahlberg. New York: Dynamo Press, 1956.

Acquired after 1940.

FEDERAL WRITERS' PROJECT. *American Stuff: An Anthology of Prose and Verse.* New York: Viking Press, 1937.

Includes Wright's essay "The Ethics of Living Jim Crow."

FEDERAL WRITERS' PROJECT. NEW YORK (CITY). *New York City Guide.* [Rev. ed.] New York: Random House, 1939.

The extent of Wright's contribution to this volume is unknown.

———. *New York Panorama: A Comprehensive View of the Metropolis, Presented in a Series of Articles.* New York: Random House, 1938.

The sources given for the "Portrait of Harlem" section Wright wrote for this WPA guide are George Washington Williams, *Story of the Negro Race in America, 1619–1880* (1883); Booker T. Washington, *Story of the Negro* (1902); and W. E. B. DuBois, *The Suppression of the African Slave Trade, 1638–1870* (1896).

The essay mentions *The Genius of Freedom* by David Ruggles and *A Text Book of the Origins and History of the Colored People* by J. C. Pennington (1841), but there is no indication that Wright really read those books. In the essay, Wright states:

"W. E. B. DuBois wrote *The Souls of Black Folk,* a sensitive interpretation of the Negroes' plight at the beginning of the 20th century. The book proved a turning point in the history of Negro thought and had a tremendous influence upon the Negroes of New York. In it, DuBois took sharp issue with the philosophy of Booker T. Washington, who at that time was the recognized leader of his race." (pp. 137–38)

FENICHEL, Otto. *The Psychoanalytic Theory of Neurosis.* London: Routledge & Kegan Paul, 1946.
Bought in Paris, 2000F.

FERENCZI, Sandor. *Further Contributions to the Theory and Technique of Psycho-analysis.* Compiled by John Rickman. Authorized Translation by Jane Isabel Suttie and Others [2d ed.] London: The Hogarth Press, 1950.
Bought in Paris, 2000F.
Quoted as epigraph to *Savage Holiday,* Part I.

FIELD, Margaret Joyce. *Akim-Kotoku: An Oman of the Gold Coast.* London: Crown Agents for the Colonies, 1948.

FINNEY, Charles G. *The Circus of Dr. Lao.* With Drawings by Boris Artzybasheff. New York: Viking Press, 1935.
Bought after 1940.

FISCHER, Louis. *Gandhi: His Life and Message for the World.* New York: New American Library, 1954.

FISHER, William. *The Waiters.* Cleveland: World Pub. Co. 1953.

FITZGERALD, F. Scott. *The Bodley Head Scott Fitzgerald.* With an Introduction by J. B. Priestley. 4 vols. London: The Bodley Head, 1958–1961. Galignani, Paris, sticker.

——. *The Crack-up. With Other Uncollected Pieces, Note-books and Unpublished Letters. Together with Letters to Fitzgerald from Gertrude Stein, Edith Wharton, T. S. Eliot, Thomas Wolfe and John Dos Passos. And Essays and Poems by Paul Rosenfeld, Glenway Wescott, John Dos Passos, John Peale Bishop, and Edmund Wilson.* Edited by Edmund Wilson. New York: New Directions, 1945.
Bought in Buenos Aires.

——. *Tender Is the Night.* New York: Scribner, 1934.
Bought before 1940.
Autograph notation "Ex Libris Richard Wright."

FLAUBERT, Gustave. *Madame Bovary.* New York: Grosset & Dunlap, 1934?

——. *Sentimental Education; Or, The History of a Young Man.* Vols. 5 and 6 of his *Works.* Chicago: Magee, 1904.
Acquired in the mid-1930s.
Autograph notation "Richard Wright, 4804 Lawrence Ave."
"Among Wright's favorite French novelists are Proust, Maupassant and Flaubert." (Interview by F. Stane, *Gavroche,* June 6, 1946)
"By which writers have you been influenced?" "In the first place by the pre-revolutionary Russians. Then Flaubert, Maupassant, Kafka, Gide,

Proust, Sartre, Camus, Thomas Mann, Joseph Conrad, Thomas Hardy, George Moore, Sherwood Anderson, and Theodore Dreiser." (Hans de Vaal, "Interview med Richard Wright," *Literair Pasport,* July-August 1953, p. 163.)

"When Flaubert wrote *Madame Bovary,* he said, 'Madame Bovary, that's me'. In the same fashion there is a psychological self-portrait in Bigger Thomas." ("Interview," Oslo *Dagbladet,* Nov. 29, 1956.)

F L A V I N, Martin. *Black and White: From the Cape to the Congo.* With Illustrations by Paul Whitman. New York: Harper, 1950.

F L O R E S, Angel, ed. *The Kafka Problem.* Norfolk, Conn.: New Directions, 1946.

F L U G E L, John C. *Man, Morals and Society: A Psycho-analytical Study.* London: Duckworth, 1948.

Bought in Paris, 655F.

A friend brought Wright Flugel's *Psycho-analytic Study of the Family* (1921) on January 19, 1945.

F L Y N N ' S   D E T E C T I V E   W E E K L Y.

According to *Black Boy,* Wright read this magazine assiduously in 1923–25.

F Ü L Ö P - M I L L E R, Rene. *Leaders, Dreamers, and Rebels: An Account of the Great Mass-Movements of History and the Wish-dreams That Inspired Them.* Translated from the German by Eden and Cedar Paul. New York: Viking, 1935.

Bought after 1940.

F O L E Y, Martha and ROTHBERG, Abraham, eds. *U.S. Stories: Regional Stories from the Forty-eight.* Selected with a Foreword. New York: Hendricks House, Farrar, Strauss, 1949.

Includes "Bright and Morning Star."

F O N T A I N E, William T.

"William T. Fontaine in the *American Journal of Sociology* for Jan. 1944 / Frazier dissents. / I take no stand in this issue but I am merely reporting that Negroes in the academic field are full of self-questioning, wanting to rid themselves of all those feelings and thought processes that stem from a purely racial identification; want to live as men."

"Conflict among Negro scholars / William T. Fontaine vs. E. Franklin Frazier / Trying to throw off even those processes of thought and feeling that stem from a purely racial role and identification. VERTICAL EXPERIENCES / The Height and Depth of the problem as seen through the eyes of two poets: Phillis Wheatley and Claude McKay." (Notes on cards for a lecture on the Negro in America, 1945–46?)

F O R D, Ford Madox.

"What happened between scenes, the writer showed through the medium of dialogue of the characters; he bridged the gap in time by having his characters, while talking to themselves, tell the reader what had transpired. Conrad, Ford Madox Ford, and many others used this device and it heightened the power of the novel still more." (Lecture on left wing literature, pp. 15–16 [1940?])

F O R D, James W. *The Negro and the Democratic Front*. Introduction by A. W. Berry. New York: International Publishers, 1938. Bought before 1940.

F O R D, Richard. *Gatherings from Spain*. London and Toronto: J. M. Dent; New York: E. P. Dutton, 1948.
Bought used in 1954.
Passages underlined.

F O R S T E R, E. M. *Aspects of the Novel*. New York: Harcourt, 1948.
Advance Copy, April 13, 1947.

———. *A Passage to India*. London: The Albatross, 1947.
Bought at Didier's, Paris.
Wright declared he had read nothing by Forster before reviewing *Aspects of the Novel*. ("E. M. Forster Anatomizes the Novel," *P.M. Magazine,* March 16, 1947, p. m3.)
See APPENDIX, pp. 201–3.

F O R S Y T H E, [?]
"Personalism will be anti-aesthetic in so far as it will seek to push art beyond mere contemplation. . . . It will seek to make those who come in contact with it take sides for or against certain *moral* issues, and these issues will be elementary ones (Forsythe)." ("Personalism," *Biblio.,* p. 167, U 62, Wright Misc. 515, p. 4.)

F O R T, Charles. *The Books of Charles Fort*. With an Introduction by Tiffany Thayer. New York: Published for the Fortean Society by H. Holt & Co., 1941.

F O R T E S, Meyer. *The Dynamics of Clanship among the Tallensi: Being the First Part of an Analysis of the Social Structure of a Trans-Volta Tribe*. London, New York: Published for the International African Institute by the Oxford University Press, 1945.

———. *The Web of Kinship among the Tellensi: The Second Part of an Analysis of the Social Structure of a Trans-Volta Tribe*. London, New York: Published for the International African Institute by the Oxford University Press, 1949.
Bought in Kumasi August 7, 1953.

FOULQUIÉ, Paul. *Existentialism.* Translated from the French by Kathleen Raine. London: D. Dobson, 1948.
Galignani, Paris, sticker.

FOWLER, Gene. *Goodnight, Sweet Prince: The Life of John Barrymore.* Philadelphia: 1945.

FOX, Ralph W. *The Novel and the People.* London: Cobbett Pub. Co., 1944.
Bought used in London, 8sh.

[FRAME, —]. *Philosophy of Insanity; By a Late Inmate of the Glasgow Royal Asylum for Lunatics at Gartnavel; with an Introduction by Frieda Fromm-Reichmann.* London, New York: Fireside Press, 1947.

FRANCE, Anatole. *The Crime of Sylvestre Bonnard.* Translated by Lafcadio Hearn. New York: H. W. Wise, 1930.

———. *The Gods Are Athirst.* New York: J. Lane, n.d.
Copy from Illinois State Library, acquired before 1940.

———. *The Revolt of the Angels.* New York: Dodd, Mead, 1914.
Autograph notation "Wright 4804 St. Lawrence"
Handwritten notes.

FRANK, Waldo. *In the American Jungle (1925–1936).* Photographic Decorations by William H. Field. New York, Toronto: Farrar & Rinehart, 1937.
Bought in 1937.

———. *South American Journey.* New York: Duell, Sloane and Pearce, 1943.
On April 9, 1945, Waldo Frank wrote Wright that he had asked his publishers to send Wright *South American Journey* after a long talk they had together regarding Wright's projected magazine, *American Pages.*
Wright quotes from *Our America* in epigraph to *Lawd Today,* Part II.

FRANKLIN, Sidney. *Bullfighter from Brooklyn: The Autobiography of Sidney Franklin, with an Evaluation of Sidney Franklin from "Death in the Afternoon" by Ernest Hemingway.* London: Hutchinson, 1952.
Bought in Paris, 300F.

FRAZER, James George. *The Golden Bough: A Study in Magic and Religion.* Abridged ed. New York: Macmillan, 1922.
Bought used before 1940.

———. *The Golden Bough: A Study in Magic and Religion*. 2 vols. of 12. London: Macmillan, 1936–37.
Bought in Paris, 1200F.

FRAZIER, E. Franklin. *The Negro Family in Chicago*. Chicago: University of Chicago Press, 1932.
Bought after 1940.

———. *The Negro Family in the United States*. Chicago: University of Chicago Press, 1940.

———. *The Negro in the United States*. New York: Macmillan, 1949.

———. *Negro Youth at the Crossways: Their Personality Development in the Middle States*. Prepared for the American Youth Commission. Washington, D.C.: American Council on Education, 1940.

"In the *American Journal of Sociology* for January, 1944, one William T. Fontaine raises the question as to the degree to which Negro scholars and scientists are determined in their studies and researches by the racial roles and identifications they hold, and the kind of truth they may seek to find.

Goodness knows, I'm not going to take sides in this quarrel; I understand that E Franklin Frazier has dissented sharply from Wm. T. Fontaine in this matter.

I merely wish to point out that such discussions are raging in Negro academic circles, and that the Negro is trying to throw off the burden of race and live as a man, as a human being . . . and think and feel freely." (Notes for a lecture)

"It was in the University of Chicago's Department of Sociology that such men as E. Franklin Frazier, who produced *The Negro Family in Chicago* and *The Negro Family in the United States,* Bertrand Doyle, who produced *The Etiquette of Race Relations in the South,* and Harold P. Gosnell, who produced *Negro Politicians* were trained and guided." (Introduction to *Black Metropolis* by St. Clair Drake and Horace Cayton [Harcourt, Brace, New York], p. xix.)

"The appearance and multiplicity of scientific social studies, of which E. Franklin Frazier's *The Negro Family in the United States* is a brilliant example, has not, of course, checked or lessened racial discrimination in America; but it has made such inhuman practices intellectually and scientifically indefensible." ("Foreword" to "Human, All Too Human," by E. Franklin Frazier, *Présence Africaine*, January–March 1949, p. 47.)

FREDERICK, John T. See DAVIS, Joe Lee.
FREUD, Anna. *The Ego and the Mechanisms of Defence.* Authorized Translation by Cecil Baines. The International Psycho-analytical

Library, no. 30. London: Hogarth Press and the Institute of Psychoanalysis, 1954.
Bought used in Paris, 500F.
F R E U D, Sigmund. *Basic Writings*. Translated and Edited, with an Introduction, by Dr. A. A. Brill. New York: Modern Library, 1938.
Bought after 1940.
―――. *Civilization, War, and Death: Selections from the Three Works by Sigmund Freud*. Edited by John Rickman. London: The Hogarth Press and the Institute of Psycho-analysis, 1939.
―――. *Collected Papers*. Authorized Translation under the Supervision of Joan Riviere. 5 vols. The International Psycho-analytical Library, nos. 7–10, 37. London: Hogarth Press and The Institute of Psychoanalysis, 1950.
―――. *The Future of an Illusion*. Translated by W. D. Robson-Scott. The International Psycho-analytical Library, no. 15. London: Hogarth Press, 1949.
―――. *Interpretation of Dreams*. Translated by A. A. Brill. The Modern Library of the World's Best Books, 96. New York: Modern Library, 1950.
―――. *Leonardo da Vinci, a Psycho-sexual Study of an Infantile Reminiscence*. Translated by A. A. Brill. Reprint of the American Edition with a Preface by Ernest Jones. London: Routledge & K. Paul, 1948.
―――. *Moses and Monotheism*. Translated from the German by Katherine Jones. London: Hogarth Press and the Institute of Psycho-analysis, 1939.
―――. *The Question of Lay Analysis: An Introduction to Psychoanalysis*. London: Imago Pub. Co., 1947.
Freud is mentioned in *Savage Holiday*, p. 73, and a quotation from *Totem and Taboo* is used as epigraph to Part I of *Savage Holiday*.

"Our conscious minds fled from this work and the words swam about in the dark of our souls, tormenting us, making us kill when we should have eaten, making us angry when we should have been delighted, making us fear when we should have been confident of lasting security.[3] [Note 3: "See Freud's *Pathology of Everyday Life,* op. cit.]" ("Let's Eat the Niggers," *Biblio.,* p. 168, U 65. [1936])

"I don't do much reading in contemporary novels. I find myself drawn more towards historians, sociologists, anthropologists. For the past few years most of my reading has been the works of Freud, Malinowski, Theodor Reik, Nietzsche, etc. Most contemporary novels are too 'cute' for me." (Interview in *L'Express,* October 18, 1955, p. 8.)

"Negro jazz music has been called over and over again by many critics the greatest surrealist music ever heard in human history. Of course, I doubt if Louis Armstrong, or Duke Ellington, or Count Basie ever talk of surrealism. Maybe, if you tried to explain surrealism to them in terms of Freud's theory of dream analysis, they might call you crazy." ("Memories of my Grandmother," *Biblio.,* p. 166, U 58, Wright Misc. 473, p. 23)

"Even Freud, after plowing up man's pleasure-ridden unconscious seemed to have reeled back in fear and began to babble of 'reality-principle', began searching for some way to reconcile man's inordinate desires with a world that contained no feasible promise for their fulfillment." (Introduction to *Black Metropolis* by St. Clair Drake and Horace Cayton [Harcourt, Brace, New York], P. xxiii).

Allusion to *Totem and Taboo* in *Pagan Spain,* 279. "I like Freud and Marx, not from a political point of view, but because they are poets." (Interview by Annie Brièrre, *France-USA* (Sept.-Oct. 1960), 2. Transl. M. Fabre)

See also BREUER, Josef.

FROMM, Bella. *Blood and Banquets: A Berlin Social Diary.* New York, London: Harper & Bros in Association with Cooperation Pub. Co., 1942.

FUNAROFF, Sol. *The Spider and the Clock: Poems.* New York: International Publishers, 1938.

Inscribed: "For the pleasure of both reading / and editing 'Bright and Morning Star' / for 'New Masses' and the novelette / in the *Caravan* / may our present editorial collaboration / widen into a firm friendship./ Fraternally / Saul Funaroff."

See also SPECTOR, Herman.

FURMAN, Abraham L., ed. *The Second Armchair Companion.* New York: Lantern Press, 1946.

Includes "Silt."

FURNEAUX, Rupert. *The Other Side of the Story: The Strange Story of Christianity, the Dark Spot of History. A Solution to an Age-old Enigma Suggested by the Long-Suppressed Evidence of Non-Christian Contemporaries.* London: Cassell, 1953.

G

GALLAGHER, Buell G. *Color and Conscience: The Irrepressible Conflict.* New York, London: Harper & Bros., 1946.

Sent to Wright for review.

GALLUP, Donald C., ed. *The Flowers of Friendship: Letters Written to Gertrude Stein.* New York: Knopf, 1953.

Wright's letter to Gertrude Stein, dated May 27, 1945, is included.

See also HAAS, Robert B.

GALSWORTHY, John. *Representative Plays.* With an Introduction by George P. Baker. New York: Scribner's, 1927.

Bought before 1940.

Plays included are *The Silver Box, Strife, Justice, The Pigeon, A Bit o' Love,* and *Loyalties.*

GARBEDIAN, H. Gordon. *Albert Einstein, Maker of Universes.* New York and London: Funk & Wagnals, 1939.

Bought used in Paris, 250F.

GARCIA LORCA, Federico. *From Lorca's Theatre: Five Plays.* In the Authorized Translation by Richard L. O'Connell and James L. Graham. With a Foreword by Stark Young. New York: C. Scribner's Sons, 1941.

Plays included are *The Shoemaker's Prodigious Wife, The Love of Don Perlimplin, If Five Years Pass, Yerma,* and *Doña Rosita, the Spinster.*

———. *Poems.* With English Translation by Stephen Spender and J. L. Gili. Selection and Introduction by R. M. Nadal. London: The Dolphin, 1939.

Bought in Paris, 200F.

GARNIER, Christine [Mrs. Kay Bret Koch].

Fetish (New York: Putnam, 1952) is listed among books bought by Wright at the Basel Mission Book Depot in Kumasi, Ghana, on August 7, 1953.

GARVEY, Marcus.
Mentioned but not quoted in *Lawd Today, White Man, Listen!,* and *American Hunger.*

GAUTIER, Théophile. *Mademoiselle de Maupin.* New York: Modern Library, 1925.
Bought used before 1940, 5¢

GEISE, John J. *Man and the Western World.* 2 vols. New York: Harcourt, Brace & Co., 1940.
Bought in October 1945.
Wright noted in his 1945 diary that he bought *The History of Modern Man* on October 17 and *Thoughts on Western World* [sic] on November 16. He apparently was referring to the two volumes of *Man and the Western World.*

GENET, Jean. *The Blacks, A Clown Show.* Translated from the French by Bernard Frechtman. New York: Grove Press, 1960.
———. *The Thief's Journal.* With a Foreword by Jean-Paul Sartre. Translated from the French by Bernard Frechtman. Paris: Olympia Press, 1954.
Inscribed: "To Dick / With thanks for the good word, / Bernie" [Bernard Frechtman]
The Thief's Journal is mentioned as "defending a cause" in Wright's "L'art est mis en question par l'âge atomique," *Arts,* no. 779, June 18, 1960, p. 1.
At Frechtman's request, Wright wrote a blurb for Genet: "Jean Genet has taken a tabooed subject and created a world that is out of this world. He is a magician, an enchanter of the first order." (Blurb for *Our Lady of the Flowers,* New York: Grove Press, 1950.)

GIBBON, Edward. *The Decline and Fall of the Roman Empire.* 3 vols. New York: Modern Library, 1946?
$1.55

GIBSON, Richard. *A Mirror for Magistrates, A Novel.* London: A. Blond, 1958.
Inscribed: "For Richard Wright, / the 'father of us all,' / with many thanks for his understanding. / Richard Gibson. / Paris, Sept. 1958."
See FABRE, 461–65, 471–72.

GIDE, André. *Corydon. With a Comment on the Second Dialogue in "Corydon"* by Frank Beach. New York: Farrar, 1950.
———. *The Counterfeiters.* Translated from the French by Dorothy

Bussy. Introduction by Raymond Weaver. New York: Modern Library, 1933.

Bought after 1940.

————. *The Fruits of the Earth: Les nourritures terrestres & Les nouvelle nourritures*. Translated from the French by Dorothy Bussy. New York: Knopf, 1949.

————. *The Immoralist*. Translated from the French by Dorothy Bussy. New York: Knopf, 1930.

Bought after 1940.

————. *Journals*. Translated from the French, with an Introduction and Notes, by Justin O'Brien. 4 vols. New York: Knopf, 1947.

————. *Strait Is the Gate*. Translated from the French by Dorothy Bussy. New York: Knopf, 1945.

————. *Travels in the Congo*. Translated from the French by Dorothy Bussy. New York: Modern Age Books, 1933.

Bought after 1940.

————. *Voyage au Congo, suivi du Retour du Tchad*. Illus. de Soixante-quartre Photographies. Inedites de March Allegret. Paris: Gallimard, 1929.

No. 494 of a numbered edition; a gift from Gide.

In 1936, *International Literature* published excerpts from *The Fruits of the Earth* in May, "An Encounter" in April and "In Defence of Culture" in August and these were available to Wright early. In an interview by Frederic Stane (*Gavroche*, June 20, 1946), Wright mentions *Travels in the Congo* as a favorite of his.

In another interview, Wright was asked: "Which French writers do you prefer? Classics or modern writers?" "I like Maupassant, Proust, Gide very much and mostly that wonderful Malraux. And I have the pleasure of knowing——and appreciating——Sartre and Simone de Beauvoir." ("Richard Wright à Paris," interview by Maurice Fleurent, *Paru*, no. 25, December 1946, p. 8. Transl. M. Fabre)

G I E D I O N, Sigfried. *Mechanization Takes Command: A Contribution to Anonymous History*. New York: Oxford University Press, 1948.

————. *Space, Time, and Architecture: The Growth of a New Tradition*. Cambridge Mass: Harvard University Press; London: H. Milford, Oxford University Press, 1947.

G I L B E R T, Douglas. *Lost Chords: The Diverting Story of American Popular Songs*. New York: Doubleday, Doran & Co., 1942.

GILBERT, William S. See SULLIVAN, Arthur S.

GILES, Janice Holt.

On April 1, 1945, Wright read Giles's *The Land Beyond the Mountains* and found it verbose (Unpublished journal).

GOBINEAU, Joseph A., comte de. *The Renaissance: Savonarola—Cesare Borgia—Julius II—Leo X—Michael Angelo.* 2d ed. London: G. Allen & Unwin, 1927.

Bought used in Paris, 300F.

GOEBBELS, Joseph. *The Goebbels Diaries, 1942–1943.* Edited by Louis P. Lochner. Garden City, N.Y.: Doubleday, 1948.

GOETHE, Johann Wolfgang.

Faust is quoted in epigraph to *Savage Holiday,* Part II.

GOETSCH, Wilhelm. *The Ants.* Translated by Ralph Manheim. Ann Arbor: University of Michigan Press, 1957.

GOGOL, Nicholas. *Dead Souls.* With an Introduction by Clifford Odets. New York: Modern Library, 1936.

Bought after 1940.

GOLD, Michael. *The Hollow Men.* New York: International Publishers, 1941.

———. *Jews Without Money.* Woodcuts by Howard Simon. New York: H. Liveright, 1930.

Bought at a reduced price, $1.00.

See also HICKS, Granville.

GOLDBERG, Isaac. *The Man Mencken: A Biographical and Critical Survey.* New York: Simon & Schuster, 1925.

Bought used after 1940, $1.00.

GOLDEN, Harry. *Only in America.* Foreword by Carl Sandburg. Cleveland: World Pub. Co., 1958.

GOLDING, William. *Pincher Martin.* New York: Capricorn Books, 1956.

GOLL, Clair. *My Sentimental Zoo: Animal Stories.* Translated by May de Huyn. Decorated by Paul McPharlin. Mount Vernon, N.Y.: Peter Pauper Press, 1942.

Inscribed: "To Richard Wright,/a great writer with a great heart./Claire Goll."

——— and GOLL, Yvan. *Love Poems.* With 8 Drawings by Marc Chagall. Brooklyn: Hemispheres, 1947.

Inscribed: "To Dick and Ellen,/the true lovers. From Claire and Yvan,/their true friends."

GOLL, Yvan. See GOLL, Clair.

GOLLOMB, Joseph.

Wright notes in his 1945 diary that he bought his *Up at City High* on March 22.

GONCHAROV, Ivan A. *Oblomov*. Translated and with an Introduction by David Magarshack. Harmondsworth, Middlesex; New York: Penguin Books, 1954.

GOODE, William J. *Religion Among the Primitives*. With an Introduction by Kingsley Davis. Glencoe, Ill.: Free Press, 1951.

GOODMAN, Ellen. *Race Awareness in Young Children*. Cambridge, Mass.: Addison-Wesley, 1952.

GOODMAN, Paul. *Kafka's Prayer*. New York: Vanguard Press, 1947.

Bought in Paris, 400F.

GORER, Geoffrey. *Africa Dances: A Book about West African Negroes*. Harmondsworth, Middlesex; New York: Penguin Books, 1945.

——. *The Americans: A Study in National Character*. London: Cresset Press, 1948.

Galignani, Paris, sticker.

——. *Life and Ideas of the Marquis de Sade*. [Enl. and rev. ed.] London: Peter Owen, 1953.

GORKY, Maxim [pseud.]. *Bystanders*. Translated from the Russian by Bernard Guilbert Guerney. New York: Literary Guild, 1930.

Bought after 1940.

——. *Culture and the People*. New York: International Publishers, 1939.

——. *Decadence*. Translated from the Russian by Veronica Dewey. New York: R. H. McBride Co., 1927.

Belonged to A. J. Aaron, Butler, Pa.

"Maxim Gorky, shortly before he died, coined a phrase to contain what he thought writers of the Left should be; Gorky thought that they should be 'engineers of the human soul.' " ("Writing from the Left," *Biblio.*, p. 170, U 74, Wright Misc. 812, pp. 8–9)

"Gorky represents to me a writer and artist whose courage and humanity towered above politics." (Interview in *L'Express*, Oct. 15, 1955, p. 5.)

See also ZHDANOV, A.

GOURDON, Françoise.

Wright wrote an introduction to her novel, *Tant qu'il aura la peur* (Paris: Flammarion, 1961, p. 1–3) shortly before he died.

See APPENDIX, pp. 203–6.

G O W, James. See D'USSEAU, Arnaud.

G R A E M E, Bruce [pseud.]. *Passion, Murder, and Mystery.* London: Hutchinson & Co., 1928.

Mistral, Paris, 350F

G R A F, Oskar M. *Prisoners All.* Translated from the German by Margaret Green. New York City: [O. M. Graf], 1943.

G R A H A M, Shirley and LIPSCOMB, George D. *Dr. George Washington Carver, Scientist.* Illustrated by Elton C. Fax. New York: J. Messner, 1944.

Inscribed: "To Richard Wright, / with sincere admiration, / Shirley Graham"

G R A V E S, Alonzo. *The Eclipse of a Mind.* New York: Medical Journal Press, 1942.

Inscribed: "To Richard Wright / with kindest compliments / from alias Alonzo Graves. / March, 1943."

G R A Y S O N, Charles, ed. *Half-a-Hundred Tales, Tales by Great American Writers.* Philadelphia: Blackiston, 1945.

Includes "Almos' a Man."

G R E E N, Julian. *The Closed Garden.* Translated from the French by Henry Longan Stuart. With an Introduction by André Maurois. New York, London: Harper & Bros., 1928.

Ricour, Paris, sticker.

G R E E N, Paul.

Hymn to the Rising Sun, published first in *New Theatre* (January 1936), was rehearsed by the Negro Unit of the Federal Theatre in Chicago, where Wright was employed in 1936. Because of his admiration for that play, he agreed to write the adaptation of *Native Son* with Paul Green in 1940. See FABRE, 137.

"I urged that our first offering [at the Chicago Negro Federal Theatre Unit] should be a bill of three one-act plays, including Paul Green's *Hymn to the Rising Sun,* a grim, poetical powerful one-acter dealing with chain-gang conditions in the South." (*American Hunger,* Harper, 1978, p. 114.)

Concerning the censorship and closing of the Federal Negro Theatre production of the play, see Wright's unpublished article, "Hymn to the Sinking Sun," *Biblio.,* U 53, p. 146.

". . . one of the straightest and most realistic plays of Negro life written by a white man was written by him, *Hymn to the Rising Sun.*" (Wright to Paul Reynolds, May 18, 1940)

GREENE, Graham. *Brighton Rock*. London and Paris: The Albatross, 1939.
 Bought used in Paris.
——. *England Made Me*. [Uniform ed.]. London: Heinemann, 1951.
——. *Gun for Sale, An Entertainment*. London: W. Heinemann, 1950.
——. *The Heart of the Matter*. London: J. Cape, 1948.
——. *Journey Without Maps*. 2d ed. London: W. Heinemann, 1950.
——. *The Lawless Roads*. Harmondsworth, Middlesex; New York: Penguin Books, 1947.
——. *The Ministry of Fear, A Novel*. New York: Penguin, 1946.
——. *The Power and the Glory*. London: Heinemann, 1950.
——. *The Quiet American*. London: W. Heinemann, 1955.
——. *Stamboul Train, An Entertainment*. [The Uniform Edition of Graham Greene's Works, 2]. London: Heinemann, 1950.
GREENWALD, Harold. *The Call Girl: A Social and Psychoanalytic Study*. London: Elek Books, 1958.
GREGORY, Horace. *Pilgrim of the Apocalypse: A Critical Study of D. H. Lawrence*. New York: Viking, 1933.
GREINER, Samuel. *Prelude to Sanity*. Ft. Lauderdale, Fla.: Master Publications, 1943.
GRENE, Marjorie. *Dreadful Freedom, A Critique of Existentialism*. Chicago: University of Chicago Press, 1948.
 Copy from the American Library in Paris.
GRIERSON, John. *Grierson on Documentary*. Edited by Forsyth Hardy. London: Collins, 1946.
 Bought used.
GRIGGS, Irwin. See KERN, Joseph D.
GRODDECK, Georg W. *The Book of the It*. London: Vision, 1950.
——. *Exploring the Unconscious*. London: Vision, 1950.
——. *The Unknown Self*. London: Vision, 1951.
——. *The World of Man*. London: Vision, 1952.
GUERARD, Albert J., Jr. *Joseph Conrad*. Directions, 1. New York: New Directions, 1947.
GUÉRIN, Daniel. *Negroes on the March: A Frenchman's Report on the American Negro Struggle*. London: New Park Publications; New York: American distributor, G. L. Weiss, 1956.
 Wright answered Guérin's questions during the preparation of the book, read the manuscript, and gave advice.

He supported Guérin when the U.S. government refused to grant him an entry visa.

GUEST, Daniel. *A Textbook of Dialectical Materialism.* With a Foreword by H. Levy. New York: International Publishers, 1939.

GUNN, Neil.

In mid-March 1945, Wright wrote a report on her book, *The Silver Darlings* (1945), for the Book-of-the-Month Club. He liked the book.

See *Biblio.,* p. 173, U 89

GUNTHER, John. *Inside Africa.* London: Hamish Hamilton, 1955.

———. *Inside U.S.A.* New York: Harper & Bros., 1947.

Wright did a review of *Inside U.S.A.* but it was never published.

See *Biblio.,* p. 173, U 87

See APPENDIX, p. 206.

——— and QUINT, Bernard. *Days to Remember: America, 1945–1955.* New York: Harper, 1956.

H

HAAS, Robert B. and GALLUP, Donald B., comps. *A Catalogue of the Published and Unpublished Writings of Gertrude Stein, Exhibited in the Yale Library, 22 February to 29 March 1941.* New Haven: Yale University Press, 1941.

A gift from Carl Van Vechten in 1945. Wright made pencil checks in front of the titles of the books he owned.

HACKETT, Clarence B. [Ten original etchings for *Native Son*, 1942.]

HAECKER, Theodor. *Kierkegaard the Cripple.* Translated by C. Van O. Bruyn. With an Introduction by A. Dru. London: The Harvill Press, 1948.

Galignani, Paris sticker.

HALL, Wynyard M. *The Great Drama of Kumasi.* With a Foreword by Field-Marshal Sir Cyril Deverell. London: Putnam, 1939.

HALLIDAY, James L. *Mr. Carlyle, My Patient: A Psychosomatic Biography.* London: Heinemann, 1949.

HALPER, Albert, ed. *This Is Chicago: An Anthology.* New York: Holt, 1952.

Includes an excerpt of *Native Son.*

HAMMETT, Dashiell.

In his 1945 diary Wright mentions buying the following titles: *Blood Money* (25¢), *The Dain Curse* (25¢), *Red Harvest* (25 ¢), *The Glass Key* (50¢), *The Maltese Falcon* (25¢), *A Man Called Spade* (25¢), and *The Thin Man* (25¢).

HAMSUN, Knut. *Growth of the Soil.* Translated from the Norwegian by W. W. Worster. 2 vols. New York: Grosset & Dunlap, 1926.

Bought after 1940 for 50¢.

———. *Hunger.* Translated from the Norwegian by George Egerton [pseud.]. With an Introduction by Edwin Björkman. New York: Grosset & Dunlap, 1924.

Bought on June 10, 1945.

HANSEN, Harry, ed. *O. Henry Memorial Award Prize Stories of 1938.* New York: Doubleday, Doran & Co., 1938.
Includes "Fire and Cloud."
———. *O. Henry Memorial Award Prize Stories of 1940.* New York: Doubleday, Doran & Co., 1940.
Includes "Almos' a Man."
HARDY, Thomas. *Far from the Madding Crowd.* Chicago: Conkey, n.d.
Bought before 1940, 5¢.
———. *The Return of the Native.* Edited with an Introduction and Notes by J. W. Cunliffe. New York, Chicago: C. Scribner's Sons, 1917.
Bought before 1940, 15¢.
———. *Tess of the d'Urbervilles, A Pure Woman Faithfully Presented.* London: Macmillan, 1957.
———. *Two on a Tower.* Conkey, n.d.
Bought before 1940, 5¢.
HARNEY, William E.
Taboo. With an Introduction by Professor A. P. Elkin. 2d ed. Sydney: Australasian Publishing Co., 1944.
HARPER, Frances Ellen.
Frances Ellen Harper's poem "Bury Me in a Free Land" is quoted in "The Literature of the Negro in the United States":

Make me a grave where'er you will
In a lowly plain, or a lofty hill

. . . . . .

I could not rest if around my grave
I heard the steps of a trembling slave, etc.

(8 lines in all, in *White Man, Listen!,* p. 117)
HARPER, Ralph. *Existentialism, a Theory of Man.* Cambridge: Harvard University Press, 1948.
HARRIS, Frank. *The Man Shakespeare and His Tragic Life Story.* London: F. Palmer, 1909.
———. *My Life and Loves.* 4 vols. Paris: Obelisk Press, 1934?
HARRIS, Sara. See MURTAGH, John M.
HART, Henry, ed. *American Writers' Congress.* New York: International Publishers, 1935.
HAWTHORNE, Nathaniel. *The Scarlet Letter.* Stockholm: Continental Book Co., 1946.

"Hawthorne posed the problem of evil, of those whom society has branded." ("Personalism" [1935–37?], *Biblio.*, p. 167, U 62.)

H A Y, John Milton.
Wright alludes to *The Bread-winners* (1884) in a 1937 lecture on American literature.

H A Y D E N, Robert E.
Twenty lines of "Gabriel" are quoted in "The Literature of the Negro in the United States" as an example of lyrical but bitter protest, expressed through the imagined testimony of the dying leader of a slave rebellion. See *White Man, Listen!*, p. 143.

H A Y E S, Dorsha [Mrs. Doris Bentley].
Wright wrote a comment on *Who Walk with the Earth* (New York: Harper, 1945), which was printed on the dust jacket.

"Dorsha Hayes handles a memorable situation with a notable degree of narrative and dramatic power. She confronts a daring and crudely individualistic East Side labor leader with a sensitive and naive Boston boy who wants to change the world, and the sparks that fly from their clash will shower upon many people. Dorsha Hayes grapples with a big and important theme and wrings from it a meaning and message that should command a wide attention. She hits hard and true." Blurb for *Who Walk with the Earth* (1945), *Biblio.*, p. 50, 1945–10.

In his journal for February 21, 1945, he noted that Hayes's book became weaker when it turned into a love story as one reached the last third of it.

H E A L Y, Anne P. *Mady: A Novel of a Negro Girl's Search for Security.* New York: Exposition Press, 1962.
Inscribed: "To Mr. Richard Wright, / from an old admirer, / Sincerely, / Anne Healy"

H E A R D, Gerald. *The Riddle of the Flying Saucers. Is Another World Watching?* London: Carroll & Nicholson, 1950.

H E G E L, Georg Wilhelm Friedrich. *Hegel's Science of Logic.* Translated by W. H. Johnston and L. G. Struthers. With an Introductory Preface by Viscount Haldane of Cloan. 2 vols. London: G. Allen & Unwin, 1929.

———. *The Logic of Hegel.* Translated from the *Encyclopaedia of Social Sciences* by William Wallace. 2d ed., rev. and augm. London: Oxford University Press, H. Milford, 1892.
Bought after 1940.

———. *The Phenomenology of Mind.* Translated with an Introduc-

tion and Notes, by J. B. Vaillie. 2d ed., rev. and cor. throughout.
London: G. Allen & Unwin; New York: Macmillan Co., 1931.
Bought almost new after 1940.

H E I D B R E D E R, Edna. *Seven Psychologies.* New York, London:
The Century Co., 1933.
Bought after 1940.

H E I D E G G E R, Martin. *Existence and Being.* With an Introduction
by Werner Brock. London: Vision Press, 1949.
Ordered for Wright by Sylvia Beach in May 1949.
"I've read Heidegger and Jaspers . . . I'm not an existentialist,
but I'm interested—together with Kafka's *Metamorphosis.* . . . "
(Interview by Fernanda Pivano, *Avanti,* May 19, 1948.)
Mentioned among Cross Damon's reading in *The Outsider.*

H É L I O N, Jean. *They Shall Not Have Me (Ils ne m'auront pas): The
Capture, Forced Labor, and Escape of a French Prisoner of War.*
New York: E. P. Dutton, 1943.
Wright was an acquaintance of the French painter who may have
given him his narrative of captivity and escape.

H E L L E R, Erich. *The Disinherited Mind: Essays in Modern German
Literature and Thought.* Cambridge [Eng]: Bowes & Bowes, 1952.

H E L L M A N, Lillian. *The Children's Hour.* New York: A. A. Knopf,
1934.
Bought used after 1940.

H E M I N G W A Y, Ernest. *Death in the Afternoon.* London: Jonathan
Cape, 1952.

———. *For Whom the Bell Tolls.* New York: Scribners, 1945.
Mistral, Paris, stamp.

———. *Men Without Women.* Sun Rise Edition, vol. 3. New York:
Scribners, 1927.
50¢

———. *The Old Man and the Sea.* London: Jonathan Cape, 1952.

———. *The Short Stories of Ernest Hemingway: The First Forty-nine
Stories and the Play The Fifth Column.* New York: Modern Li-
brary, 1927.
Bought on December 28, 1945.

———. *The Sun Also Rises.* Introduction by Henry Seidel Canby. New
York: Modern Library, 1926.

———. In his 1945 diary Wright mentions buying *In Our Time* on
June 10, 1945.

The Chicago Southside Writers' Club discussed Hemingway: "All of us young writers were influenced by Hemingway. . . . We liked the simple, direct way in which he wrote, but a great many of us wanted to write about social problems. . . . Hemingway's style is so concentrated upon naturalistic detail that there is no room for social comment." ("How Uncle Tom's Children Grew," *Columbia University Writers Club Bulletin*, 2 May, 1938, p. 18.)

Wright had already read Hemingway [*A Farewell to Arms* (?)] at the Chicago Post Office (*Book-of-the-Month Club News*, February 1940, p. 4).

"Ernest Hemingway, looking in person like a retired Illinois business man, brought vivid word-pictures of battles between the loyalists and fascists in Spain. For once disdaining his favorite mode of understatement, Hemingway openly branded fascism as a bully and a bluff. . . . [He] cited in dramatic detail how the trained fascist armies of Germany and Italy were beaten to a standstill time and again on the battlefields of Spain. It was the first time the sensitive and legendary Hemingway had ever faced an audience from a platform, and his determination to tell the truth about fascism was apparent in his impassioned sincerity." ("The Barometer Points to Storm," *Biblio.*, p. 164, U 45, Wright Misc. 271, p. 2.)

"American literature now offers a desolating panorama. It is full of mystics and psychoanalysts. We are going through a crisis; there is no one who deserves the respect and the universal consideration due to great values. . . . The best: Hemingway. . . . I am of Malraux's opinion: the writer in my country is fundamentally a designer of plots. Generally he does not deal with ideas, but with images and feelings." (Interview by R. A. Castro, *Vea y Lea*, October 1949, transl. M. Fabre)

Hemingway's depiction of bullfights is mentioned in *Pagan Spain*, 193, 174.

See APPENDIX, pp. 207–8.

Wright commented on *To Have and Have Not* in notes for a lecture on left-wing literature in 1940.

HENRY, O. [William Sydney Porter]. *The Best Short Stories of O. Henry.* Selected, and with an Introduction, by Bennett A. Cerf and Van H. Cartmell. New York: The Modern Library, 1945.

Ricour, Paris, stamp.

HERNDON, Angelo. *Let Me Live.* New York: Random House, 1937.

Bought before 1940.

HERODOTUS. *The Histories*. Newly Translated and with an Introduction by Aubrey de Selincourt. Harmondsworth, Middlesex; Baltimore: Penguin Books, 1954.

HERSKOVITS, Melville J. *The Myth of the Negro Past*. New York, London: Harper & Bros., 1941.

HEYWARD, DuBose. *Porgy*. New York: Modern Library, 1934.

HICKS, Granville et al., eds. *Proletarian Literature in the United States: An Anthology*. Edited by Granville Hicks, Joseph North, Michael Gold, Paul Peters, Isidore Schneider [and] Alan Calmer. With a Critical Introduction by Joseph Freeman. New York: International Publishers, 1935.

Includes Wright's poem "Between the World and Me."

HILER, Hilaire; MILLER, Henry; and SAROYAN, William. *Why Abstract?* New York: J. Laughlin, 1951. "A new directions book."

HIMES, Chester B. *Lonely Crusade*. New York: A. A. Knopf, 1947. (Agent's copy)

Inscribed: "To Ellen Wright and Helene Bokanowski. / Author's regards"

———. *The Primitive*. A Signet Book, 1264. New York: New American Library, 1956.

Inscribed: "For Richard Wright/—a great writer and as great a man/—a true pioneer in both literature and life, / whom I am proud to call my friend. / Chester. Paris, 1956."

———. *The Third Generation*. Cleveland: World Pub. Co., 1954.

Himes is mentioned in *White Man, Listen!*

Wright wrote a review of *If He Hollers Let Him Go* (1945) in "Two Novels of the Crushing of Men, One White, One Black," *P.M. Magazine*, Nov. 25, 1945, p. m7–m8. (*Biblio.*, p. 170, U 75). He also wrote a blurb for *Lonely Crusade* (1947) and an introduction to *La Croisade de Lee Gordon* (Paris: Corréa, 1952), its French translation.

APPENDIX, pp. 208–13.

On their friendship, see Fabre, 290–91, 471–72. See also HIMES in *The Quality of Hurt* and *My Life of Absurdity*.

HITLER, Adolf. *Mein Kampf*. Complete and Unabridged, Fully Annotated. Editorial Sponsors: John Chamberlain, Sidney B. Fay [and others]. New York: Reynal & Hitchcock, 1941.

"Hitler has admirably analyzed this resistance *to my plan* [replaced by 'the ? nature of the Negro'] in his notable work, *Mein*

Kampf.[7] [Note 7: *Mein Kampf,* pp. 639–40, op. cit.]" ("Let's Eat the Niggers," *Biblio.,* p. 168, U 65.)

"We are in a race with fate and disaster. One nation after another is falling to the Nazis, who today possess the offensive. The issues and the ground of struggle are being stated and projected by men who are destructionists, men who will use any scheme to enlist the loyalties and sympathies of men. Are we Communist writers to be confined merely to the political and economic spheres of reality and leave the dark and hidden places of the human personality to the Hitlers and Goebbels? I refuse to believe such. Hitler yells about 'strength through joy, organic satisfactions,' 'the organic state,' 'a solidarity of ideals,' etc. Well, the old fascist butcher in Berlin has some good points, but he is twisting them for his own bloody ends. And, unfortunately, there are millions of Bigger Thomases in all lands with starved bodies and sensibilities who will follow the Hitlers. The Nazi movement in Germany proves it. I, for one, am not going to leave the field to Hitler and his cohorts. Not to plunge into the complex jungle of human relationships and analyze them is to leave the field to the fascists and I won't and can't do that. If I should follow Ben Davis's advice and write of Negroes through the lens of how the Party views them in terms of political theory, I'd abandon the Bigger Thomases. I'd be tacitly admitting that they are lost to us, that fascism will triumph, because it alone can enlist the allegiance of those millions whom capitalism has crushed and maimed. No! I say, wherever the fascists go with their doctrines, I go. Wherever they seek to claim the souls of men with their rot and noise, I, too, make my claim. Paraphrasing Walt Whitman: 'Not until the sun excludes Bigger Thomas, will I exclude him.'" (Letter to Mike Gold, May 1940.)

"Hitler saw and cynically exploited the weak spots in our society perhaps more clearly than any politician of modern times." On Hitler as a social critic see "Introduction" to *Black Metropolis,* by St. Clair Drake and Horace Cayton (New York: Harcourt, Brace, 1945), pp. xxiv–xxv, xxvi–xxvii.

H O G B E N, Lancelot. *Mathematics for the Million: A Popular Self Educator.* Illustrated by J. F. Horrabin. London: Allen & Unwin, 1947.

H O L T, Rackham. *George Washington Carver: An American Biography.* Garden City, N.Y.: Doubleday, Doran & Co., 1943.

H O R N E, Frank.

Five lines of "Nigger" are quoted in "The Literature of the Negro in the United States" as an image by the black man of himself, seen through white eyes in "a mood of self-laceration." See *White Man, Listen!,* p. 141.

H O R T O N, George M.
George Horton's life story is briefly recalled in "The Literature of the Negro in the United States." Eight lines are quoted from his "On Liberty and Slavery":

Alas! and am I born for this,
to wear this slavish chain?
Deprived of all created bliss,
Through hardship, toil and pain!
. . . .
Oh, Heaven! and is there no relief
This side the silent grave—
To soothe the pain—to quell the grief
And anguish of a slave?

Horton is seen as having somewhat broken away from his culture, as a "split man." *White Man, Listen!*, pp. 116–17.

H O U S M A N, A. E. *A Shropshire Lad.* Illustrated by Elinore Blaisdell. New York: Concord Books, 1932.
Bought used.

H O Y L E, Fred, Sir. *The Nature of the Universe: A Series of Broadcast Lectures.* Oxford: Blackwell, 1950.

H U D S O N, W. H. *Green Mansions: A Romance of the Tropical Forest.* With an Introduction by John Galsworthy. New York: A. A. Knopf, 1927.

H U G H E S, Dorothy B. *Mystery Reader, Containing Two Complete Novels: "The So Blue Marble," and "The Fallen Sparrow."* Cleveland: World Pub. Co., 1944.

H U G H E S, Langston. *The Dream Keeper and Other Poems.* With Illustrations by Helen Sewell. New York: Alfred A. Knopf, 1945.

———. *Simple Speaks His Mind.* New York: Simon and Schuster, 1950.
Mistral, Paris, stamp.

———. *The Weary Blues.* With an Introduction by Carl Van Vechten. New York: Alfred A. Knopf, 1945.

——— and BONTEMPS, Arna, eds. *The Book of Negro Folklore.* New York: Dodd, Mead, 1958.
Inscribed: "To Dick Wright-/A souvenir of my first visit to Paris/ which he helped to make memorable./ Arna and Alberta./29 Sept. 1960."

——— and ———. *The Poetry of the Negro, 1746–1949: An Anthology.* Garden City, N.Y.: Doubleday, 1949.

Wright lectured on Hughes's *The Weary Blues* and *The Ways of White Folks* (1934) as early as November 1934 at the Indianapolis John Reed Club.

Wright attended a performance by the Harlem Suitcase Theatre of Langston Hughes's *Don't You Want to Be Free?* on June 10, 1938. He reviewed *The Big Sea* (1940) twice: (1) "Forerunner and Ambassador," *The New Republic*, 103 (Oct. 24, 1940), 600; and (2) Chicago *News*, Dec. 4, 1940, p. 10. He refused to review *I Wonder as I Wander* (1956), which he didn't like.

"What are in your opinion other Negro writers of high caliber?"
"There are many. Langston Hughes, Claude McKay, Countee Cullen and others of undoubtable value." ("Richard Wright à Paris," interview by Maurice Fleurent, *Paru*, no. 25, December 1946, p. 8. Transl. M. Fabre.)

"Langston Hughes' 'On the Way Home' gives us the portrait of a young Negro who receives news of his mother's imminent death. There are no racial overtones; it could have been any man lost and living alone in a great city. The young man cannot endure the thought of losing his mother, that mother who made him promise that he would never drink, for his father had died a drunkard. Thus, upon the news of his mother's death, the boy takes to the bottle, duplicating his father's drinking and falls under the influence of a prostitute, thereby finding another mother and another home." ("Foreword to *Lest We Forget*," *Biblio.*, p. 175, U 94, Wright Misc. 456 [July 30, 1955])

Four lines of "Let America Be America Again . . ." are quoted in "The Literature of the Negro in the United States," followed by three lines from "Good morning, Revolution." Hughes's voice is one of the first "lyrical-sounding voices of the new period," dealing not in complaints and pleas but in demands and statements. See *White Man, Listen!*, p. 142.

See also DE CARAVA, Roy.

On their friendship, see Fabre, 57 *passim*.

See APPENDIX, pp. 213–16.

HUME, David. *An Abstract of A Treatise of Human Nature, 1740, a Pamphlet Hitherto Unknown*. Reprinted with an Introduction by J. P. Keynes and P. Sraffa. Cambridge [Eng.]: The University Press, 1938.

Bought remaindered in London for 4sh., 6.

HUMPHREYS, Christmas. *Zen Buddhism*. London: Allen & Unwin, 1957.

H U N E K E R, James. *Iconoclasts*. New York: Scribner, 1905?
Ricour, Paris, sticker.
———. *The Pathos of Distance: A Book of a Thousand and One Moments*. New York: C. Scribner's Sons, 1913.
Bought after 1940, $1.95.
———. *Steeplejack*. 2 vols. in 1. New York: Scribner, 1920.
Bought on December 9, 1945.
According to Jack Conroy, Wright must have read *Ivory Apes and Peacocks* by the late 1930s. Huneker is mentioned in *Black Boy.*
H U N T O N, William Alpheus. *Decision in Africa: Sources of Current Conflict*. New York: International Publishers, 1960.
H U R S T O N, Zora Neale.
Wright reviewed *Their Eyes Were Watching God* (1937) adversely in "Between Laughter and Tears," *New Masses,* 25 (Oct. 5, 1937), 22–25.

"Zora Neale Hurston's 'The Gilded Six-Bits' shows how a black man, living in that same No Man's Land, rides out the affront to his manhood and resumes living, accepting a sexual violation of his wife as a temporary and unimportant matter. In this man Africa lingers on in America. . . ." ("Foreword to *Lest We Forget*," Biblio., p. 175, U 94, Wright Misc. 456 [1955])

"A few years ago, the Negro woman writer, Zora Neale Hurston wrote an article which was published in the *American Mercury* under the title 'The Pet Nigger System.' The late Miss Hurston, with admirable honesty, described how American whites, spurred by guilt, would select an individual Negro for special attention and friendship." ("The Position of the Negro Artist and Intellectual in American Society," Biblio., p. 168, U 63, Wright Misc. 622, p. 6 [1960]).

See APPENDIX, pp. 250–51.
H U S S E R L, Edmund.
In 1947, Wright had a copy of Husserl's *Ideas: General Introduction to Pure Phenomenology* (1931) rebound in black leather so that he could take it wherever he went.

"The last point I'd like to touch upon is something that came out of Europe, out of Germany and France, and that is the phenomenology of Sartre, Husserl, and others. William James as much as any of the Europeans called our attention to the fact that we could view the world as innocent people, and Husserl developed a method to make the world be for us something that we could not 'let be,' something that we could contemplate." (Notes for a lecture in Bandung, 1955.)

Husserl is mentioned among Cross Damon's reading in *The Out-sider. Ideas* is quoted as epigraph to *Black Power,* Part III, "The Brooding Ashanti."

HUXLEY, Aldous. *Brave New World.* The Vanguard Library, no. 2. London: Vanguard Press, 1952.

I

IBSEN, Henrik. *Works*. One Vol. Ed. New York: Black's Readers Service, 1928.
Bought in Chicago in 1932.
IDDON, Don. *Don Iddon's America*. Edited by Charles Sutton. With a Preface by Sir Alan Herbert. Illustrated by Trog. London: Falcon Press, 1951.
Bought in Paris, 860F.
ILLINOIS LABOR NOTES. (National Research League. Chicago Chapter). 4, no. 3 (March 1936).
This is a special issue devoted to the National Negro Congress held in Chicago. Wright wrote a "Foreword" for the issue.
See *Biblio.*, p. 3, 1936–4 JWJ Wright Misc. 377.
INMAN, Mary. *In Woman's Defence*. Los Angeles: The Committee to Organize the Advancement of Women, 1940.
INTERNATIONAL LITERATURE. (International Union of Revolutionary Writers).
Wright had the few issues of the magazine to which he contributed poetry (1934–36).
INTRO. Vol. 1, no. 3–4, 1951.
IRVING, Washington. *Tales of the Alhambra*. With an Introduction and Notes by Ricardo Villa-Real. Granada: Editorial Padre Suarez, 1950.
ISHERWOOD, Christopher. *Prater Violet*. 2d ed. New York: Random House, 1944.
"Yes, I've got *Prater Violet;* I've not read it but hope to during the holidays." (To Carl Van Vechten, December 20, 1945)

J

JACKS, Lawrence P. *The Revolt Against Mechanism.* Hibbert Lectures, 1933. London: G. Allen & Unwin, 1934.
Bought after 1940.
JACKSON, Joseph Henry, ed. *The Portable Murder Book.* Selected and Introduced by Joseph Henry Jackson. New York: Viking Press, 1945.
JACOB, Lewis. *The Rise of the American Film: A Critical History.* New York: Harcourt, Brace & Co., 1939.
Bought after 1940.
JAMES, C. L. R.
Wright read *The Black Jacobins* (1938) in 1951, when he was thinking of writing on Toussaint L'Ouverture. He quoted *The Black Jacobins* to emphasize the importance of L'Ouverture in Haitian history when he sought to induce the Secretary of the Embassy of Yugoslavia in Paris to help him with a film on L'Ouverture. (To Streten Maric, October 12, 1950).
JAMES, Henry. *The Ambassadors.* New York: Harper & Bros., 1902?
Bought after 1940.
———. *The American.* London: Nelson, n.d.
Bought after 1940.
———. *The Art of the Novel, Critical Prefaces.* With an Introduction by Richard P. Blackmur. New York, London: C. Scribner's & Sons, 1934.
Acquired before 1940.
———. *Daisy Miller.* New York: Mentor Books, 1947.
———. *The Portrait of a Lady.* New York Public Library copy. (Last stamped: October 25, 1936)
———. *The Tragic Muse.* London: Rupert Hart-Davis, 1948.
———. *The Two Magics; The Turn of the Screw; Covering End.* New York: Macmillan, 1929.
New York Library copy acquired before 1940.

―――. *The Wings of the Dove.* New York: Modern Library, 1946.
Wright was fond of discussing *The Portrait of a Lady, Daisy Miller,* and *Roderick Hudson* with Joyce Gourfain around 1935– 37 in Chicago.
"Experiments in words, Stein; experiments in dialogues, James; experiments in scenes, James; experiments in moods, Conrad." (Notes for a lecture)
In Chicago, when Wright wrote his first short stories around 1932–34, he noted that he took his cue from Henry James, especially from the technique of *The Awkward Age* so that his dialogue "should carry as heavy a burden of reference possible." He adapted the "lush prose" of Conrad to describe the landscape of the South and used it in his writing about poverty, death, fear, and hysteria in gloomy writings.

"Still another principle which writers subscribed to was the so-called dramatic present. . . . Henry James brought this principle to its highest point of perfection. In order to show the character's past life and still maintain that illusion of the present, they introduced the principle of foreshortening, which they borrowed from painting, the stage, music." ("Lecture on Proletarian Literature," p. 20)

"Henry James and Nathaniel Hawthorne complained bitterly about the bleakness and flatness of the American scene. But I think that if they were alive, they'd feel at home in modern America. . . . We do have in the Negro the embodiment of a past tragic enough to appease the spiritual hunger of even a James; and we have in the oppression of the Negro a shadow athwart our national life dense and heavy enough to satisfy even the gloomy broodings of a Hawthorne. And if Poe were alive, he would not have to invent horror; horror would invent him." ("How 'Bigger' Was Born," *Saturday Review of Literature,* June 1, 1940, p. 20.)

JAMES, William. *On Vital Reserves; The Energies of Men; The Gospel of Relaxation.* New York: H. Holt, 1911?
Acquired after 1940.
―――. *The Philosophy of William James.* Selected from His Chief Works. With an Introduction by Horace M. Kallen. New York: Modern Library, n.d.
Bought on December 3, 1945.
―――. *A Pluralistic Universe: Hibbert Lectures at Manchester College on the Present Situation in Philosophy.* London: Longmans, Green & Co., 1890.
Bought used after 1940 for $2.00.

———. *Pragmatism; A New Name for Some Old Ways of Thinking: Popular Lectures on Philosophy.* London: Longmans, 1910. Librairie anglaise, Paris.

"The philosophies of William James and John Dewey, and all the pragmatists in between, are but intellectual labors to allay the anxieties of modern man; adjuration to the white men of the West to accept anxiety as a way of life, to live within the vivid, present moment and let the meaning of that moment suffice as a rationale of life and death." (Introduction to *Black Metropolis* by St. Clair Drake and Horace Cayton [New York: Harcourt, Brace, 1945], p. xxiii)

". . . white men once left the slumberous feudal world and eagerly took the risks of, as William James phrased it, an 'unguaranteed existence.'" (*Ibid.*, p. xxv)

"William James, in discussing the way in which the 'social self' of man exists in society, says: '. . . a man has as many social selves as there are individuals who recognize him and carry an image of him in their minds.' Then, in speculating upon what a man would feel if he were completely socially excluded, he says: 'No more fiendish punishment could be devised, were such a thing physically possible, than that one should be turned loose in society and remain absolutely unnoticed by all the members thereof. If no one turned round when we entered, answered when we spoke, or minded what we did, but if every person we met "cut us dead," and acted as if we were non-existent things, a kind of rage and impotent despair would ere long well up on us, from which the cruelest bodily tortures would be a relief; for these would make us feel that, however bad might be our plight, we had not sunk to such a depth as to be unworthy of attention at all.'"[1] (Note: *The Philosophy of William James,* Modern Library Edition, p. 128) 1 (*Ibid.*, p. xxxii)

J A N O U C H, Gustan. *Conversations With Kafka: Notes and Reminiscences.* With an Introduction by Max Brod. Translated by Goronwy Rees. London: D. Verschoyle, 1953.
J A S P E R S, Karl. *Man in the Modern Age.* Translated by Eden and Cedar Paul. London: G. Routledge & Sons, 1933.
   Bought after 1940.
———. *The Origin and Goal of History.* London: Routledge & K. Paul, 1953.
   Bought in Accra on July 30, 1953.
———. *The Perennial Scope of Philosophy.* Translated by Ralph Manheim. London: Routledge & K. Paul, 1950.

————. *Reason and Existenze: Five Lectures.* Translated with an Introduction by William Earle. London: Routledge, 1956.

————. *The Way to Wisdom: An Introduction to Philosophy.* Translated by Ralph Manheim. London: Gollancz, 1951.

JEFFERSON, Thomas.

"It has long been one of the basic tenets of our political faith that all powers that are not entrusted to Congress must reside in the people.[4] [Note 4: See the writings of Thomas Jefferson]" ("Let's Eat the Niggers," *Biblio.*, p. 168, U 65.)

JERVIS, William H. *A History of France from the Earliest Times to the End of the Great European War, 1918.* With Additional Chapters by W. J. N. Griffith. New and Rev. Ed. London: J. Murray, 1926.

Bought in Paris for 100F.

JESSUP, M. K., ed. *1956 UFO Annual.* London: Acre Publishers, 1957.

JÜNGER, Ernst. *On the Marble Cliffs, A Novel.* Translated from the German by Stuart Hood. London: J. Lemann, 1947.

JOHNSON, Charles S. *Growing Up in the Black Belt: Negro Youth in the Rural South.* Prepared for the American Youth Commission. Washington, D.C.: American Council on Education, 1941.

————. *Patterns of Negro Segregation.* New York, London: Harper & Bros., 1943.

————; EMBREE, Edwin R.; and ALEXANDER, W. W. *The Collapse of Cotton Tenancy: Summary of Field Studies & Statistical Surveys, 1933–1935.* Chapel Hill: University of North Carolina Press, 1935.

New York Public Library copy acquired after 1940.

JOHNSON, Fenton.

"Tired" by Fenton Johnson is quoted in "The Literature of the Negro . . ." as a testimony of the black man's dissatisfaction with American civilization. See *White Man, Listen!*, p. 138.

JOHNSON, James Weldon. *Black Manhattan.* New York: A. A. Knopf, 1940.

————. *God's Trombones: Seven Negro Sermons in Verse.* Drawings by Aaron Douglas. Lettering by C. B. Falls. New York: Viking Press, 1929.

Bought used in Paris.

Copy inscribed by Johnson to Violette Mura.

Wright reviewed *Black Manhattan* for the Chicago *News*, May
22, 1940, p. 10.
James Weldon Johnson is described, in "The Literature of the
Negro in the United States," as a conservative who neverthless con-
sistently fought lynchings. Thirteen lines of "Saint Peter Relates an
Incident" are quoted. See *White Man, Listen!*, pp. 135–36.
See APPENDIX, pp. 216–17.
J O L A S, Eugène. *Wanderpoem; Or, Angelic Metamorphosis of the
City of London.* [Paris]: Transition Press, 1946.
J O N E S, Ernest. *Hamlet and Oedipus.* London: Gollancz, 1949.
———. *On the Nightmare.* The International Psycho-analytic Library,
no. 20. London: The Hogarth Press and the Institute of Psycho-
analysis, 1949.
J O W I T T, William Allen Jowitt, 1st earl. *The Strange Case of Alger
Hiss.* London: Hodder and Stoughton, 1953.
Galignani, Paris, sticker.
J O Y C E, James. *Finnegans' Wake.* New York: Viking, 1939.
Bought after 1940.
———. *A Portrait of the Artist as a Young Man.* Introduction by Her-
bert Gorman. New York: Modern Library, 1928.
Bought after 1940.
———. *Stephen Hero: Part of the First Draft of "A Portrait of the
Artist as a Young Man."* Edited with an Introduction by Theodore
Spencer. London: Cape, 1944.
———. *Ulysses.* With a Foreword by Morris L. Ernst and the Decision
of the United States District Court Rendered by Judge John M.
Woolsey. New York: Modern Library, 1934.
Bought probably after 1940 since Wright said he borrowed it
from the Chicago Public Library in the 1930s.
"*Wasteland* by Jo Sinclair, has thrilled Richard Wright more than
anything he has read since Joyce's stories about Dublin." (*Time
Magazine*, February 18, 1946). "The Dead" in *Dubliners* certainly
influenced the end of "Bright and Morning Star" (See KENETH KIN-
NAMON, *The Emergence of Richard Wright*, Urbana: University of
Illinois Press, 1972, p. 116.)
J U N G, Carl G. *Modern Man in Search of a Soul.* London: Kegan
Paul, Trench, Trübner, 1933.
Bought used in Paris.
———. *Psychology of the Unconscious: A Study of the Transforma-*

tion and Symbolisms of the Libido. Authorized Translation with Introduction by Beatrice M. Hinkle. New York: Dodd, Mead, 1944.
Bought on February 13, 1945.
————. *The Undiscovered Self.* Translated from the German by R. F. C. Hull. New York: New American Library, 1959.
JUNKER, Buford H. See WARNER, W. Lloyd.

K

KAFKA, Franz. *The Castle.* With an Introduction by Thomas Mann. Translated from the German by Edwin and Willa Muir. New York: Knopf, 1946.

———. *The Country Doctor: A Collection of Short Stories.* Translated from the German and Illustrated in Black and White by Vera Leslie. Oxford: Counterpoint Publications, 1945.

———. *Diaries.* Edited by Max Brod. 2 vols. London: Secker & Warburg, 1948–49.

———. *A Franz Kafka Miscellany: Pre-fascist Exile.* [Rev. Enl. 2d ed.] New York: Twice a Year Press, 1946.

Wright mentions Kafka's hero, K., in *Black Boy,* comparing his ordeal with his own grandfather's quest for a pension; he mentions Kafka in his review of Michel Del Castillo, *The Disinherited* (Saturday Review, April 16, 1960).

———. *The Great Wall of China: Stories and Reflections.* Translated by Willa and Edwin Muir. New York: Schocken, 1946.

———. *The Metamorphosis.* New York: Vanguard Press, 1946.

———. *Selected Short Stories.* Translated by Willa and Edwin Muir. Introduction by Philip Rahv. New York: Modern Library, 1952.

KALAR, Joseph. See SPECTOR, Herman.

KAMPMEIER, Rudolph H. *The Essentials of Syphilology . . . with Chapters by Alvin Z. Keller and J. Cyril Peterson.* 2d ed. Oxford: Blackwell, 1946.

KARAKA, D. F. *Betrayal in India.* London: Gollancz, 1950.

KARPMAN, Ben. *Case Studies in the Psychopathology of Crime.* 3 vols. [Washington, D.C.: Printed by Mimeoform Press, 1944–48].

Inscribed: "To Dick Wright,/with deepest personal regards./Ben Karpman./August 1944."

———. *The Individual Criminal: Studies in the Psychogenetics of Crime.* Washington, D.C.: Neuroses and Mental Diseases Publications, 1940.

Inscribed: "To Richard Wright,/with kindest personal regards./ Ben Karpman."

KAUFMANN, Walter A., ed. *Existentialism from Dostoevsky to Sartre.* Edited with an Introduction, Prefaces, and New Translations. New York: Meridian Books, 1956.

KAZIN, Alfred. *On Native Grounds: An Interpretation of Modern American Prose Literature.* New York: Overseas Editions, 1942. Bought in Paris, 35F.

KEFAUVER, Estes. *Crime in America.* Edited and with an Introduction by Sidney Shalett. London: Landsborough Publications, 1958.

KERN, Joseph D. and GRIGGS, Irwin, eds. *This America.* New York: Macmillan, 1942.
Includes "Down by the Riverside."

KEROUAC, Jack. *On the Road.* New York: A Signet Book published by the New American Library, 1958.

KIELTY, Bernadine, ed. *A Treasury of Short Stories: Favorites of the Past Hundred Years from Turgenev to Thurber, from Balzac to Hemingway; With Biographical Sketches of the Authors.* New York: Simon & Schuster, 1947.
Includes "Almos' a Man."

KIERKEGAARD, Søren. *Attack Upon "Christendom," 1854– 1855.* Translated with an Introduction by Walter Lowrie. London: Geoffrey Cumberlege, Oxford University Press, 1946.

———. *The Concept of Dread.* Translated with Introduction and Notes by Walter Lowrie. Princeton: Princeton University Press, 1944.
Bought on June 11, 1945.

———. *Consider the Lilies: Being the Second Part of "Edifying Discourses in a Different Vein," Published in 1847 in Copenhagen.* Translated from the Danish by S. Aldworth and W. S. Ferrie. London: C. W. Daniel Co., 1940.

———. *Either/Or: A Fragment of Life.* Translated by David F. Swenson and Lillian Marvin Swenson. 2 vols. Princeton: Princeton University Press, 1946.

———. *Fear and Trembling: A Dialectical Lyric by Johannes de Silentio* [pseud.] Translated from the Danish by Robert Payne. Oxford: Oxford University Press, 1946.

———. *For Self Examination and Judge for Yourselves! And Three Discourses, 1851.* Translated by Walter Lowrie. Princeton: Princeton University Press; London: H. Milford, Oxford University Press, 1944.

———. *Kierkegaard's Concluding Unscientific Postscript.* Translated from the Danish by David F. Swenson, Completed after His Death and Provided with an Introduction and Notes by Walter Lowrie. Princeton: Princeton University Press for the American Scandanavian Foundation, 1944.

———. *Philosophical Fragments, Or, A Fragment of Philosophy by Johannes Climacus* [pseud.]. Responsible for publication, S. Kierkegaard. Translated from the Danish with Introduction and Notes by David F. Swenson. Princeton: Princeton University Press, 1946. Bought in London for 2 sh.

———. *The Point of View, Etc.; Including "The Point of View for My Work as an Author," "Two Notes about 'The Individual'" and "On My Work as an Author."* Translated, with Introduction and Notes, by Walter Lowrie. London, New York: Oxford University Press, 1939. Bought in Paris after 1940 for $2.50.

———. *Purify Your Hearts: A "Discourse for a Special Occasion,"* The First of Three "Edifying Discourses in a Different Vein," Published in 1847 at Copenhagen. Translated from the Danish by A. S. Aldworth and W. S. Ferrie. London: C. W. Daniel, 1937. Bought in London, 7 sh., 6

———. *Repetition: An Essay in Experimental Psychology.* Translated with an Introduction and Notes by Walter Lowrie. With a Bibliographical Essay: How Kierkegaard Got into English. Princeton: Princeton University Press, 1946.

———. *The Sickness Unto Death.* Translated with an Introduction by Walter Lowrie. Princeton: Princeton University Press, 1944.

———. *Stages on Life's Way.* Translated by Walter Lowrie. London: Oxford University Press, 1945.

———. *Training in Christianity and The Edifying Discourse Which "Accompanied" It.* Translated with an Introduction and Notes by Walter Lowrie. Princeton: Princeton University Press, 1944.

———. *Works of Love.* Translated from the Danish by David F. Swenson and Lillian Marvin Swenson. With an Introduction by Douglas V. Steere. Princeton: Princeton University Press, 1946.

Wright noted in his diary that he bought *Sickness Unto Death* on June 11, 1945.

The Concept of Dread is quoted as epigraph to *The Outsider,* Part I; and Kierkegaard is mentioned among the reading of Cross Damon in *The Outsider.* "I'm bringing a good deal of the work of Kierkegaard, English translations, of course. Also I'll bring Korzybski's *Science and Sanity.*" (To Gertrude Stein, March 15, 1946.)

KILLENS, John Oliver. *Youngblood.* New York: Pocket Books, 1955.

KING, Martin Luther, Jr. *Stride Toward Freedom: The Montgomery Story.* New York: Harper, 1958.
Inscribed: "To Richard Wright, / with best wishes / and warm personal regards. / Martin Luther King, Jr. / Feb. 7, 1959."
"Now, I don't agree all the way with King but I like and admire him, and above all he tells the truth." (To Paul R. Reynolds, Jr., March 2, 1959.)

KINGSTON, Charles. *Law-breakers.* London: John Lane, 1930.
Bought after 1940.

KINSEY, Alfred C.; POMEROY, Wardell B.; and MARTIN, Clyde E., eds. *Sexual Behavior in the Human Male.* Philadelphia: W. B. Saunders, 1948.

KIPLING, Rudyard. *Departmental Ditties, And Other Verses.* With Illustrations by Dudley Cleaver. London: G. Newnes, 1899.
Bought after 1940.

KLEIN, Melanie. *The Psycho-analysis of Children.* Authorized Translation by Alix Strachey. The International Psycho-analytical Library, no. 22. London: The Hogarth Press and the Institute of Psycho-analysis, 1950.

KLINEBERG, Otto, ed. *Characteristics of the American Negro.* New York, London: Harper & Bros., 1944.
See "Acknowledgements" in introduction to *White Man, Listen!.* Wright often met Klineberg in Paris.

KÖHLER, Wolfgang. *The Place of Value in a World of Facts.* New York: Liveright Publications, 1938.
Bought after 1940.
"I began reading Köhler's *The Place of Value in a World of Facts.* It starts hard and I must get used to the terminology." (Unpublished journal, September 6, 1947.)

KOESTLER, Arthur. *The Age of Liberty.* A Signet Giant, S985. New York: New American Library, 1953?
———. *Arrival and Departure.* London: Jonathan Cape, 1947.

————. *Darkness at Noon.* Translated by Daphne Hardy. New York: Macmillan, 1941.
  Bought used in 1942.
————. *The Yogi and the Commissar, and Other Essays.* New York: Macmillan, 1946.
  Ricour, Paris, stamp.
  Mentioned in review of Michel Del Castillo's *The Disinherited* (*Saturday Review,* April 16, 1960). Koestler was a contributor to *The God That Failed* (1949).
K O R N G O L D, Ralph. *Citizen Toussaint.* Boston: Little, Brown, 1944.
K O R Z Y B S K I, Alfred, count. *Science and Sanity: An Introduction to Non-Aristotelian Systems and General Semantics.* 2d ed. Lancaster, Pa.; New York: The International Non-Aristotelian Library Publishing Co., The Science Press Printing Co., distributors, 1941.
K O S S A, Ethol Sexton. See SEXTON, Ethol.
K O U P E R N I K, Cyrille. *L'Equilibre Mental.* La Maladie et nous, v. 1. [Nancy: Fayard, 1959].
  Inscribed: "A Richard Wright, / sans crainte de la concurrence / qu'il peut me faire / en tant que 'lay psychoanalyst' / et en témoignage de ma sincère affection."
K R A F F T - E B I N G, R. von. *Psychopathia Sexualis: With Especial Reference to the Antipathic Sexual Instinct; A Medico-Forensic Study.* Only Authorized English Adaptation of the 12th German Ed. by F. J. Rebman. London: Rebman, 1906.
  Bought in Paris, 1000F.
K R E Y, A. C. See SELLERY, C. G.
K R E Y M B O R G, Alfred. *Man and Shadow, An Allegory.* New York: E. P. Dutton, 1946.
————; MUMFORD, Lewis; and ROSENFELD, Paul, eds. *The New Caravan.* New York: W. W. Norton, 1936.
  Includes Wright's story "Big Boy Leaves Home."
K R O L L, Harry Harrison.
  Wright wrote a review of *I Was A Share-cropper* (1937). ("A Sharecropper's Story," *New Republic,* 93 [Dec. 1, 1937], 109.)
  See APPENDIX, pp. 218–19.
K R O P O T K I N, Petr A. *Memoirs of a Revolutionist.* Boston and New York: Houghton Mifflin, 1899.
  Bought used after 1940.
K R U E G E R, Kurt. *I Was Hitler's Doctor.* From the German. Fore-

word by Upton Sinclair. Introduction by Otto Strasser. Preface by
K. Arvid Enbind. New York: Biltmore Pub. Co., 1943.

KRUTCH, Joseph Wood.

Wright referred to "the tragic fallacy" alluding to a book by
Krutch in the late 1930s. The only written reference to Krutch is:
"The New Deal provided no certain solution for the American intellectuals, artists and students. Disillusioned and facing a future
that is wholly uncertain, they have manifested in their thought and
works of art a new degree of pessimism as will be seen in such
works as *The Modern Temper* (1929) by Joseph Wood Krutch and
The Disinherited by Jack Conroy." (Paper written for his old Jackson friend Essie Lee Ward for a sociology class in 1935.)

KUHN, Helmut. *Encounter with Nothingness, An Essay on Existentialism.* The Humanist Library, 11. Hinsdale, Ill.: Regnery, 1949.

L

LA FARGE, Oliver. *As Long as the Grass Shall Grow.* Photographs by Helen M. Post. New York, Toronto: Alliance Book Corp., Longmans, Green & Co., 1939.
> Used as a model for the format of *Twelve Million Black Voices.*

LAIRD, John. *Recent Philosophy.* Home University of Modern Knowledge, 181. London, New York: Oxford University Press, 1945.

LAMB, Charles. *Essays of Elia.* With Introduction and Notes by H. J. Robins. New York: Macmillan, 1907.
> Bought before 1940.

——— and LAMB, Mary. *Tales from Shakespeare.* London: Collins Clear-type Press, 190-?.
> Bought after 1940.

LAMB, Mary. See LAMB, Charles.

LAMMING, George. *The Emigrants.* New York: McGraw-Hill, 1955.
> Wright wrote an introduction to *In the Castle of My Skin* (New York: McGraw-Hill, 1953, ix-xii.) On his association with Lamming, see Fabre, 400–01.
> See APPENDIX, pp. 219–21.

LANGE, Johannes. *Crime and Destiny.* Translated by Charlotte Haldane. New York: C. Boni, 1930.
> Bought after 1940.

LANGER, Susanne K. *Philosophy in a New Key: A Study in the Symbolism of Reason, Rite, and Art.* New York: Penguin Books, 1948.

LARDNER, Ring W. *The Big Town; How I and the Mrs. Go to New York to See Life and Get Katie a Husband.* New York: Bantam Books, 1949.
> Mistral, Paris, stamp.

92   *Laski—Leeuw*

L A S K I, Harold J. *The American Presidency, An Interpretation*. New
York, London: Harper & Bros., 1940.
Ricour, Paris, sticker.
L A S K Y, Victor. See DE TOLEDANO, Ralph.
L A U X, John J. *Church History: A Complete History of the Catholic
Church to the Present Day*. New York: Benzinger Bros., 1932.
L A V I N E, Emanuel H. *Secrets of the Metropolitan Police*. Garden
City, N.Y.: Garden City Pub. Co., 1937.
Bought after 1940.
L A V R I N, Janko. *Dostoevsky, A Study*. London: Methuen, 1943.
Bought used.
———. *Nietzsche, An Approach*. London: Methuen, 1948.
Bought after 1940.
L A W R E N C E, D. H. *Aaron's Rod*. New York: T. Selzer, 1922.
Bought after 1940.
———. *D. H. Lawrence*. [Poems Selected from Mr. Lawrence's Two
Volumes *Love Poems* and *Amores*, by Humbert Wolfe. London:?
Benn, 1932].
———. *Fantasia of the Unconscious*. New York: A & C Boni, 1930.
Bought after 1940.
———. *The Fox*. Penguin Books, Hammondsworth: 1946.
———. *Glad Ghosts*. London: E. Benn, 1926.
Bought in London.
———. *Lady Chatterley's Lover*. Hamburg: Odyssey Press, 1933.
Bought before 1940.
———. *The Lost Girl*. London: T. Seltzer, 1921.
Bought in Paris, 150F.
———. *The Lovely Lady*. Hamburg: The Albatross, 1935.
Bought in Paris, 200F.
———. *The Plumed Serpent*. Hamburg: The Albatross, 1933.
Bought in France.
———. *The Rainbow*. New York: Modern Library, 1916.
Bought after 1940.
———. *Sons and Lovers*. Introduction by John Macy. New York:
Modern Library, 1922.
Bought after 1940.
———. *The Virgin and the Gipsy*. Cleveland: World Pub. Co., 1944.
———. *The Woman Who Rode Away, And Other Stories*. Hamburg:
The Albatross, 1934.
Bought after 1940.

———. *Women in Love.* With a Foreword by the Author. New York: Modern Library, 1937.

> Bought before 1940.
> D. H. Lawrence is mentioned in regard to the English landscape in *Black Power,* p. 7. *Sons and Lovers* is described as "an old favorite of mine" in an October 10, 1944, letter to Philip Wylie. See APPENDIX, p. 191; Fabre, 85, 112.

L A W R E N C E, T. E. *Seven Pillars of Wisdom, A Triumph.* [New ed.]. London: Jonathan Cape, 1946.

L A W S O N, Elizabeth. See CAYTON.

L A W S O N, John Howard. *Theory and Technique of Playwriting.* New York: G. P. Putnam's, 1936.

> Bought after 1940.

"John Howard Lawson, in his *Theory and Technique of Playwriting* sought to apply Marxist aesthetics to the theatre in terms of an expression of man's will to change the social scene; he posed the premise that dreams came into being at the moment when men intentionally threw the weight of their will against that of society." ("Writing from the Left," *Biblio.,* p. 170, U 74, Wright Misc. 812, p. 8.)

L A Y E, Camara. *The Dark Child.* With an Introduction by Philippe Thoby-Marcelin. Translated by James Kirkup, Ernest Jones and Elaine Gottlieb. London: The Noonday Press, 1954.

L E A G U E O F A M E R I C A N W R I T E R S. *Writers Take Sides: Letters about the War in Spain from 418 American Authors.* New York: The League, 1938.

> Wright was one of the contributors.

L E B O N, Gustave. *The Crowd: A Study of the Popular Mind.* London: Benn, 1947.

L E D E R E R, William J. and BURDICK, Eugene.

> "Did you read *The Ugly American?* It is badly written but a true novel and it makes you wonder and wonder." (To Margarit de Sabloniere, June 13, 1960.)

L E E, Sidney, Sir. *A Life of William Shakespeare.* With Portraits and Facsimiles. New Ed., Rewritten and Enlarged. London and New York: Macmillan, 1916.

> Bought after 1940 for $2.50.
> Inscribed: "Richard Wright—best life"

L E E U W, Gerardus van der. *Religion in Essence and Manifestation:*

A *Study in Phenomenology*. Translated by J. E. Turner. London: G. Allen & Unwin, 1938.
Galignani, Paris, sticker.

LEFT FRONT.
Wright had the 1933–1934 issues of the magazine to which he contributed poetry.

LEIRIS, Michel. *Race and Culture*. UNESCO Publication, 894. Paris: UNESCO, 1951.
Inscribed: "A Richard Wright, / Hommage très amical. / Michel Leiris"

LENIN, V. I. *Imperialism, the Highest Stage of Capitalism: A Popular Outline*. New, Rev. Translation. Little Lenin Library, v. 15. New York: International Publishers, 1939.
Bought before 1940.

————. *State and Revolution: Marxist Teaching about the Theory of the State and Tasks of the Proletariat in the Revolution*. Revised Translation. Little Lenin Library, v. 14. New York: International Publishers, 1935.
Bought before 1940.

————. *What Is to Be Done? Burning Questions of Our Movement*. Little Lenin Library, v. 4. New York: International Publishers, 1935.
Bought before 1940.

————. *Women and Society*. With an Introduction by N. Krupskaya. Little Lenin Library, v. 23. New York: International Publishers, 1938.
Lenin is mentioned in "Blueprint for Negro Writing" (*New Challenge*, Fall 1937, 54), on oppressed minorities reflecting the techniques of the bourgeoisie.
Mentioned in *How Bigger Was Born*, reprinted as a 39 pp. pamphlet by Harper's in 1940. "Freedom belongs to the strong" is quoted as a conclusion to *Fire and Cloud*.
"Wright inscribes *Black Boy* for me in his large handwriting. He writes 'Freedom belongs to the strong.'" (Michel Gordey, "Deux heures avec un grand américain," New York City, [1945 or 1946]).
Wright inscribed *Black Boy* to Sylvia Beach on June 15, 1946: "Freedom belongs to the strong. (These words of Lenin influenced me more than any other words in my life). Sincerely yours"
Wright alludes to carrying Lenin's *What Is to Be Done?* in his luggage when returning from Mexico to the United States in the

summer of 1940. ("How Jim Crow Feels," *Negro Digest*, v, January 1947, 44.)

L E N T Z, Emil E. *A Spanish Vocabulary*. London and Glasgow: Blackie & Son, 1928.

The words most used by Wright are underlined in the first sections.

L E S S I N G, Gotthold E. *Lakoon; Nathan the Wise & Minna von Barnhelm*. Translated with an Introduction by William A. Steel. Everyman's Library, no. 843. London, Toronto: J. M. Dent & Sons; New York: E. P. Dutton & Co., 1930.

Bought before 1940.

L E S U E U R, Meridel.

"I would like here to call to mind some brilliant pieces of Left writing of that period which because of their transitional nature and because critics failed to see the wider context of life which gave them birth, were completely misunderstood. Meridel Le Sueur wrote an article in the *New Masses* entitled 'I Was Marching'. Her piece dealt with the emotional experiences of a midwestern woman marching in her first outdoor demonstration. It was branded by many as an expression of mob emotion, of mass drunkenness, and many critics accused Le Sueur of wanting to lose the individual in the crowd. On the face of it, it seemed to many at the time that this criticism was correct, despite the fact that Le Sueur as an individual writer had come Left precisely because she felt capitalist society had crushed the individual. . . . Rebecca Pitts wrote an article for the *New Masses* called 'Something to Believe In,' a philosophical attempt on her part to identify herself with the Marxist position. This piece, like Le Sueur's, was branded as being tainted with religious emotion despite the fact that Rebecca Pitts, of all the Left critics, stood four-square for personality and individualism. I, too, wrote an article for the *New Masses* along similar lines, called 'Joe Louis Uncovers Dynamite,' which, too, was branded as catering to the mob spirit among Negroes." ("Writing from the Left," *Biblio.*, p. 170, U 74, Wright Misc. 812, p. 6.).

L E U B A, James H. *The Psychology of Religious Mysticism*. London: Kegan Paul; New York: Harcourt, 1929.

L E V I, Carlo. *Of Fear and Freedom*. Translated from the Italian by Adolphe Gourevitch. London: Cassel, 1950.

Bought used.

In a June 6, 1957, clipping from an unidentified Italian newspaper, Wright is reported as saying that he has read *Fontamara* (1934?) by Ignazio Silone, almost all of Carlo Levi, and some Elio Vittorini.

L E V I N, Harry. *Toward Stendahl: An Essay . . . , to Which Is Appended an "Open Letter" to the Publisher of the Modern Library.* Pharos, no. 3. Murray, Utah, 1945.

L E V I N, Meyer.

Wright defended Levin's protest play *Model Tenements* against censorship when Mayor Dawson had prevented its performance on the stage of Chicago's Federal Theatre in 1936. In his "Letter to the Editors" (*Partisan Review and Anvil*, 3, June 1936, p. 30), Wright defended Levin who had been branded as a reactionary in an article published in a previous issue of the magazine.

L E W I S, C. S. *The Screwtape Letters.* London: G. Bles, Centenary Press, 1950.

Galignani, Paris, sticker.

L E W I S, Sinclair. *Cass Timberlane, a Novel of Husbands and Wives.* London: J. Cape, 1946.

———. *Gideon Planish, A Novel.* Ljus English Library, v. 18. Stockholm. Ljus Förlag, 1944.

———. *Kingsblood Royal.* New York: Random House, 1947.

———. *The Prodigal Parents.* New York: The American Mercury, Inc., 1938.

Bought after 1940, 15¢

"Sinclair Lewis, at heart a reformer, laughed and sneered. Abruptly there ends the major attempts of literary artists to deal with their time and age." ("Personalism" [1935–37?], *Biblio.*, p. 167, U 62.)

Babbitt (1922) and *Main Street* (1920) are mentioned in *Black Boy: "Main Street* made me see my boss, Mr. Gerald, and identify him as an American type. . . . I felt that now I knew him, that I could feel the limits of his narrow life." (*Black Boy*, New York: Harper, 1945, p. 219.)

"Strangely, America has but little literature dealing with religious emotion per se, despite our proud boast that we are a religious people. I exclude such books as Sinclair Lewis' *Elmer Gantry;* they are satires upon institutional religion and criticism of the hypocrisy of much religious conduct rather than descriptions of the living inner springs of religious emotions. . . . And the descriptions of James, Mencken, Frank, *et al,* are couched in philosophical rather than concrete, unique terms." ("Memories of My Grandmother," *Biblio.*, p. 166, U 58, Wright Misc. 473, p. 3.)

"One must not forget—as I was stupid enough to do when I went on a lecture tour last year—that the hinterland is just about what it was when

Sinclair Lewis wrote his *Main Street.* I was shocked, not by race hate, but by the vast and appalling ignorance and indifference." (To Mr. Scanton, June 15, 1946)

"First books. / Lewis' *Mainstreet.* I'd tell my fellow workers about these books, urge them to read them. / Mencken's books. Why I liked them / Out of all this I had one pretty set idea. I'd say to myself: 'I understand that emotion. I could write that down.' / In Memphis, after work, I first seriously began to write, not for publication but for myself, playing with words. . . .

In Chicago, I left off writing and began reading again; I could get hold of more books: Anderson, Dreiser, Dostoevsky, Turgenev, Mencken's *Prefaces,* Chekhov, Joyce, Conrad. / I tried again to write, express my attitude / The labor movement / Stein's book, *Three Lives.* / Experiments in words: Stein / Experiments in dialogue: James / Experiments in scenes: James / Experiments in moods: Conrad / Yet I had nothing to say / Self-discovery: reading of non-fiction. . . ." (Notes for a lecture on writing, undated.)

L E W I S, Wyndham. *The Lion and the Fox: The Role of the Hero in the Plays of Shakespeare.* London: G. Richards, 1927.
Sylvia Beach, ex libris, Paris.
————. *Time and Western Man.* London: Chatto & Windus, 1927.
Bought used after 1940.
————. *The Writer and the Absolute.* London: Methuen, 1952.
Galignani, Paris, sticker.
L I E P M A N N, Heinz. *Murder——Made in Germany: A True Story of Present-day Germany.* Translated by Emile Burns. New York, London: Harper, 1934.
Bought before 1940.
L I N, Yutang. *The Importance of Understanding: Translations from the Chinese.* Cleveland: World Pub. Co., 1960.
L I N D G R E N, Ernest. *The Art of the Film: An Introduction to Film Appreciation.* London: G. Allen & Unwin, 1949.
L I N D S A Y, Vachel.
"White America has reduced Negro life in our great cities to a level of experience of so crude and brutal a quality that one could say of it in the words of Vachel Lindsay's *The Leaden Eyed:*

It is not that they starve, but they starve so dreamlessly,
It is not that they sow, but that they seldom reap,
It is not that they serve, but they have no gods to serve,
It is not that they die, but that they die like sheep.

(Introduction to *Black Metropolis,* by St. Clair Drake and Horace Cayton, New York: Harcourt, Brace, 1945, p. xxxiv.)
L I P S C O M B, George D. See GRAHAM, Shirley.
L I P T O N, Lawrence.
Wright recommended Lipton's *Brother, the Laugh Is Bitter* (1942) as "an excellent novel about Chicago" in "Readers and Writers," an interview by Edwin Seaver, Dec. 23, 1941.
L O C K E, Alain.
On November 19, 1938, Wright went with Alain Locke to attend a debate on "The Negro, a Force in American Literature," with Langston Hughes, Sterling Brown, Jessie Fauset, and Genevieve Taggard participating.

"The movement [of the Harlem Renaissance] was in large part initiated by the publication of the *Survey Graphic's* special 'Harlem number' and of Alain Locke's interpretative anthology entitled *The New Negro.* A host of young writers made their appearance in the middle and late 1920's, among them Walter White, Eric Walrond, Rudolph Fisher, Jean Toomer, Claude McKay, Countee Cullen, Langston Hughes, Wallace Thurman, Jessie Fauset, Nella Larsen, Zora Neale Hurston, George Schuyler and Arna Bontemps. . . . For a few years Negro writers created more than ever before. . . . Joyce's *Ulysses* influenced some of them and even the gospel of Gertrude Stein claimed a number of Negro adherents. Some members of the movement were apotheosized in Carl Van Vechten's *Nigger Heaven,* a novel that New York read with avidity. The poetry of McKay, Cullen and Hughes expressed in new rhythms and beauty and vigor the bitterness and despair of Negro life in America. Toomer, in *Cane,* sounded a new and lyric note in American prose; and Walter White, in *The Fire in the Flint* and *Flight,* dealt with the Negro's struggle in both South and North. Against the barriers of color, Jessie Fauset, Nella Larsen and Claude McKay frequently depicted Harlem life in their novels. James Weldon Johnson, long a Harlem resident and later a professor at Fisk and New York Universities, elaborated in *Black Manhattan* the description of Harlem that was a permanent feature of his earlier *Autobiography of an Ex-Colored Man.* Rudolph Fisher, Wallace Thurman, George Schuyler and W. E. B. DuBois wove fantasy and satire into their descriptions of Negro life." ("Portrait of Harlem" in *New York Panorama,* Random House, New York, 1938, pp. 142–43.)

L O C K E, Louis. See ARMS, George W.
L O G A N, Rayford W. *The Negro in American Life and Thought: The Nadir, 1877–1901.* New York: Dial Press, 1954.

———, ed. *What the Negro Wants*. Chapel Hill: University of North Carolina Press, 1944.

L O M A X, John A.

"In most blues songs the verses have no meaning or relationship to each other. . . . The same is true of many Negro folk songs. I quote seven verses of 'Dink's Blues,' from *American Ballads and Folks Songs,* collected by John A. Lomax:

Some folks say that the worry blues ain't bad
It's de wors' ol' feeling I ever had

Git you two three men, son one won't worry you' min',
Don't they keep you worried and bothered all de time?

I wish to God Eas' bound train would wreck,
Kill the engineers, break the fireman's neck
I'm gwine to de river, set down on de groun'.
Ef de blues overtake me, I'll jump overboard and down.

Ef trouble was money, I'd be a millioneer,
Ef trouble was money, I'd be a millioneer.

My chuck grindin' every hole but mine,
My chuck grindin' every hole but mine.

Come de big *Kate Adams* wid headlight turn down de stream,
An' her sidewheel knockin', "Great-God-I-been-redeemed!"

("Memories of My Grandmother," *Biblio.,* p. 166, U 58, Wright Misc. 473, p. 12.)

L O N D O N, Jack. *The Sea-Wolf.* New York: Grosset & Dunlap, 1935.

Ricour, Paris, stamp.

London is mentioned in *The Color Curtain,* concerning the "yellow scare."

L O N D O N, Louis S. *Sexual Deviations in the Female: Case Histories of Frustrated Women.* London, New York: Thomas Yoseloff, 1957.

L O N D R E S, Albert. *The Road to Buenos Ayres.* With an Introduction by Theodore Dreiser. The Translation is by Eric Sutton. London: Constable & Co., 1928.

Mistral, Paris, stamp.

L O N G F E L L O W, Henry Wadsworth. *The Poetical Works of Henry Wadsworth Longfellow.* New York: W. P. Nimmo, 1876.

Bought after 1940.

L O T I, Pierre. *The Iceland Fisherman*. Translated from the French by Anna Farwell de Koven. Chicago: A. C. McClurg & Co., 1889.

Bought before 1940.

L O W E S, John Livingston.

In my notes for the biography of Wright, I have found reference to a volume on "Xanadu," by one "Love." On checking, the title seems to be *The Road to Xanadu, A Study in the Ways of Imagination (1927)* by John L. Lowes. If this is the correct title, Wright read it in 1937 or '38.

L O W R I E, Walter. *Kierkegaard*. London, New York: Oxford University Press, 1938.

Bought after 1940.

———. *A Short Life of Kierkegaard*. Oxford: H. Milford, Oxford University Press, 1944.

L U D O V I C I, Anthony M. *Who Is to Be Master of the World? An Introduction to the Philosophy of Friedrich Nietzsche*. With an Introduction by Dr. Oscar Levy. Edinburg & London: T. N. Foulis, 1914.

Bought used in Paris for 300F.

L U D W I G, Emil. *Napoléon*. Translated by Eden and Cedar Paul. New York: Boni & Liveright, 1926.

Bought before 1940.

L U N D B E R G, Ferdinand and FARNHAM, Marynia L. *Modern Woman: The Lost Sex*. New York: Harper, 1947.

L Y N D, Helen M. *On Shame and the Search for Identity*. London: Routledge & Kegan Paul, 1958.

L Y T T O N, Edward Bulwer Lytton, baron. *The Last Days of Pompei*. Complete in one volume. New York: American Publishers Corporation, 189?.

M

MACAULAY, Thomas Babington, 1st baron. *Lays of Ancient Rome and Other Poems.* Edited, with Notes, by William J. Rolfe and John C. Rolfe. New York: American Book Co., 1916.
Bought before 1940.
Notes on fly-leaves.

McCULLERS, Carson. *A Member of the Wedding.* Boston: Houghton Mifflin & Co., 1946.
Inscribed: "For Dick and Ellen, / with my love, / Carson"
———. *Reflections in a Golden Eye.* Boston: Houghton Mifflin, 1941.
Inscribed: "For Richard Wright / with my great admiration—/ Carson McCullers./ (also for Dick/I have wanted to see you for a long time/but you are so exclusive./I look forward to seeing you again/and send my love and best wishes./Carson)
Wright reviewed *The Heart Is a Lonely Hunter* (1940) in "Inner Landscape,"*New Republic,* 103 (August 5, 1940), 195.
On their friendship, see Fabre, 244–45, 314. See APPENDIX, pp. 221–23.

McGARRETT, Vincent. *Toward Better Photography.* Boston: American Photographic Publishing Co., 1947.

MACHIAVELLI, Niccolo. *The Prince and The Discourses.* With an Introduction by Max Lerner. New York: Modern Library, 1940.

McKAY, Claude.
Claude McKay's sonnet "White House" is quoted in its entirety in "The Literature of the Negro in the United States" as an instance of black rebellion. (See *White Man, Listen!,* p. 139); "If We Must Die" is quoted in Wright's introduction to *Black Metropolis.* In his essay, "Black Boy in France" (*Ebony,* July 1953) William Gardner Smith said Wright found first editions of James Weldon Johnson's *God's Trombones* and Claude McKay's *Banjo* (1929) in the Paris bookstalls along the Seine.

McKAY, Herbert C. *Movie Making for the Beginner.* Chicago: Ziff-Davis, 1939.

MacKINLEY, Helm. *Angel Mo' and Her Son, Roland Hayes.* Boston: Little, Brown & Co., 1942.
"Compliments of the Publishers."
McLANE, Mary. *I, Mary McLane: A Diary of Human Days.* New York: Stokes, 1917.
Acquired after 1940.
Inscribed: "To Margaret Hammond from Mary McLane. / Along of a good luncheon. / Feb., 1918 in Chicago."
MacLEISH, Archibald.

"In opening the [June 1937 American Writers] Congress, Archibald MacLeish, Pulitzer Prize poet and editor of *Fortune,* pled for the support of the Spanish anti-fascists 'who are now fighting our future battles on the battlefields of Spain.'" ("The Barometer Points to Storm," *Biblio.,* p. 164, U 45, Wright Misc. 271, p. 2)

McLEOD, Norman.

"The scene of Left poetry was in a like position. Edwin Rolfe, William Pillin, Norman McLeod, and many others were searching for images and symbols on the American scene to express their sense of a rapidly changing world." ("Writing from the Left," *Biblio.,* p. 170, U 74, Wright Misc. 812, p. 7)

McMEEKIN, Claré.
Wright did a reader's report for the Book-of-the-Month Club on her novel *Black Moon* (1945). See *Biblio.,* p. 171, U 78.
MACMILLAN, William M. *Africa Emergent: A Survey of Social, Political, and Economic Trends in British Africa.* Rev. and Exp. Ed. with New Appendix. Harmondsworth, Middlesex: Penguin Books, 1949.
MADARIAGA, Salvador de. *Spain.* London: J. Cape, 1946.
Inscribed: "A little token of a most pleasant meeting / and delightful journey Madrid-Paris. / From Skip. / Sept. 1954"
MAILER, Norman. *The Deer Park.* New York: New American Library, 1957.
————. *The Naked and the Dead.* New York: Rinehart, 1948.
MALINOWSKI, Bronislaw. *Crime and Custom in Savage Society.* London: Routledge K. Paul, 1951.
The Dynamics of Culture Change (Yale University Press, 1945) seems to be the book to which the title "Dynamics" refers on Wright's receipt from the Kumasi Basel Mission Book Depot dated August 7, 1953. Meyer Fortes's *Dynamics of Clanship among the*

Tallensi had appeared in 1945. Malinowski's book was not found in Wright's library.

MALRAUX, André. *Days of Wrath.* Translated by Haakon M. Chevalier with a Foreword by Waldo Frank. New York: Random House, 1936.

———. *Man's Fate* [*La Condition humaine*]. Translated by Haakon M. Chevalier. New York: Modern Library, n.d.
   Bought after 1935.

———. *Man's Hope.* Translated from the French by Stuart Gilbert and Alistair Macdonald. New York: Modern Library, 1938.

———. *Voices of Silence.* Translated by Stuart Gilbert. London: Secker & Warburg, 1953.

"Already on the Left there are tendencies to frame the goal of writing in terms of a New Humanism, such as that which guides the work of André Malraux. It was Malraux who first provided a framework in which the problem could be conceived in psychological terms. Malraux contended that men were most human when they were engaged in a conflict which called forth all their qualities of hope and courage; it was he who first introduced the highly intelligent and self-conscious character in revolutionary fiction. In order to arrive at a Marxist aesthetics, Malraux went back to a concept of the individual closely resembling the Greeks. He framed a premise that justified the class struggle in artistic terms; he contended that the class struggle was in itself transitory, that his character engaged in it with the view of ending class conflict, in order that they might face the task of subjugating natural forces. Malraux's work embodies by far the most elaborate effort to humanize Marxism in literature." ("Writing from the Left," *Biblio.*, p. 170, U 74, Wright Misc. 812, p. 8)

"I like the work of Hemingway, of course, who does not? But the two writers whose works I like most today are André Malraux and William Faulkner. I think both of them in their respective fields are saying important things.
   As a fellow Mississippian, I know that Faulkner deals with a phase of the real South. He is the only white writer I know of living in Mississippi who is trying to tell the truth in fiction.
   . . . What Faulkner is to the small area, Malraux is to the progressive movement all over the world, that is, an interpreter.
   Faulkner shows how human beings are taunted and degraded in Mississippi, while Malraux shows how millions all over the world are trying to rise above a degraded status. I value Malraux higher than I do Faulkner because of the quality of heroic action Malraux depicts in his novels." ("An Editorial Conference," WNYC, April 13, 1938). See FABRE, 146, 176, 304, 426 on Wright reading Malraux.

MALTZ, Albert.
Wright saw *Black Pit* (1935) performed in New York in May 1935.

"A good writer like Albert Maltz, for instance, can take his city cultural background for granted. A Negro writer can take nothing for granted. He comes up against things our white writers never hear of." ("Readers and Writers," an interview by Edwin Seaver, December 23, 1941.)

In his 1945 diary Wright mentions buying *The Cross and the Arrow* (1944) on February 13, 1945.

MANN, Thomas. *The Magic Mountain*. London: Secker & Warburg, 1946.

MANNHEIM, Herman. *War and Crime*. London: Watts & Co., 1941.
Bought in Paris, 150F.

MANNHEIM, Karl. *Ideology and Utopia: An Introduction to the Sociology of Knowledge*. With a Preface by Louis Wirth. Translated from the German by Louis Wirth and Edward Shils. New York: Harcourt, Brace; London: Kegan Paul, 1946.
Copy belonging to Professor Louis Wirth.

MANNONI, Dominique O. *Prospero and Caliban: The Psychology of Colonization*. Translated by Pamela Powesland. With a Foreword by Philip Mason. New York: Praeger, 1956.
Many passages underlined.
Wright wrote a review of Mannoni's book *Prospero and Caliban* in "Neurosis of Conquest," *The Nation*, 183 (Oct. 20, 1956), 330–31. He used many concepts from the book in lectures later gathered in *White Man, Listen!* See APPENDIX, pp. 223–25.

MANOUKIAN, Madeline. *Tribes of the Northern Territories of the Gold Coast*. Ethnographic Survey of Africa: Western Africa, pt. 5. London: International African Institute, 1951.
Bought in Accra in 1953.

MANSFIELD, Katherine. *The Garden Party and Other Stories*. Brussels: W. Collins, 1922.
Bought used after 1940.

MANTLE, Burns, ed. *The Burns Mantle Best Plays and the Yearbook of the Drama in America*. New York: Dodd, Mead, 1941.
Includes a summary of *Native Son: The Biography of a Young American, A Play in Ten Scenes*.

————. *The Burns Mantle Best Plays of 1942–43.* New York: Dodd, Mead, 1943.
Includes a summary and excerpts of *Native Son: . . . A Play.*
MANVELL, Roger. *Film.* Rev. and Enl. Edition. Harmondsworth, Middlesex: Penguin Books, 1946.
MAO, Tse-tung. *On the Correct Handling of Contradictions among the People. Text of a Speech Made on February 27, 1957, at the Eleventh Session (Enlarged) of the Supreme State Conference.* London: Communist Party, 1957.
MARAN, René. *Batouala.* New York: Selzer, 1922.
Bought on February 17, 1945, for $1.75.
Wright met Maran, who reviewed two of his books, in the late 1940s in Paris.
MARCEL, Gabriel. *Being and Having.* Translated by Katharine Farrar. Westminster [London]: Daere Press, 1949.
————. *The Mystery of Being.* 2 vols. London: The Harvill Press, 1950–51.
————. *The Philosophy of Existence.* Translated by Manya Harari. London: The Harvill Press, 1949.
MARCH, Richard and TAMBIMUTTA, eds. *T. S. Eliot: A Symposium from C. Aiken (and Others).* London: Editions Poetry, 1948.
MARIE-THÉRÈSE [pseud.]. *Vie d'une prostituee, version intégrale.* Paris: A mes dépens, 1950.
Given by Simone de Beauvoir in the early 1950s. Wright read it with great interest.
MARITAIN, Jacques. *The Dream of Descartes.* London: Editions Poetry, 1946.
————. *Existence and the Existent.* English Version by Lewis Galantieri and Gerald P. Phelan. New York: Pantheon? 1949.
MARKS, John. *To the Bullfight: A Guide to the Spanish National Pastime.* London: D. Verschoyle, 1954.
Galignani, Paris, sticker.
MARLOWE, Christopher.
A quotation from *Dr. Faustus* is used as epigraph to *Savage Holiday,* Part III.
MARTEN, Edward. *The Doctor Looks at Murder . . . As Told to Norman Cross* [pseud]. New York: Doubleday, Doran & Co., 1935.
Bought used after 1940, 49¢.

MARTIN, Clyde E. See KINSEY, Alfred.

MARTIN, John B. *Break Down the Walls: American Prisons, Present, Past, and Future.* New York: Ballantine Books, 1954.

MARX, Karl. *Capital.* 3 vols.
Bought used on October 16, 1945.

———. *Capital: A Critique of Political Economy.* Edited by Frederick Engels. 3 vols. Chicago: C. H. Kerr & Co., 1932–33.
New Copy.

———. *Selected Works.* Prepared by the Marx-Engels-Lenin Institute, Moscow, under the Editorship of V. Adoratsky. 2 vols. Moscow, Leningrad: Co-operative Publishing Society of Foreign Workers in the USSR, 1935.
Acquired before 1940. Inscribed: "Best wishes—/Bob Campbell"

——— and ENGELS, Friedrich. *The Civil War in the United States.* 2d ed. Marxist Library: Works of Marxism-Leninism, v. 30. New York: International Publishers, 1940.

——— and ———. *Manifesto of the Communist Party.* Authorized English Translation. Edited and Annotated by Friedrich Engels. New York: International Publishers, 1934.
In his essay "How Jim Crow Feels" (1946), Wright alludes to traveling from Mexico back to the southern United States with *Capital* in his luggage. The book is also mentioned in *Black Power* (pp. 100 and 358) and in Wright's introduction to Françoise Gourdon's *Tant qu'il y aura la peur* (1960). See Fabre, 452.

MASTERS, Edgar Lee.
Mentioned in *Black Boy,* 252, 262.

MAUGHAM, W. Somerset. *The Moon and Sixpence.* London: W. Heinemann, 1925.
Bought used.

MAURINA, Zenta. *A Prophet of the Soul: Fyodor Dostoievsky.* Translated from the Latvian by C. P. Finlayson. London: J. Clarke, 1940.
Bought after 1940 for $3.00.

MAWSON, Christopher O. *Roget's Thesaurus of the English Language in Dictionary Form; Being a Presentation of Roget's Thesaurus of English Words and Phrases in a Modernized, More Complete, and More Convenient Dictionary Form, Together with Briefer Synonymies for the Busy Writer, the Whole Comprised in One Alphabetical Arrangement, with an Appendix of Foreign*

Words and Expressions. New York: Garden City Publishing Co., 1937.

M A Y E R, Jacob P. *Sociology of the Film: Studies and Documents.* London: Faber & Faber, 1946.

M E A D, Margaret. *From the South Seas: Studies of Adolescence and Sex in Primitive Societies.* New York: William Morrow, 1941.

M E C K L E N B U R G - S C H W E R I N, Duke of. See ADOLF FRIEDRICH, Duke of Mecklenburg-Schwerin.

M E I S S N E R, Hans Otto. *The Man with Three Faces.* London: Pan Books, 1950.

"Un manuscript de 29 pages, ecrit a la main. . . .
20th century novel by Joseph Warren Beach
Repetition by Kierkegaard
The Man with Three Faces by Hans Otto Meissner et des autres livres."
(Notes)

M E L V I L L E, Herman. *Moby Dick, Or, the Whale.* Illustrated by Rockwell Kent. New York: Modern Library, 1930.
Bought after 1940 for $1.95.

———. *Omoo.* New York: Editions for the Armed Services, 194–?
Bought in Paris, 12F.

———. *Romances: Typee, Omoo, Mardi, Moby Dick, White Jacket, Israel Potter, Redburn.* New York: Pickwick Publishers, 1929.
Copy belonged to A. J. Aaron.

———. *Selected Writings of Herman Melville: Complete Short Stories, Typee, [and] Billy Budd, Foretopman.* New York: Modern Library, 1952.
Melville is mentioned in "How 'Bigger' Was Born." On *Moby Dick* as one of Wright's favorite novels, see FAULKNER.
"Melville dramatized his conflict with society in emotional terms, basically pessimistic." ("Personalism" (1935–37?), *Biblio.*, p. 167, U 62)

"As an American Negro, I must admit that we American Negroes have no monopoly upon the concept of freedom or its various means of expression. Herman Melville, Thoreau, Whitman came before us, fired by the desire to express it." (Fragment on "How the French See American Negroes," undated, probably 1946, *Biblio.*, p. 165, U 50)

M E M M I, Albert.
Wright probably read his *Portrait du colonise, precede du portrait du colonisateur* (1957).

MENCKEN, H. L. *The American Language: An Inquiry into the Development of English in the United States. Supplement I—.* New York: A. A. Knopf, 1945—.
Bought on November 11, 1945.
————. *A Book of Prefaces.* Garden City, N.Y.: Garden City Pub. Co., 1927.
Bought before 1940.
————. *In Defence of Women.* New York: A. A. Knopf, 1924.
Bought before 1940.
The first leaf bears "aphrodisiacal," "asphodel" in Wright's handwriting.
————. *Minority Report: H. L. Mencken's Notebooks.* New York: Knopf, 1956.
Bought after 1940.
————. *Notes on Democracy.* New York: Knopf, 1926.
Bought on November 11, 1945.
————. *Prejudices: First Series.* New York: A. Knopf, 1924.
Bought on November 11, 1945.
————. *Prejudices: Second Series.* New York: A. A. Knopf, 1924.
Bought on November 11, 1945.
————. *Prejudices: Third Series.* New York: A. A. Knopf, 1922.
Bought on November 11, 1945.
————. *Prejudices: Fourth Series.* New York: A. A. Knopf, 1924.
Bought on November 11, 1945.
————. *Prejudices: Fifth Series.* New York: A. A. Knopf, 1926.
Bought on November 11, 1945.
————. *Prejudices: Sixth Series.* New York: A. A. Knopf, 1927.
Bought after 1940.
————. *Treatise on Right and Wrong.* New York: Knopf, 1934.
Bought after 1940.
————. *The Treatise on the Gods.* New York, London: A. A. Knopf, 1930?
Bought on November 11, 1945.

"One day I came across a second-hand edition of *A Book of Prefaces.* Mencken's book served as a literary Bible for me for years. I read all the books he mentioned that I could lay hands on." (*Book-of-the-Month Club News,* Feb. 1940, p. 4).

"I developed the habit of reading everything that fell into my hands. Accidentally, I came across H. L. Mencken's *Book of Prefaces,* which served as a literary Bible for me for some years." (Interview by June Greenwall, Mercury Theatre, 1941)

See CHARLES SCRUGGS, *The Sage in Harlem*, Baltimore: Johns Hopkins University Press, 1984, pp. 25, 166–69, 172.
See FABRE, 68–69, 84.

MERCIER, Charles A. *Criminal Responsibility*. Oxford: At the Clarendon Press, 1905.
Bought used in Paris, 200F

MEREJKOWSKI, Dmitri S. *Death of the Gods: Julian the Apostate*. Translated from the Original Russian by Bernard Guilbert Guerney. New York: Modern Library, 1929.
Bought after 1940.

———. *Peter and Alexis*. Translated by Bernard Guilbert Guerney. New York: Modern Library, 1931.
Bought after 1940.

MEYEROWITZ, Eva. *The Sacred State of the Akan*. London: Faber & Faber, 1951.

MICHAUX, Henri.
Wright attended a party given at Sylvia Beach's on the occasion of the publication of *A Barbarian in Asia* (1949) on July 4, 1949. Beach had translated the book into English.

MILL, John Stuart.
"You probably know what John Stuart Mill (a century ago) wrote about this in *Principles of Political Economy:* '. . . of all vulgar modes of escaping from the consideration of the effect of moral and social influences on the human mind, the most vulgar is that of attributing the diversities of conduct and character to inherent natural differences.'" (Hans de Vaal, "Interview med Richard Wright," *Literair Pasport*, July-August 1953, p. 162.)

MILLER, Arthur. *Focus*. New York: Reynal and Hitchcock, 1945.
Wright reviewed *Focus* in "Two Novels of the Crushing of Men, One White, One Black," *P.M. Magazine*, Nov. 15, 1945, p. m7–m8. See APPENDIX, pp. 210–13.

MILLER, Henry. *The Air-conditioned Nightmare*. New York: New Directions, 1945.

———. *Black Spring*. Paris: Obelisk Press, 1937.
Bought used in Paris.

———. *The Colossus of Maroussi*. Norfolk, Ct.: New Directions, 1931.
Bought after 1940.

—————. *The Cosmological Eye.* Norfolk, Ct.: New Directions, 1939.
Bought on March 3, 1945.

—————. *Max and the White Phagocytes.* Paris: Obelisk Press, 1943.

—————. *Murder the Murderer: An Excursus on War from "The Air-conditioned Nightmare."* [Fordingbridge, Hants]: The Delphic Press, 1946.
Wright first bought a copy in New York on March 8, 1945.

—————. *The Plight of the Creative Artist in the United States of America.* Haulton, Me.: Ben Porter Press, 1943.
Bought on March 8, 1945.

—————. *Remember to Remember.* Vol. 2 of his *The Air-conditioned Nightmare.* Norfolk, Conn.: New Directions, 1947.

—————. *Sunday After the War.* London: Editions Poetry, 1945.

—————. *Tropic of Cancer.* Preface by Anaïs Nin. Paris: The Obelisk Press, 1939.
Bought in Paris.

—————. *The Wisdom of the Heart.* Norfolk, Conn.: New Directions, 1941.
See also HILER, Hilaire.

MILLER, Richard R. *Slavery and Catholicism.* Durham, N.C.: North State Publishers, 1957.
Inscribed: "With best wishes to Richard Wright / from the author"

MILLIGAN, Robert H. *The Fetish Folk of West Africa.* New York, Chicago: Fleming H. Revell Co., 1912.
Bought in England.

MILLIN, Sarah Gertrude.

"In Sarah Gertrude Millin's 'I Did This Thing' there is presented in story form the difference between the sexual mores of African tribal life and the sexual codes of the Western world. . . . Western codes of law are besides the point to this murderer who freely, even proudly, admits his crime. A free confession of guilt is his way of saving face, of asserting his own dignity." (Foreword to *Lest We Forget, Biblio.,* p. 175, U 94, Wright Misc. 456 [1955])

MILLS, C. Wright. *White Collar: The American Middle Classes.* New York: Oxford University Press, 1956.

MILTON, John. *Milton's L'Allegro, Il Penseroso, Comus, and Lycidas.* Edited by Martin W. Sampson. New York: H. Holt, 1912.
Bought before 1940.

————. *Paradise Lost*. With Illustrations by William Blake Printed in Color for the First Time, and with Prefaces by Philip Hofer and John T. Winterich. New York: Heritage Press, 1940.
Inscribed: "To Richard Wright / with great appreciation. / Rosetta Felsman (Toshka)."

————. *Poetical Works*. New York: John Winston Co.
Bought used before 1940, $1.00.

MITCHELL, Joseph. *McSorley's Wonderful Saloon*. New York: Duell, Sloan, and Pearce, 1943.

MÜGGE, M. A. *Nietzsche: Who He Was and What He Stood For*. Girard, Kan.: Haldeman-Julius Co., 19—.
Bought after 1940.

MOHOLY-NAGY, László. *Vision in Motion*. Chicago: P. Theobald, 1947.

MOLINERO, Alcalde. *La trágica emoción del toro de "Chamaco."* 35 dibujos inédibos del natural. [Barcelona]: Graf. Radial, 1954?
Bought in 1954.

MONEY-KYRLE, Roger E. *The Meaning of Sacrifice*. The International Psycho-analytical Library, no. 16. London: L. & V. Woolf and the Institute of Psycho-Analysis, 1930.
Acquired used after 1940.

MOON, Bucklin. *The Darker Brother*. Garden City, N.Y.: Doubleday, Doran & Co., 1943.

————. *The High Cost of Prejudice*. New York: J. Messner, 1947.
Inscribed: "To Richard Wright / with the best of wishes. / April 16, 1947. / Buck"

————, ed. *A Primer for White Folks*. Garden City, N.Y.: Doubleday, Doran & Co., 1945.
Includes "The Ethics of Living Jim Crow."

MOORE, George. *Celibates*. New York: Macmillan & Co., 1895.
Bought used after 1940, 50¢.

————. *Confessions of a Young Man*. Introduction by Floyd Dell. New York: Modern Library, 1917.
Bought before 1940.

————. *Esther Waters, A Novel*. Chicago: Henneberry, n.d.
Bought used before 1940.

————. *Sister Teresa*. New York: Brentano's, 1918.
Bought after 1940, 60¢.
The book was recommended by Mencken in *A Book of Prefaces* and Wright probably read it before buying it.

"The next principle to which most serious writers subscribed was the character in the foreground, the story of a single line of development. This principle, too, was not imposed. Writers took it up avidly and voluntarily, feeling that they could gain greater power in writing by doing this. And they did. Witness George Moore's *Esther Waters* and *The Mummer's Wife*. The gap between life and fiction began to close." (Lecture on left wing literature, p. 15 [1940?])

M O O R E H E A D, Alan. *The Traitors: The Double Life of Fuchs, Pontecorvo, and Nunn May.* London: Hamish Hamilton, 1952. Galignani, Paris, sticker.

M O R R I S, Edita. *The Flowers of Hiroshima.* New York: Viking Press, 1959.
    Inscribed: "For Richard Wright, / the fighter, the writer, / who is making this a better world. / Sept. 1959. / Edita Morris."

M O R R I S, Ira V. *The Paper Wall, A Novel.* London: Chatto & Windus, 1960.
    Inscribed: "For that fine writer, Dick Wright, / who knows something about walls / and how to break them down. / 19–6–60."

M O T L E Y, Willard. *Knock on Any Door.* New York, London: Appleton-Century Co., 1947.

M O T T, Frank Luther. See DAVIS, Joe Lee.

M U L L E R, Herbert J. *The Loom of History.* New York: Harper, 1958.
    Inscribed: "Best wishes from / Mac, J. Appleton, Ben." (Gift from Harper)

M U M F O R D, Lewis. *The Condition of Man.* New York: Harcourt, Brace & Co., 1944.
    Bought on March 28, 1945.

———. *Herman Melville.* New York: The Literary Guild, 1929.
    Bought before 1940.

"In the third story [of *Uncle Tom's Children*], "Long Black Song," I had borrowed heavily from Sherwood Anderson, D. H. Lawrence, and of all people for a story writer to borrow from, from Lewis Mumford. In Mumford's *The Golden Day* he spoke of the introduction of clocks into medieval society, of how this affected the life of the peasant. I seized upon this to show the difference between how a northern-born white boy might feel and how it would contrast with the feelings of a peasant Negro woman in the Deep South, on plantations." (Unpublished journal, January 3, 1945)

See also KREYMBORG Alfred.

MUNSON, Gorham B.
Destinations (1928) is mentioned in Wright's notes.
MURTAGH, John M. and HARRIS, Sara. *Cast the First Stone.* New York: McGraw-Hill, 1957.
LE MUSÉE VIVANT. *1848: abolition de l'esclevage: 1948: evidence de la culture négre.* Numero special, no. 36–37. Paris: Le Musée vivant, Nov., 1948.
This special issue on African art, edited by Madeleine Rousseau and Anta Diop, has an introduction by Wright.
MUSEUM OF MODERN ART (New York, N.Y.). *The Sense of Abstraction: An Exhibition.* Contemporary Photographer, v. 1, no. 2. [Oberlin, Ohio: T. M. Hill, 1960].
MUSMANNO, Michael A. *After Twelve Years.* New York: A. A. Knopf, 1939.
Bought after 1940.
MYRDAL, Gunnar. *Beyond the Welfare States: Economic Planning in the Welfare States and Its International Implications.* London: Duckworth, 1960.
———. *An International Economy, Problems and Prospects.* New York: Harper, 1956.
Inscribed: "To Richard and Ellen / from Gunnar / June 1956."
"Discrimination in America" quotes Myrdal's *An American Dilemma* (1944).

"[*Black Metropolis*] supplements and endorses the conclusions arrived at by Gunnar Myrdal in his *American Dilemma,* that monumental study of race relations in the United States." (Introduction to *Black Metropolis* by St. Clair Drake and Horace Cayton, New York: Harcourt, Brace, 1945, xxix)

"We have the testimony of a Gunnar Myrdal but we know that this is not all. What would life on the Chicago Southside look like when seen through the eyes of a Freud, a Joyce, a Proust, a Pavlov, a Kierkegaard? It should be recalled in this connection that Gertrude Stein's *Three Lives,* the first long serious literary treatment of Negro life in the United States, was derived from Stein's preoccupation with Jamesian psychology." (*Ibid.,* p. xxxi)

"I also knew that he [Myrdal] had with one volume, *An American Dilemma,* made millions of white Americans acutely conscious of their racial policies, had so prodded their moral stance that, belatedly, they had moved to square their practices with their preachment." ("The Heart Is on Both Sides," *Biblio.,* p. 165, U 54)

"It is almost impossible for a white man to determine just what a Negro is really feeling, unless that white man, like a Gunnar Myrdal, is gifted with a superb imagination. In a recent literary interview, William Faulkner, Nobel Prize Winner, declared that he could not imagine himself a Negro for two minutes." (*White Man, Listen!*, p. 43)

Wright also quotes Gunnar Myrdal as recommending state intervention in industrializing Third World countries. (*White Man, Listen!*, p. 59)

Pagan Spain is dedicated to Alva and Gunnar Myrdal. *An American Dilemma* is often mentioned by Wright in his 1945 journal. *An International Economy* is quoted in *White Man, Listen!*.

N

N A B O K O V, Vladimir. *Lolita.* New York: Putnam, 1955.
———. *Nabokov's Dozen: Thirteen Stories.* Harmondsworth: Penguin Books, 1960.
N A R B O R O U G H, Fred. *Murder on My Mind.* London: A. Wingate, 1959.
   Bought remaindered at 55oF.
N E G R O D I G E S T. Wright had a few issues of the magazine from 1942 to 1945.
T H E N E G R O H A N D B O O K. New York: W. Malliet & Co., 1942—. Wright bought a copy of the title in January 1945.
N E H R U, Jawaharlal. *Toward Freedom: The Autobiography of Jawaharlal Nehru.* New York: John Day, 1941.
N E I D E R, Charles. *Kafka: His Mind and Art.* London: Routledge, Kegan Paul, 1949.
   Galignani, Paris, sticker.
N E L S O N, John H. and CARGILL, Oscar, eds. *Contemporary Trends: American Literature Since 1900.* New York: Macmillan, 1949.
   Reprints "Bright and Morning Star."
N E M I L O V, Anton V. *The Biological Tragedy of Woman.* Translated from the Russian by Stephanie Ofental. London: G. Allen Unwin, 1932.
   Mistral, Paris, stamp.
N E W C H A L L E N G E.
   Wright had issue No. 2 (Fall 1937) to which he had contributed "Blueprint for Negro Writing."
N E W M A N, John Henry. *Apologia Pro Vita Sua: Being a History of His Religious Opinions.* London: Longmans, 1890.
   Bought before 1940, 5¢.
N E W M A S S E S.
   Wright had some 50 issues in his library. He contributed to the magazine from 1934 to 1941.

NICHOLS, Edward J.
Wright did a reader's report for the Book-of-the-Month Club on Nichols' novel *Hunky Johnny* (1945). See *Biblio.*, p. 172, U 81.

NIEHBUR, Reinhold. *The Nature and Destiny of Man: A Christian Interpretation.* 2 vols. in 1. New York: C. Scribner's Sons, 1946.

NIETZSCHE, Friedrich. *The Antichrist.* Translated from the German with an Introduction by H. L. Mencken. New York: Knopf, 1927.
Bought after 1940.

———. *The Dawn of Day.* Translated by J. M. Kennedy. Vol. 9 of his *Complete Works.* London: Allen & Unwin, 1924.

———. *Ecce Homo (Nietzsche's Autobiography).* Translated by Anthony M. Ludovici. Poetry Rendered by Paul V. Cohn, Francis Bickley [and others]. "Hymn to Life" (composed by F. Nietzsche). Vol. 17 of his *Complete Works.* London, New York: Macmillan, 1924.
Bought on December 3, 1945.

———. *Human, All Too Human: A Book for Free Spirits.* 2 vols. With an Introduction by J. M. Kennedy. Vols. 6–7 of his *Complete Works.*
London: Allen & Unwin, 1924.
Bought on November 16, 1945.

———. *The Philosophy of Nietzsche.* New York: Modern Library, n.d.
Bought after 1940.

———. *Selected Letters of Friedrich Nietzsche.* Edited, with a Preface, by Dr. Oscar Levy. Authorized Translation by Anthony M. Ludovici. London: Heinemann, 1921.
Bought in Paris, 400F.

———. *Thoughts out of Season.* 2 vols. Vols. 4–5 of his *Complete Works.* London: Allen & Unwin, 1924.
Bought used after 1940.

———. *The Will to Power: An Attempted Transvaluation of All Values.* 2 vols. Translated by Anthony Ludovici. Vols. 14–15 of his *Complete Works.* [3d ed.] London: Allen & Unwin, 1924.
Bought used after 1940.

Wright mentioned in his diary buying *Thus Spake Zarathustra* and *The Genealogy of Morals* on November 16, 1945.

Nietzsche is mentioned among Damon's readings in *The Outsider,* 268. "Man is the only being who makes promises" is quoted as epigraph to Book 5 of *The Outsider.* Nietzsche is quoted in epigraph to Part II *Savage Holiday,* quoted in epigraph to *Pagan Spain,* and mentioned in both *Black Power* and in *White Man, Listen!.*

" 'Frog Perspectives' . . . is a phrase I've borrowed from Nietzsche to describe someone looking from below upward, a sense of someone who feels himself lower than others." (*White Man, Listen!,* p. 27).

"I began to read. I suppose some of you college students are expecting me to tell you that I read Nietzsche or Herbert Spencer. No; I went to second-hand magazine stores and purchased huge bundles of Smith and Street detective story magazines! I didn't learn anything, but I enjoyed myself. But while browsing around in second-hand bookstores, I did eventually run across magazines of nation-wide circulation, good ones. I read them and thought that I, and I alone, had discovered the world." ("Adventure and Discovery," *Biblio.,* p. 163, U 41, Wright Misc. 226, p. 4)

Thus Spake Zarathustra is often quoted as one of Wright's favorite books. (Interview, *L'Express,* Oct. 18, 1955, p. 8)
"Nietzsche, a great prophet whose questions are actual and everlasting." (Interview, *Dagens Nyheter,* Nov. 25, 1956.)

NIN, Anaïs. *Ladders to Fire.* With Engravings by Ian Hugo. New York: Dutton, 1946.
Inscribed: "For Dick, / who revealed to me / the deeper level of American life, / who is for me a symbol / of the most human and the wisest."

———. *Solar Barque.* Illustrated by Peter Loomer. [Ann Arbor, Mich.: Edwards Bros., 1958].
Inscribed: "For the Wrights, / with friendship"

———. *A Spy in the House of Love.* Paris, New York: British Book Centre, 1954.
Inscribed: "For the Wrights, / with my friendship"

———. *Under a Glass Bell.* Line engravings on copper by Ian Hugo. [New York: Gemor Press, 1944].
Inscribed: "To Dick and Ellen, / with the deepest friendship. / Anais + Hugo. / N.Y.: June, 1944."

———. *Winter of Artifice.* Line Engravings on Copper by Ian Hugo. [London: The Author, n.d.].

Inscribed: "For Ellen and Richard Wright, / with gratitude / for being initiated by 'Native Son' / to the deepest, most tragic and most lovable / people of America. Anais Nin."

N O R D A U, Max. *Degeneration*. Translated from the 2d ed. of the German Work. New York: D. Appleton, 1895.

Bought used in Paris, 100F.

N O R M A N, Dorothy. *Dualities*. New York: Privately Printed for An American Place, 1933.

Inscribed: "To Dick / I give this to you / with warmest feelings / but without words. / Dorothy." (After 1940)

N O R R I S, Frank. *Blix; Moran of the Lady Letty; Essays on Authorship*. Vol. 4 of his *Complete Works*. New York: Collier, 1893.

Bought before 1940.

Mentioned in *Black Boy*, 262. Reading *McTeague* was one of Wright's early incursions into American realism.

N O R T H, Joseph. See HICKS, Granville.

N O R T H C O T T, Cecil. *Voice Out of Africa*. London: Edinburgh House, 1952.

N O R T H U P, Solomon. *Twelve Years a Slave. Narrative of Solomon Northup, Citizen of New York, Kidnapped in Washington City in 1841 and Rescued in 1853, from a Cotton Plantation near the Red River, in Louisiana*. Auburn: Derby and Miller; Buffalo: Derby, Orton and Mulligan, 1853.

Bought after 1940.

N U R N B E R G, Walter.

Lighting for Photography: Means and Methods. London, New York: Focal Press, 1945.

Bought in Buenos Aires.

With 30 pages of handwritten formulas.

N U T T, Howard. *Special Laughter: Poems*. With an Introduction by Richard Wright. Prairie City, Ill.: Press of J. A. Decker, 1940.

Inscribed: "Dear Dick, / I'm proud that you shared / the venture with me. / Howard."

Wright wrote the introduction in the form of a letter dated Spring 1940. See APPENDIX, pp. 225–27.

O

OATES, Whitney J. and O'NEILL, Eugene, Jr. *The Complete Greek Drama: All the Extant Tragedies of Aeschylus, Sophocles, and Euripedes and the Comedies of Aristophanes and Menander, in a Variety of Translations*. 2 vols. New York: Random House; Toronto: Macmillan, 1938.
  Bought used after 1940.
  Euripedes is quoted as epigraph to Part III of *Savage Holiday*.
OBENG, R. E.
  Eighteen Pence. Willner Bros., 1950.
O'BRIEN, Edward J., ed. *The Best American Short Stories, 1938*. Boston: Houghton Mifflin, 1938.
  Includes Wright's "Bright and Morning Star."
———. *Best American Short Stories, 1941*. Boston: Houghton Mifflin, 1941.
  Reprint of "Almos' A Man" included.
O'CONNOR, Flannery.
  Mentioned by Wright in a lecture on American literature given in January 1951 in Rome.
ODETS, Clifford.
  "I also had time to see some of the plays on Broadway: *Till the Day I Die; Waiting for Lefty; Tobacco Road; Black Pit; Awake and Sing*, etc. The whole thing was very enjoyable." (To Mary Wirth, May 10, 1937).
ODUM, Howard C. *Wings on My Feet: Black Ulysses at the Wars*. Indianapolis: Bobbs-Merrill, 1929.
  Bought after 1940.
OGDEN, Charles K. *The System of Basic English*. New York: Harcourt, Brace & Co. [1934]
  Bought after 1940.
O'HARA, John. *Appointment in Samarra, A Novel*. New York: Grossett & Dunlap, 1935.
  Wright read the book on April 4, 1945 (Unpublished journal).

———. *Butterfield Eight, A Novel.* New York: Harcourt, Brace & Co. 1935.
   Wright read the book on March 30, 1945, and "liked it" (Unpublished journal).
———. *The Doctor's Son and Other Stories.* New York: New Avon Library, 1943.
   Wright read the book on April 7, 1945 (Unpublished journal).
———. *Hope of Heaven.* New York: Harcourt, Brace & Co., 1938.
   Wright read the novel on April 4, 1945 (Unpublished journal).
———. *Pal Joey.* New York: Duell, Sloan & Pearce, 1940.
   Bought in 1945.
———. *Pipe Night.* With a Preface by Wolcott Gibbs. New York: Duell, Sloan & Pearce, 1945.

Inscribed: "To Richard Wright, / Who never did this before / -well hardly ever -/ thanks and good wishes / for the good wishes. / 16 April 1946."

Wright did a radio review of *Pipe Night* in 1945. He read the novel on April 8, 1945, and also O'Hara's *Files on Parade* for that purpose.
   Wright wrote notes on four index cards for discussion of O'Hara's short stories in *Hellbox* for an "Author Meets the Critics" broadcast. See *Biblio.*, p. 192, U 13.
   Pal Joey reminded Wright of Dostoevsky's *Poor Folk* and Samuel Richardson's *Clarissa* and gave him the idea of reworking *Lawd Today* in epistolary form. (Unpublished journal, April 16, 1945).
OLIVER, Paul. *Bessie Smith.* London: Cassell, 1959.
   Wright wrote a foreword to Oliver's *Blues Fell This Morning* (London: Horizon Press, 1960, vii-xii).

"It is a history of the blues; Paul Oliver wrote it and it is *very good*. It is an indictment of racial conditions in America shown through the Negro's songs, something a little in the line of my 'Literature of the Negro in the United States.'" (To Margrit de Sablonière, March 19, 1960).

See APPENDIX, pp. 227–31.
O'NEILL, Eugene. *The Emperor Jones; The Straw.* Introduction by Dudley Nichols. New York: Modern Library, 1928.
   Bought before 1940.

"Willis Richardson's one act plays were produced in some of the little and commercial theatres; and, in 1925, Garland Anderson's *Appearances* ran at the Frolic Theatre. Wallace Thurman collaborated on *Lulu Belle* and

Harlem, both well known on Broadway. In 1937, Langston Hughes entered the field with his *Mulatto.* . . .
Prominent among those plays written by whites in which Negro actors have had an opportunity to depict the lives of their people are Eugene O'Neill's *The Emperor Jones* and *All God's Chillun Got Wings* . . . Edward Sheldon and Charles McArthur's *Lulu Belle* . . . Paul Green's Pulitzer Prize Play, *In Abraham's Bosom* . . . Marc Conelly's *The Green Pastures* . . . and Paul Peters and George Sklar's *Stevedore.* . . ." ("Portrait of Harlem," in *New York Panorama,* New York: Random House, 1938, p. 146.)

"In 1936, the Federal Theatre, working with a Negro cast, opened the Lafayette again to legitimate drama, producing Frank Wilson's *Walk Together Chillun,* Rudolph Fisher's *The Conjure Man Dies* and Orson Welles' production of *Macbeth* . . . followed by Gus Smith's and Peter Morell's *Turpentine,* Carlton Moss's adaptation of Obey's *Noah,* George Kelly's *The Show Off,* George McEntee's *The Case of Philip Lawrence,* Dorothy Hailpern's *Horse Play,* four of Eugene O'Neill's one-act plays of the sea, and William DuBois' *Haiti.*" (*Ibid.,* p. 148)

O N S T O T T, Kyle. *Mandingo.* Richmond, Va.: Denlinger, 1957?

"*Mandingo* . . . is the most wonderfully horrible description of American slavery on record. Let me know if you have not heard of it or read it, for it is a must." (To Margrit de Sablonière, Sept. 1, 1960)

Wright was instrumental in getting the novel translated and published in Paris.

O R T E G A Y G A S S E T, José. *Concord and Liberty.* Translated from the Spanish by Helene Weyl. New York: W. W. Norton, 1946.
    Bought in Buenos Aires.
———. *The Revolt of the Masses.* Authorized Translation from the Spanish. New York: New American Library, 1950.
    According to Ralph Ellison, Wright discussed the book with him around 1937.

O R W E L L, George [Eric Arthur Blair]. *Coming Up for Air.* [New ed.] London: Secker & Warburg, 1948.
———. *Keep the Aspidistra Flying, A Novel.* New York: Popular Library, 1956.
———. *1984.* Secker, 1951.

O S W A L D, Marianne.
    Comments by Wright are printed on the dust jacket of *One Small Voice* (New York: Whittlesey House; London: McGraw Hill, 1945).

"If there ever came out of France a voice that America ought to understand, love and accept for her own, surely it is the astounding and human voice of that remarkable woman rebel, Marianne Oswald. In her book *One Small Voice,* the story of her incredible childhood, she tells how she grew up as an ugly duckling, an unwanted and rejected child; how she was cheated, scolded, raped, and cast into the world to live or die. But she emerged unbent, vibrant, a free spirit, with a will to fight against every illusion and obstacle that encroach upon people who are trying to exercise their natural and acquired powers. Her book is one more bit in the mounting mass of evidence that proves that scientists do not yet really quite know how we came to be human beings. One cannot read *One Small Voice* without being confounded, shocked and yet elated over the fact that there are still people who can speak the truth, who can crawl even out from under stones with a soul strong and essentially virginal enough to reject every compromise that does not square with a deep sense of integrity. Enclosed is the book of Miss Marianne Oswald. . . . I'm convinced that she knows a lot and can write as well as sing." (To Paul Reynolds, December 12, 1945)

O T T L E Y, Roy. *"New World A-coming": Inside Black America.* Boston: Houghton Mifflin, 1943.

O U S P E N S K Y, Petr D. *Tertium Organum, The Third Canon of Thought: A Key to the Enigmas of the World.* Translated from the Russian by Nicholas Bessaraboff and Claude Bragdon. With an Introduction by Claude Bragdon. London: Kegan Paul, 1923.
     Bought after 1940.

P

PADMORE, George. *Africa: Britain's Third Empire.* London: Dobson, 1949.

———. *The Gold Coast Revolution: The Struggle of an African People from Slavery to Freedom.* London: Dobson, 1953.

Inscribed: "To my good friend Dick, / with affection, / George. / 17–4–53."

———. *Pan-Africanism or Communism? The Coming Struggle for Africa.* London: Dobson, 1956.

Inscribed:

". . . your eulogistic foreword makes me / feel guilty of the cult of the personality. / Well, we shall wait / and see the public reactions. / Yours ever / George / London, July 26, 1956."

On March 2, 1956, Wright wrote an introduction to *Pan Africanism or Communism?*, pp. 11–14, which was revised as a preface to *Panafricanisme ou communisme?* (Paris: Presence Africaine, 1960), on September 10, 1960.

" 'George Padmore, a West Indian, and W. E. B. DuBois, American, first gave to the world the idea of Pan-Africanism. Padmore, after becoming disillusioned with Soviet politics, and DuBois, shortly after the first World War dreamed the dream which today has aroused Africa. . . .' At this point Wright removed his glasses and put away his prepared notes." (Edward Reeves, "Richard Wright Hits U. S. Racial Hypocrisy," Chicago *Defender,* Nov. 29, 1960, p. 13)

On Wright and the Padmores as friends, see Fabre, 311 to 496, *passim.*

See APPENDIX, pp. 231–34.

PALGRAVE, Francis Turner. *The Golden Treasury of the Best Songs and Lyrical Poems.* A Modern Edition, Revised, Enlarged, and Brought Up to Date by Oscar Williams. New York: New American Library, 1953.

P A N C O A S T, Henry S. *English Prose and Verse from Beowulf to Stevenson.* New York: Holt, 1923.

P A N N I K A R, Sandar K. M. *Asia and Western Dominance: A Survey of the Vasco da Gama Epoch of Asian History, 1498–1945.* London: G. Allen & Unwin, 1955.
     Mistral, Paris, stamp.
     Sandar K. Pannikar gave a talk on black Africa at the American Cultural Center in Paris on April 24, 1958, and Wright participated in the debate that followed.

P A R A P S Y C H O L O G Y   F O U N D A T I O N ,   N E W   Y O R K. *Proceedings of Four Conferences of Parapsychological Studies.* New York: The Foundation, 1957.
     Bought in Paris, 400F

P A R K, Robert E.

"In *Native Son*, I said, I had used the concepts of sociology as devised by some of the guys at the University of Chicago. . . . Also I had used there for the first time some of the psychoanalytic concepts I had picked up. . . . I had used them all in *Black Boy*." (Unpublished journal, January 2, 1945)

"Critical examinations of the daily habits of white and Negro urban people, the ritual of their lives (à la *The City*)." ("Suggestions for the Launching of American Pages," *Biblio.*, p. 177, U 100, Wright Misc. 238, p. 11.)

"Robert E. Park's view of the Negro / Impulse-ridden Negroes of the South vs. valid human personalities; the Negro is now conscious of this. What kind of feelings does this consciousness engender?" (Notes on cards for a lecture on the Negro in America, 1945–46?)

"I had the honor of meeting the Dean of American sociologists, Dr. Robert E. Park, while on a visit to Chicago [in 1941]. . . . Cayton arranged that I should meet Dr. Park."("The Position of the Negro Artist and Intellectual in American Society," *Biblio.*, p. 168, U 63, Wright Misc. 622, p. 7 [1960])

See CARLA CAPETTI, "The Sociology of an Existence; Richard Wright and the Chicago School," *MELUS*, 12 (Summer 1985), 25–44.

P A R T I S A N   R E V I E W ;   P A R T I S A N   R E V I E W   A N D   A N V I L. (John Reed Club, New York). Wright had a number of issues of the magazine, from 1935 to 1940; he contributed a few items.

P A S C A L, Blaise. *Pensées: The Provincial Letters.* New York: Modern Library, 1941.

PASTERNAK, Boris. *Doctor Zhivago.* Translated from the Russian by Max Hayward and Manya Harari. London: Collins, and Harvill Press, 1958.

PATTERSON, Frances T. *Cinema Craftsmanship: A Book for Photoplaywrights.* New York: Harcourt, Brace & Howe, 1920. Bought secondhand after 1940 for $1.75.

PATTERSON, Haywood and CONRAD, Earl. *Scottsboro Boy.* Garden City, N. Y.: Doubleday, 1950.

PAUL, Louis.

"In Louis Paul's 'No More Trouble for Jedwick,' [the protagonist is] seemingly halfway between the tribal life of Africa and the mores of the Western world, fleeing the law, slugging, killing. . . . Yet this desperate man is at bottom friendly; he fears that he will be killed and so he kills first." ("Foreword to *Lest We Forget*," *Biblio.*, p. 175, U 54, Wright Misc. 456 [1955])

PEDLER, Frederick J. *West Africa.* London: Methuen, 1951. G. Padmore's copy.

PÉGUY, Charles. *Basic Verities: Prose and Poetry.* Rendered into English by Anne and Julian Green. [4th ed.] New York: Pantheon Press, 1945.

———. *Men and Saints: Prose and Poetry.* Rendered into English by Anne and Julian Green. New York: Pantheon Press, 1944.

PERKINS, Maxwell E. *Editor to Author: Letters of Maxwell E. Perkins.* Selected and Edited with Commentary and an Introduction by John Hall Wheelock. New York: Scribner, 1950.
   Inscribed: "A good trip to you Dick,/and do not worry/about Alexander."

PERRIN, Porter G. *Writer's Guide and Index to English.* Chicago, Atlanta: Scott, Foresman, 1942.

PETERMANN, Bruno. *The Gestalt Theory and the Problem of Configuration.* Translated by Meyer Fortes. New York: Harcourt, Brace, 1932.
   Bought in Paris, 300F.

PETERS, J. *The Communist Party: A Manual on Organization.* New York: Workers Library Publishers, 1935.

PETERS, Paul. See HICKS, Granville.

PETRY, Ann. *The Street.* Boston: Houghton Mifflin, 1946.

"Not enough perspective exists for me to feel the new trends. Yet the sheer absence of some of the old qualities is enough to allow some inferences.

For example, in the work of Chester Himes, Ralph Ellison, James Baldwin, Ann Petry, Frank Yerby, Gwendolyn Brooks, etc. one finds a sharp loss of lyricism, a drastic reduction of the racial content, a rise in preoccupation with urban themes and subject matter both in the novel and the poem." ("The Literature of the Negro in the United States," in *White Man, Listen!*, p. 147.)

PHILLIPS, William and RAHV, Philip, eds. *The Partisan Reader: Ten Years of Partisan Review, 1934–1944, An Anthology.* Introduction by Lionel Trilling. New York: The Dial Press, 1946.
Includes Wright's poem "Between the World and Me."

PHYFE, William H. P. *Ten Thousand Words Often Mispronounced . . . A Complete Handbook of Difficulties in English Pronunciation.* New York and London: G. P. Putnam's Sons, 1903.
Bought before 1940.

PITKIN, Walter B. *A Short Introduction to the History of Human Stupidity.* New York: Simon & Schuster, 1938.
Bought in Paris, 200F

PLATO. *The Dialogues of Plato.* Translated into English by B. Jowett. With an Introduction by Professor Raphael Demos. 2 vols. New York: Random House, 1937.
Bought after 1940.

PLAYFAIR, Giles and SINGTON, Derrick.
The Offenders: Society and the Atrocious Crime. London: Secker and Warburg, 1957.

PLEKHANOV, George. *Art and Society.* Translated from the Russian. Introduction by Granville Hicks. New York: Critics Group, 1936.
Bought after 1940.

POE, Edgar Allen.
Poems and Tales. Edited with an Introduction, Explanatory Notes, and Questions for Class Study by Joseph Paxton Simmons. Lincoln, Chicago: The University Publishing Co., 1924.
Copy stamped "Alexander Hamilton High School"
Acquired before 1940.
———. *Works* (Vol. 4); *Criticism.* New York: Harper, n.d.
Bought before 1940.
———. *The Works of Edgar Allen Poe.* Vol. 3 of 4 vols. New York: W. J. Widdleton, 1876.
Bought after 1940.
"Poe hid in the shadows of a dream world, a region almost akin to

the Heaven of the surrealists." ("Personalism" (1935–37?), *Biblio.*, p. 167, U 62.)
Mentioned at the end of "How Bigger Was Born."
For Poe's influence on *Native Son* and "Superstition," see Fabre, 84–85 and *World,* 27–33, 217–28.

POINTS. No. 1, February-March 1949 and no. 2, April-May 1949.

POLAND. MINISTERSTWO INFORMACJI. *The Black Book of Poland.* New York: G. P. Putnam's Sons, 1942.
Inscribed: "For Richard Wright, / in admiration and respect / and with very best wishes, / Vladimir Murny, / Le Harve, May 9, 1946."

POMEROY, Wardell B. See KINSEY, Alfred C.

PORTER, Katherine Anne. *Noon Wine.* Detroit: Schuman's, 1937.

PORTFOLIO. v. 1—(no. 1—.); Summer, 1945—[Paris]: Black Sun Press.

POWDERMAKER, Hortense. *After Freedom: A Cultural Study in the Deep South.* New York: Viking Press, 1939.
Bought after 1940.

POWELL, A. Van Buren. *The Photoplay Synopsis.* Foreword by J. Berg Esenwein. Springfield, Mass.: The Home Correspondence School, 1919.
Bought used after 1940 for $4.50.

PRESCOTT, Frederick C. *Poetry & Myth.* New York: Macmillan Co. 1927.
Bought before 1940.

PRESCOTT, William H. *History of the Conquest of Mexico; and, History of the Conquest of Peru.* New York: Modern Library, n.d.
The story of Montezuma and Cortez was used by Wright as a basis for the outline of a novel, "When the World Was Red" *Biblio.*, p. 163, U 40.

PRÉSENCE AFRICAINE.
Wright was one of the founders of the magazine in 1947 and a frequent contributor, as well as the adviser on Afro-American affairs until 1956. The magazine was sent to him until his death.

PREUVES.
Wright had only a few copies of this magazine, 1953–58.

PREYRE, E. A. *The Freedom of Doubt: Reflections of a Natural Sceptic.* Revised and Translated under the Author's Supervision. London: The Harvill Press, 1953.
Bought in Paris.

PRITCHETT, V. S. *The Spanish Temper.* London: Chatto & Windus, 1954.

PROUST, Marcel. *Remembrance of Things Past.* Translated by C. K. Scott Moncrieff. Introduction by Joseph Wood Krutch. 10 pts. in 4 vols. New York: Random House, 1934.
Bought new in 1935.

"The writer can now begin to project himself——objectively, of course——more and more into his work. I add hastily that I am not arguing for the return of the subjectivism of a Proust or a Joyce——I realize that one must be on the defense in opening up such a subject as this." ("Lecture on Left-wing Literature" [1940?], p. 6)

"I spent my nights reading Proust's *Remembrance of Things Past,* admiring the lucid, subtle but strong prose, stupefied by its dazzling magic, awed by the vast, delicate intricate and psychological structure of the Frenchman's epic of death and decadence. But it crushed me with hopelessness, for I wanted to write of the people in my environment with an equal thoroughness and the burning example before my eyes made me feel that I never could." (*American Hunger,* p. 24)

"This neighborhood in which I'm living is the one in which Proust lived and laid many of his scenes." (Unpublished journal, August 24, 1947.)

"I think that there can be a union of the theoretical and aesthetic components of the human outlook. Many works of art have demonstrated this; I refer to Marcel Proust's *Remembrance of Things Past* which is a truly enchanting, magical piece of work, a series of novels whose appeal to the senses excludes any message; yet it does carry a deep and meaningful moral lesson. . . . The fact is that Joyce, Proust, Kafka, Stein, have made brilliant contributions in the realm of combining the aesthetic and the moral in great art." (Notes for a lecture in Bandung, 1955.)

"Well, I don't know what you mean by 'the pure novel'. In my opinion all novels, of necessity, possess an autobiographical base. The work of Marcel Proust was surely anchored firmly in autobiographical material. The same is true of the novels of James Joyce. I could say the same thing of the tremendous novels of American life written by Theodore Dreiser." (Radio interview by Raymond Barthes, 1956.)

PUSHKIN, Alexandr. *Pushkin's Poems.* A Selection Translated by Walter Morison. With an Introduction and Notes by Janko Lavrin. London: Published for Prague Press, Ltd. by G. Allen & Unwin, 1945.
In "Literature of the Negro in the United States," a passage

from a short story by Pushkin about a duel is quoted to show that he was more a Russian than a Negro. "Pushkin wrote out of the rich tradition of Russian realism and he helped to further and enrich that tradition. He was one with his culture." (*White Man, Listen!*, p. 112)

See Wright's unpublished "Notes on Reading" (*Biblio.*, p. 182, U 13) which includes comments on Alexander Pushkin's "The Shot."

Q

QUINN, Kerker and SHATTUCK, Charles, eds. *Accent Anthology: Selections from Accent, a Quarterly of New Literature, 1940–1945.* New York: Harcourt, Brace & Co., 1946.
Includes "The Man Who Lived Underground."
QUINT, Bernard. See GUNTHER, John.

R

RABELAIS, François. *The Works of Mr. Francis Rabelais, Doctor in Physick. Containing Five Books of the Lives, Heroick Deeds & Sayings of Gargantua and His Sonne Pantagruel Together with the Pantagrueline Prognostication, the Oracle of the Divine Bachuc, and Response of the Bottle. Hereunto Are Annexed the Navigations unto the Sounding Isle and the Isle of the Apedefts; As likewise the Philosophical Cream with a Limosin Epistle.* Now Faithfully Translated into English. Illustrated by W. Heath Robinson. 2 vols. New York: Privately Printed for Rarity Press, 1932.
   Bought before 1940.
RADCLIFFE, Cyril John Radcliffe, baron. *The Problem of Power.* London: Secker & Warburg, 1952.
RADEK, K. See ZHDANOV, A.
RADIN, Paul, ed. *African Folktales & Sculpture.* Selected and Edited by Paul Radin with the Collaboration of Elinore Marvel. Introduction to the Tales by Paul Radin. Sculpture Selected with an Introduction by James Johnson Sweeney. New York: Pantheon Books, 1953.
RAHV, Philip. See PHILLIPS, William.
RAJAN, Balachandra, ed. *T. S. Eliot: A Study of His Writings by Several Hands.* London: D. Dobson, 1948.
RAMUZ, C. F. *The Triumph of Death.* London: Routledge, 1946.
   Ricour, Paris, sticker.
———. *When the Mountain Fell.* Translated by Sarah Fisher Scott. New York: Pantheon, 1947.
   Ricour, Paris, sticker.
RAPER, Arthur F. and REID, Ira de A. *Sharecroppers All.* Chapel Hill: University of North Carolina Press, 1941.
   Mentioned as background reading for *Twelve Million Black Voices.*

RATCLIFFE, A. J. J. *A History of Dreams: A Brief Account of the Evolution of Dream Theories, with a Chapter on the Dream in Literature.* With an Introduction by Godfrey Hilton Thomson. London: G. Richards, 1923.
Bought after 1940.

RATTRAY, R. S., Captain. *Ashanti.* Oxford: Clarendon Press, 1923.
Bought in the Gold Coast.

READ, Herbert E. *Existentialism, Marxism and Anarchism: Chains of Freedom.* London: Freedom Press, 1949.

————. *Form in Modern Poetry.* London: Vision, 1948.

READE, Winwood. *The Martyrdom of Man.* With an Introduction by F. Legge. London: Watts, 1928.
Bought before 1940.

RECKLESS, Walter C. *The Crime Problem.* New York: Appleton-Century-Crofts, 1950.
Bought used in Paris, 500F.

————. *Criminal Behavior.* New York, London: McGraw-Hill, 1940.
U.S.I.S. Library copy, March, 1952.

REDDICK, Lawrence D. *Crusader Without Violence: A Biography of Martin Luther King, Jr.* New York: Harper, 1959.
Inscribed: "For Dick and Ellen / and those wonderful daughters / who have never known / the bad taste we know. / Larry Reddick."

REDDING, J. Saunders. *No Day of Triumph.* With an Introduction by Richard Wright. New York, London: Harper & Bros., 1942.
For Wright's introduction to the book, see APPENDIX, pp. 234–35.

————. *On Being Negro in America.* Indianapolis: Bobbs-Merrill, 1951.

————. *Stranger and Alone, A Novel.* New York: Harcourt, Brace, 1950.
Wright recommended Redding for a Guggenheim Fellowship in 1947:

"There are in the United States today two young writers in whose work I have the greatest faith, Nelson Algren and Jay S. Redding. A few years ago I gave you my opinion of Algren, and I now gladly give you my opinion of Redding.

For sheer prose writing, I feel that Redding has none but few equals among Negro writers today. His prose is sensitive but strong, and is backed by an informed sensibility. His earlier book, *No Day of Triumph,* for which I was proud to write an introduction, revealed a unique knowledge of Negro life. I am convinced that if he were given the opportunity to execute the enclosed plan, America would gain a valuable work of art." (To Mr. Moe, John S. Guggenheim Fellowship Board, New York City, 1947)

REDFIELD, Robert.
On February 26, 1945, Wright bought *Tepoztlan* and *The Folk Culture of Yucatan* and read them that same week. (Unpublished journal)

"It was from the scientific findings of men like the late Robert E. Park, Robert Redfield and Louis Wirth that I drew the meanings for my documentary book *12,000,000 Black Voices*, for my novel *Native Son;* it was from their scientific facts that I absorbed some of that quota of inspiration necessary for me to write *Uncle Tom's Children* and *Black Boy*." (Introduction to *Black Metropolis* by St. Clair Drake and Horace Cayton [Harcourt, Brace, New York, 1955] p. xviii.)

"Scientific volumes characterized by brilliant insight and feeling are Robert Redfield's *Tepoztlan*, Louis Wirth's *The Ghetto*, Everett V. Stonequist's *The Marginal Man*, Frederic M. Thrasher's *The Gang*, Park's and Burgess's *The City* and Harvey W. Zorbaugh's *The Gold Coast and the Slum*." (*Ibid.* p. xvx)

"As Robert Redfield has pointed out: holy days became holidays, clocks replaced the sun as a symbolic measurement of time." (*Ibid.*, p. xxii)

REED, John. *Daughter of the Revolution, and Other Stories.* Edited, with an Introduction, by Floyd Dell. New York: Vanguard Press, 1929.
Bought after 1940.
Wright discussed *Ten Days That Shook the World* with Jack Conroy around 1935.

REICH, Wilhelm. *Character-analysis: Principles and Techniques for Psychoanalysts and in Training.* Translated by Theodore P. Wolfe. 2d ed. New York: Orgone Institute Press, 1945.
———. *The Function of the Orgasm: Sex-economic Problems of Biological Energy.* Vol. 1 of his *The Discovery of the Orgone.* New York: Orgone Institute Press, 1942.
Bought on March 3, 1945.
———. *The Mass Psychology of Fascism.* Translated from the German Manuscript by Theodore P. Wolfe. 3d. rev. and enl. ed. New York: Orgone Institute Press, 1946.

————. *The Sexual Revolution: Toward a Self-governing Character Structure*. Translated by Theodore P. Wolfe. New York: Orgone Institute Press, 1945.

REID, Ira De Augustine. *In a Minor Key: Negro Youth in Story and Fact*. Washington, D. C.: American Council on Education, 1940.
See also RAPER, Arthur.

REIK, Theodor. *Fragment of a Great Confession: A Psychoanalytic Autobiography*. New York: Farrar, Straus, 1949.

————. *Listening with the Third Ear: The Inner Experience of a Psychoanalyst*. New York: Farrar, Straus 1949.

————. *Masochism in Modern Man*. Translated by Margaret H. Beigel and Gertrud M. Kurth. New York: Farrar, Straus, 1949.
Bought in London, 45 sh.

————. *Myth and Guilt: The Crime and Punishment of Mankind*. London: Hutchinson, 1958.
Bought in Paris, 1900F.

————. *Psychology of Sex Relations*. New York, Toronto: Farrar & Rinehart, 1945.

————. *Ritual: Psycho-analytic Studies*. With a Preface by Sigmund Freud. Translated from the Second Edition by Douglas Bryan. International Psycho-analytical Library, no. 19. London: Leonard & Virginia Woolf, 1931.
Bought after 1940.

————. *The Unknown Murderer*. Translated from the German by Dr. Katherine Jones. New York: Prentice-Hall, 1945.
A quotation from *The Unknown Murderer* is used as epigraph to *Savage Holiday*, Part II.

REINDORF, Carl C. *History of the Gold Coast and Asante, Based on Traditions and Historical Facts, Comprising a Period of More than Three Centuries from about 1500 to 1860*. Basel: The Author, 1899.

REITMAN, Ben L. *The Second Oldest Profession: A Study of the Prostitute's "Business Manager."* New York: Vanguard Press, 1931.
Bought after 1940.

REIWALD, Paul. *Society and Its Criminals*. Translated and Edited by T. E. James. London: Heinemann, 1949.

REPLANSKY, Naomi. *Ring Song: Poems*. New York: Scribner, 1952.

Replansky was a friend of the Wrights; Richard wrote a blurb for her *Poems (Biblio.,* p. 170, U 76).

REYBURN, H. A. *Nietzsche: The Story of a Human Philosopher.* In Collaboration with H. E. Hinderks and J. G. Taylor. London: Macmillan, 1948.

RHINE, J. B. *The Reach of the Mind.* New York: Sloane Assocs., 1947.

Royvaux, Paris, 600F.

RHODES, Henry T. *The Criminals We Deserve: A Survey of Some Aspects of Crime in the Modern World.* London: Methuen, 1937. Bought after 1940.

RICHMOND, Anthony H. *The Colour Problem. A Study of Racial Relations.* Hammondsworth, Middlesex: Penguin Books, 1955.

RICK, Pierson.

"Pierson Rick's 'Swamp Maze' introduces the white world as a protagonist, revealing the psychological gulf existing between an old, simpleminded Negro, but uncannily wise, baffling and elusive, and a scheming white man." ("Foreword to *Lest We Forget," Biblio.,* p. 175, U 94, Wright Misc. 456 [1955])

RICOEUR, Paul. See DUFRENNE, Mikel.

RIESMAN, David. *The Lonely Crowd: A Study of the Changing American Character.* With Nathan Glaszer and Reuel Denney. Garden City, N. Y.: Doubleday, 1953.

RILKE, Rainer Maria. *Letters to Benevenuta.* With a Foreword by Louis Untermeyer. London: The Hogarth Press, 1953.

Mistral, Paris, 775f.

———. *Poems.* Translated from the German by J. B. Leishman. London: L. & Virginia Woolf at the Hogarth Press, 1934.

Acquired after 1940———Sophie Reagan.

———. *Poems of the Book of Hours: "Das Studenbuch."* Translated by Babette Deutsch. Norfolk, Conn.: New Directions, 1941.

———. *Translations from the Poetry of Rainer Maria Rilke.* By M. D. Herter Norton. New York: W. W. Norton & Co., 1938.

Acquired after 1940—Sophie Reagan.

" 'But can you write in Paris, so far from your subject matter?' is flung at me with frequent unctuousness. . . . A few other writers, among whom are Rilke, Joyce, Turgenev, D. H. Lawrence managed to create in French exile." ("I Choose Exile," *Biblio.,* p. 166, U 57 [1952])

RIMBAUD, Arthur. *A Season in Hell*. In a New English Translation by Louise Varése. Norfolk, Conn.: New Directions, 1945.

ROBERTS, Elizabeth Madox. *The Time of Man*. With an Introduction by J. Donald Adams. New York: Modern Library, 1935.
Bought after 1940.

ROCHE, Philip Q. *The Criminal Mind: A Study of Communication Between the Criminal Law and Psychiatry*. New York: Grove Press, 1959.

ROEDER, Bill. *Jackie Robinson*. New York: Barnes, 1950.
Inscribed: "To Richard Wright, / with my best, best wishes / to a real writer."

ROGERS, J. A. *100 Amazing Facts About the Negro: With Complete Proof: A Shortcut to the World History of the Negro*. 18th and revised edition. New York: J. A. Rogers Publication, 1934.
Wright mentions in his unpublished journal having bought the book on February 17, 1945. On February 24, he noted that he found *Sex and Race* badly written.

ROGET'S THESAURUS. See MAWSON, Christopher O.

ROHEIM, Géza. *Psychoanalysis and Anthropology: Culture, Personality, and the Unconscious*. New York: International University Press, 1950.

ROLFE, Edwin. See SPECTOR, Herman.

ROLLAND, Romain. *Jean Christophe*. Translated from the French by Gilbert Cannan. New York: Modern Library, 1938.
Inscribed "Dear Dick / Please will you write / one this size? / Lee and Kit / 25 dec. 1938."

ROLLINS, William, Jr.
Wright wrote a review of *The Wall of Men* (1938) in "Adventure and Love in Loyalist Spain," *New Masses*, 26 (March 8, 1938), 25–26. See APPENDIX, pp. 235–36.

ROLPH, C. H., ed. *Women of the Streets: A Sociological Study of the Common Prostitute*. Edited by C. H. Rolfe For and On Behalf of the British Social Biology Council. London: Secker & Warburg, 1955.
Bought in Paris, 1365F.

ROMAINS, Jules. *Men of Good Will*. Vols. 1 and 2 of 14 vols. New York: A. A. Knopf, 1933–46. Terminal Bookshop, 3337 Lawrence Ave., Chicago.
Bought before 1937, 35¢.

ROSENFELD, Paul. See KREYMBORG, Alfred.

ROTHA, Paul. *The Film Till Now: A Survey of World Cinema with an Additional Section by Richard Griffith.* Rev. and enl. ed. New York: Funk & Wagnalls, 1949.

ROTHBERG, Abraham. See FOLEY, Martha.

ROUGEMONT, Denis de. *The Devils's Share.* New York: Pantheon, 1940.

———. *Love in the Western World.* Translated by Montgomery Belgion. New York: Harcourt, Brace, 1940.

ROUGHEAD, William. *Famous Crimes.* London: Faber & Faber, 1935.

ROUSSET, David. *A World Apart.* Translated by Yvonne Moyse and Roger Senhouse. London: Secker & Warburg, 1951.

RUGGIERO, Guido de. *Existentialism.* Edited and Introduced by Rayner Heppenstall. London: Secker & Warburg, 1946.

———. *Modern Philosophy.* Translated by A. Howard Hannay and R. G. Collingwood. London: Allen & Unwin; New York: Macmillan, 1921.

RUNES, Dagobert D., ed. *Twentieth Century Philosophy: Living Schools of Thought.* New York: Philosophical Library, 1947.

RUSSELL, Bertrand. *Power, A New Social Analysis.* London: Allen, 1948.

RUTHERFOORD, Peggy, ed. *African Voices: An Anthology of Native African Writing.* New York: Vanguard Press, 1960.

S

SADE, marquis de. *The Bedroom Philosophers. Being an English Rendering of "La philosophie dans le boudoir."* Done by Pieralessandro Casavini. Paris: Olympia Press, 1953.
Inscribed: "A mon ami Richard Wright, / l'homage du traducteur / Bernard Casavini. (Paris, 1953)."

SAGARRA, José Mariá de. *Montserrat.* Barcelona: Noguer, 1954.

SAINT-EXUPERY, Antoine de. *Night Flight.* Preface by Andre Gide. Translated by Stuart Gilbert. Paris: Crosby Continental Editions, 1932.
Bought in Paris.

SAKI [H. H. Munro]. *The Novels and Plays of Saki (H. H. Munro), Complete in One Volume.* London: J. Lane, 1949.

SALINGER, J. D. *The Catcher in the Rye.* New York: New American Library, 1953.

SANDBURG, Carl.
"I am an American . . . that is to say without traditions and looking towards the future resolutely. Carl Sandburg renders such attitude thus:

The past is a bucket of ashes
A fallen wind
A sun

(Interview by Jeanine Delpech, *Les Nouvelles Littéraires*, March 8, 1958. Transl. M. Fabre)
Quoted as epigraph to *Pagan Spain.*

SAN LAZZARO, Guitieri di. *Painting in France, 1895–1949.* Translated by Baptista Gilliat-Smith and Bernard Wall. New York: Philosophical Library; Toronto: George J. McLeod, 1949.
Bought after 1940, $3.75.

SAPIN, Louis.
Papa Bon Dieu (1958), Sapin's play on a black religious theme, appealed to Wright and he wrote an introduction to it in French—

"Une pièce qui aurait ravi Voltaire," *L'Avant-Scène*, No. 168 (1958), 3–4—before preparing an adaptation of the play under the title *Daddy Goodness*.

"About a month ago, a young Frenchman, Louis Sapin, came to me with a play that he had written. The play was not very good, but the idea was, it seemed to me, good. He suggested that I translate and adapt it to Negro life in America." (To Paul Reynolds, June 14, 1956.)

"Sapin knows that there lurks deep in the heart of most people a reverence for their fathers, for authority, for the miraculous, and that this psychological trait is summed up under the name: God. Yet Sapin knows that this hunger for God is never really appeased nor finds fulfilment in real life. Out of this universal contradiction, Sapin has proceeded to weave a fantastic play wherein a drunken French peasant about to be interred as dead comes to life and is taken by his naive neighbors as God. No doubt this incident happened more than once in history, but Sapin's treatment of the Risen Messiah varies sharply from other similar histories in that his Messiah is too compassionate toward mankind to wish to fool men into thinking that he is God, yet at the same time too merciful to deny that he is God. . . ." (*American Theatre Association of Paris Newsletter*, no. 1, February 1959, p. 1)

S A R O Y A N, William. *The Human Comedy*. New York: World, 1955.
———. *Love, Here Is My Heart*. New York: Modern Age Books, 1938.
    Bought before 1940.
    Titles of short stories, except number 2, checked in pencil.
———. *My Name Is Aram*. Illustrated by Don Freeman. New York: Harcourt, Brace, 1940.
    New York Public Library stamp, 1942.
    See also HILER, Hilaire.
S A R T R E, Jean-Paul. *Age of Reason*. Vol. 1 of his *The Roads to Freedom*. From the French by Eric Sutton. New York: A. A. Knopf, 1947.
———. *Baudelaire*. Translated from the French by Martin Turnell. Directions, v. 17. Norfolk, Conn.: New Directions, 1950.
———. *Being and Nothingness: An Essay on Phenomenological Ontology*. Translated and with an Introduction by Hazel E. Barnes. London: Methuen & Co., 1957.
    Bought in Paris, 3050F.

――. *The Chips Are Down (Les jeux sont faits)*. Translated by Louise Varése. London, New York: Rider, 1951.
Galignani, Paris, sticker.

――. *The Diary of Antoine Roquentin*. Translated from the French "La nausée" by Lloyd Alexander. London: Lehman, 1949.

――. *The Emotions: Outline of a Theory*. Translated from the French by Bernard Frechtman. New York: Philosophical Library, 1948.
Mistral, Paris, stamp.

――. *Existentialism*. Translated by Bernard Frechtman. New York: Philosophical Library, 1947.

――. *The Flies (Les mouches) and In Camera (Huis clos)*. Translated by Stuart Gilbert. London: H. Hamilton, 1946.

――. *Intimacy, and Other Stories*. Translated by Lloyd Alexander. London, New York: P. Nevill, 1949.

――. *Iron in the Soul*. Translated from the French by Gerard Hopkins. London: Hamish Hamilton, 1950.

――. *Le Mur*. With Etchings by Prassinos. Paris: Gallimard, 1945.
Inscribed: "Avec les hommages sympathiques de / Jean-Paul Sartre."

――. *Portrait of the Anti-Semite*. New York: Partisan Review, 1946.

――. *The Psychology of Imagination*. London, New York: Rider, 1950.

――. *The Reprieve*. Vol. 2 of his *The Roads to Freedom*. Translated from the French by Eric Sutton. New York: Knopf, 1947.

――. *Three Plays*. Translated from the French by Kitty Black. London: H. Hamilton, 1949.
The plays are *Crime Passionnel (Les mains sales); Men Without Shadows (Morts sans sepulture);* and *The Respectful Prostitute (La putain respecteuse)*.

――. *What Is Literature?* Translated from the French by Bernard Frechtman. New York: Philosophical Library, 1949.

"I am extremely interested in Sartre's *The Respectful Prostitute*. Sartre's literary expression is of great interest to me because he seems to feel deeply the reality of my own country. . . . No foreign visitor has felt so accurately the incredible naivety of American civilization. In particular, the character of the prostitute is basically true, from the human point of view as well as from that of America today." (Michel Gordey, "L'Amérique n'est pas le Nouveau Monde" [interview], *Les Lettres Françaises*, January 10, 1947, p. 7. Transl. M. Fabre)

Wright wrote a translation of Sartre's introduction to his *L'Etre et le Néant* [*Being and Nothingness*], called "In Pursuit of Being." See *Biblio.*, p. 184, U 146.

"Read Sartre's article [in *Twice A Year*] this morning about revolution and freedom; and also read the Beauvoir's article on freedom. How those French boys and girls think and write; nothing like it exists anywhere on earth today. How keenly they feel the human plight. Read Camus's article, but, though I liked it, it did not possess the sharpness and sense of urgency that the other articles possessed." (Unpublished journal, August 5, 1947)

"I agree with Sartre on several points. Our mission as writers is to tell the truth at whatever cost. We must not fear reprisals, whether Russian or American." ("Entrevista con Richard Wright," *Revista Branca*, Buenos Aires, 1960. Transl. M. Fabre)

"One of the most remarkably gifted men I've met in Paris is Jean-Paul Sartre, playwright, novelist and philosophical spokesman for atheistic existentialism. Sartre feels that it is his right rather than his duty to defend, on purely humanistic grounds, the interests of workers, to castigate anti-Semites, racism and imperialism. Albert Camus, Jean Cocteau, Simone de Beauvoir and a host of other French writers share the same humanistic passion to defend the dignity of man." ("I Choose Exile," *Biblio.*, p. 166, U 57. [1952])

"Why is the reality of race so vivid an experience among them [colored people of whatever race or nationality] now?. . . . As usual the French have a word for this reality; the African intellectuals of Paris have a strong word for this feeling, a word that goes much deeper than race consciousness. They call it negritude. As the black poets and Jean-Paul Sartre have analyzed it, it means this: when a vast group of colored people are made aware that the color of their skin is the justification for the domination, exploitation, and oppression that is meted out to them by whites, these people cannot escape feeling that their humanity has been denied, and denied on a strange basis they cannot control: color." *Typescript on Africa and Communism, unpublished, 1955–56?*

Wright wrote an introduction to *The Respectful Prostitute* in *Art and Action* (New York: Twice A Year Press, 1948), pp. 14–16. Upon reading the play in manuscript form, he sent Sartre several pages of remarks on its accuracy, insofar as American life and habits were concerned.

On Wright's relationship with Sartre, see Fabre, 520–27; *World*, 158–63, 171.

See APPENDIX, pp. 236–44.

SCHAPIRO, Jacob S. *Modern and Contemporary History (1815–1923)*. Boston, New York: Houghton Mifflin, 1923.
Bought before 1940, 25¢.

SCHAPPES, Morris U. *Letters from the Tombs*. Edited with an Appendix, by Louis Lerman. Foreword by Richard Wright. Drawings by James D. Egleson. New York: Schappes Defense Committee, 1941.
For Wright's foreword to this collection of letters from the Communist militant to his wife, see APPENDIX, pp. 244–45.

SCHERMAN, Harry. *The Promises Men Live By: A New Approach to Economics*. New York: Random House, 1944.
Inscribed: "To my good friend Richard Wright / with regards and admiration - 9/19/1944 / Harry Scherman"

SCHMALENBACH, Werner. See SCHMIDT, Georg.

SCHMIDT, Georg; SCHMALENBACH, Werner; and BÄCHLIN, Peter. *The Film: Its Economic, Social, and Artistic Problems*. English version: Hugo Weber and Roger Manvell. London: Falcon Press, 1948.
Galignani, Paris, sticker.

SCHMULLER, Aaron. *Man in the Mirror*. With a Foreword by Alfred Kreymborg. New York: Harbinger House, 1945.

SCHNEIDER, Isidor. *The Temptation of Anthony; A Novel in Verse, and Other Poems*. New York: Boni & Liveright, 1928.
Bought before 1940, $2.00.
See also HICKS, Granville.

SCHNITZLER, Arthur. *Bertha Garlan*. New York: Modern Library, 1918?
(R.E.W.)
———. *Theresa, the Chronicle of a Woman's Life*. Translated by William A. Drake. New York: Simon & Schuster, 1928.
Bought before 1940.

SCHOPENHAUER, Arthur.
The Art of Literature: A Series of Essays. Selected and Translated by T. Bailey Saunders. New York: S. Sonnenschein & Co., 1891.
Bought before 1940, 50¢.

SCHREINER, Olive. *The Story of an African Farm*. Introduction by Francis Brett Young. New York: Modern Library, 1927.
Bought after 1940.

SEABROOK, William B. *No Hiding Place: An Autobiography*. Philadelphia, New York: J. B. Lippincott, 1942.

————. *Witchcraft: Its Power in the World Today.* New York: Harcourt, Brace, 1940.

Bought in London, 8 sh. 6.

S E A V E R, Edwin, ed. *Cross Section: A Collection of New American Writing.* New York: L. B. Fischer, 1944.

Includes "The Man Who Lived Underground" and novellas by other black authors.

————. *Cross Section: A Collection of New American Writing.* New York: L. B. Fischer, 1945.

Includes "Early Days in Chicago."

S E L L E R Y, C. G. and KREY, A. C., eds. *Medieval Foundations of Western Civilization.* New York:Harper & Bros., 1929.

Bought after 1940, $2.00.

S E L S A M, Howard. *What Is Philosophy? A Marxist Introduction.* New York: International Publishers, 1938.

Bought after 1940.

S E N G H O R, Léopold Sédar.

Although Wright met Senghor several times, there is no indication that he read any of his works other than his contributions to *Présence Africaine.* On their relationship, see *World,* pp. 200–10.

S E R V I C E, Robert W.

Wright did a reader's report for the Book-of-the-Month Club on his novel *Ploughman of the Moon.* See *Biblio.,* p. 172, U 82.

S E X T O N, Ethol (Ethol Sexton Kossa). Wright wrote a blurb for *Count Me Among the Living,* which appears on the dust jacket of the book (1946). See *Biblio.,* p. 63, 1946–15.

"I've just finished reading the galleys of a novel called *Wasteland* by Jo Sinclair, which I predict will create some talking when it is published. It's great! Also read Ethol Kossa's *Count Me Among the Living,* which will also, I think, create some talk after the first of the year." (To Carl Van Vechten, December 20, 1945.)

S H A K E S P E A R E, William. *The Complete Works of William Shakespeare . . . Also the History of His Life . . . With a Contribution on the Shakespeare and Bacon Controversy by the Late Sir Henry Irving.* New York: World Syndicate Co., 1927.

Bought before 1940.

————. *Complete Works.* Edited with a Glossary by W. J. Craig. London, New York: Oxford University Press, 1944.

Bought used, 1944.

————. *The Tragedies of Shakespeare.* New York: The Modern Library, 1943.
Bought in Québec City on June 9, 1945.
Shakespeare is mentioned in *Black Boy*, as being among Wright's early reading, and is quoted as epigraph to *The Outsider*, Book IV, "Despair": "The wine of life is drawn and the mere lees / Is left this vault to brag of." (*Macbeth*). Shakespeare is quoted as epigraph to *The Long Dream*, Part III, "Waking Dream": "The dream's here still; even when I wake it is / Without me, as within me: not imagined." (*Cymbeline*).
Willard Maas and Marie Mencken took Wright to see a performance of *Hamlet* in 1939. This was the first time Wright saw a play by Shakespeare. He exclaimed "Gee, if I could write like that!" (Interview of Marie Mencken and Willard Maas by Michel Fabre, 1963)
On November 16, 1942, Wright, John Hammond, Horace Cayton, and Vandi Haygood went to a performance of *Macbeth*. On January 30, 1945, Wright saw a performance of *The Tempest* in New York, in the company of Ellen, Herbert Klein, Mark Marvin, June Goodman, and others. He thought that Shakespeare was "tops."

"Many migrants like us were pursued, in the manner of the characters in a Greek play, down the paths of defeat. . . . [F]or those of us who did not come through, we are trying to do the bidding of Hamlet who admonished of Horatio:

If thou didst ever hold me in thy heart,
Absent thee from felicity awhile
And in this harsh world draw thy breath in pain,
To tell my story."

(Preface to *Black Metropolis* by St. Clair Drake and Horace Cayton, New York: Brace, Harcourt, 1955, p. xvii)

Wright alluded to the Negro middle-class writers saying "if you prick me, I bleed; if you put fire to me, I burn; I am like you who exclude me" in "The Literature of the Negro in the United States." He does not footnote his allusion to Shakespeare's *Merchant of Venice*. He goes on:

"Perhaps the most graphic and lyrical of those men was W. E. B. DuBois; indeed, one might say that it was with him that the Negro complaint reached almost religious heights of expression."

Eleven lines of "A Litany in Atlanta" are quoted as instances of public prayer and Old Testament style apostrophizing. See *White Man, Listen!*, pp. 134–35.

In the French version of this lecture, Wright explains he borrowed the phrase "shapes of the unknown" from Theseus' speech in *Midsummer Night's Dream. (Les Temps Modernes,* August 1948, p. 208)

The Outsider was called "I did but dream," in May 1952, from a line in *Richard III* by Shakespeare. Some time later, a new title, "Innocence at Home," was suggested by Twain's *Innocents Abroad.*

SHATTUCK, Charles. See QUINN, Kerker.

SHAW, George Bernard. *Getting Married, and The Shewing-up of Blanco Posnet.* Copyright ed. Leipzig: B. Tauchnitz, 1914.
Bought after 1940.
Only the preface and the first 30 pages are cut.

———. *Pygmalion: A Romance in Five Acts.* With Over a Hundred Drawings by Feliks Topolski. Toronto: Penguin Books, 1942.

SHAW, Irwin. *The Troubled Air.* New York: New American Library, 1952.

SHEA, J. Vernon, ed. *Strange Barriers.* New York: Lion Library Editions, 1955.
"Almos' A Man" is included.

SHELDON, William H. *Philosophy of the Promethean Will.* New York: Harper, 1936.
Bought after 1940.

———. *The Varieties of Temperament: A Psychology of Constitutional Differences. . . .* With the Collaboration of S. S. Stevens. New York, London: Harper & Bros., 1942.

SHERIDAN, Richard Brinsley. *The Dramatic Works of Richard Brinsley Sheridan.* With Introduction and Notes by Joseph Knight. London, New York: H. Frowde, Oxford University Press, 1906.
Bought used in Paris, 150F.

SHESTOV, Lev. *In Job's Balances: On the Sources of the Eternal Truths.* Translated by Camilla Coventry and C. A. Macartney. London: J. M. Dent and Sons, Ltd., 1932.

SHILS, Edward A. *The Torment of Secrecy: The Background and Consequences of American Security Policies.* Melbourne: Heinemann, 1957.

SHOLOKOV, Mikhail A.
Wright read *And Quiet Flows the Don* in *International Literature*.
SHRODES, Caroline. See CAMPBELL, Oscar J.
SILONE, Ignazio. *And He Hid Himself: A Play in Four Acts*. Translated by Darina Tranquilli. New York: Harper & Bros., 1948.
Inscribed: "A Richard Wright. / Avec une grande admiration / pour son talent et son honnêteté./ Ignazio Silone. / Rome, 3 Mars 1949."
———. *Fontamara*. New York: Modern Age Books, 1938.
Bought after 1940.
———. *The School for Dictators*. Translated from the Italian by Gwenda David and Eric Mosbacher. London: Jonathan Cape, 1939.
Bought after 1940.
———. *The Seed Beneath the Snow*. Translated from the Italian by Frances Frenaye. New York: Harper & Bros., 1942.
SIMMONS, Ernest. *Dostoevski: The Making of a Novelist*. London, New York: Oxford University Press, 1940.
SIMMONS, Herbert. *Corner Boy, A Novel*. Boston: Houghton Mifflin, 1957.
SIMPSON, Louis. *The Arrivistes: Poems, 1940–1949*. New York: Fine Editions Press, 1949.
SINCLAIR, Jo [Ruth Seid].
Wright wrote a review of *Wasteland* (New York: Harper, 1946) in "Wasteland Uses Psychoanalysis Deftly," *P.M. Magazine*, Feb. 17, 1946, p. m8. See APPENDIX, pp. 245–47.
SINCLAIR, Upton.
In mid-March 1945, Wright did a reader's report for the Book-of-the-Month Club on Sinclair's novel *Dragon's Harvest* (1945). See *Biblio.*, p. 171, U 79.
SINGTON, Derrick. See PLAYFAIR, Giles.
SITWELL, Osbert, Sir. *Left Hand, Right Hand: An Autobiography*. London?: Macmillan, 1957.
SLOCHOWER, Harry.
Wright mentions in his diary buying *No Voice Is Wholly Lost* on September 4, 1945.

"Harry Slochower, an exile from Nazi Germany and author of *Three Ways of Modern Man*, gave a report on culture under Hitler. Slochower pointed out that, anti-cultural as the Nazi regime is, it is dialectically producing a culture, that is, an *anti*-Nazi culture. . . . Slochower pointed out further that the recent forthright anti-fascist stand taken by Thomas Mann, Germany's foremost contemporary writer, was heartening the friends of democracy throughout the world." ("The Barometer Points to Storm," *Biblio.*, p. 164, U 45, Wright Misc. 271, p. 3)

S M I T H, Bernard. *Forces in American Criticism: A Study in the History of American Literary Thought*. New York: Harcourt, Brace, 1939.
Inscribed: "For Dick / from Ket and Lee. / 12/25/39"

S M I T H, Edward H., ed. *Mysteries of the Missing*. New York: L. McVeagh Dial Press, 1927.
Bought in Paris, 500F.

S M I T H, Lillian. *Killers of the Dream*. New York: W. W. Norton, 1949.
Inscribed: "For Dick Wright, / with my warm regards / Lillian Smith. / Clayton, Ga."

———. *Strange Fruit, A Novel*. New York: Reynal & Hitchcock, 1944.
Wright recommended *Strange Fruit* and *An American Dilemma* in a November 11, 1945, Washington *Star* interview.

"In Lillian Smith's 'Talk with the Preacher' we get a cogent statement of the old-time Christian outlook upon Negroes." ("Foreword to *Lest We Forget*," *Biblio.*, p. 175, U 94, Wright Misc. 456 [1955])

Smith is mentioned in Wright's introduction to Françoise Gourdon's *Tant qu'il y aura la peur* (1960).

S M I T H, William Gardner.
Smith presented Wright with his novels, in particular *Last of the Conquerors* (1948), in the mid-1950s. He wrote an essay on Wright, "Black Boy in France," for *Ebony* in July 1953.

S N E L L, Bruno. *The Discovery of the Mind*. Oxford: Blackwell, 1953.

S O L O V I E V, Vladimir S. *The Meaning of Love*. London: G. Bles, The Centenary Press, 1945.

S O N T A G, Raymond James and BEDDIE, James Stuart, eds. *Nazi-Soviet Relations, 1939–1941: Documents from the Archive of the German Foreign Office as Released by the Department of State*. Washington, D.C.: Department of State, 1948.

S O P H O C L E S. *The Tragedies of Sophocles*. Translated into English Prose by Sir Richard E. Jebb. Cambridge: Cambridge University Press, 1905.

SOUPAULT, Philippe.
Wright wrote a blurb for *Age of Assassins* (1946), which is printed on the dust jacket. See *Biblio.*, p. 63, 1946–18.

"Philippe Soupault's *Age of Assassins* is yet another example of the brilliant resurgence of French genius in post-war literature, that genius that knows how to create directly out of experience. *Age of Assassins* is a picture of men under pressure, of their resistance to and transcendence of the Nazi tide that sought to blot out their humanity. The book deals with extreme situations——imprisonment, loneliness, and death——situations which have become too familiar to far too many men during the last 12 years. The relentless psychological analysis will remind you of Dostoyevsky. *Age of Assassins* proves that great living is necessary to produce writing that breathes the spirit of truth and rekindles in us a sense of the irreducibly human." (April 22, 1946)

SPAETH, Sigmund G. *The Art of Enjoying Music.* New York: Garden City Pub. Co., 1938.
Inscribed: "To Richard, / with sincere regards. / Ellen."

SPECTOR, Herman *et al. We Gather Strength: Poems by Herman Spector, Joseph Kalar, Edwin Rolfe, and Saul Funaroff.* Introduction by Michael Gold. New York: Liberal Press, 1933.
Acquired before 1940.

SPENCER, Herbert. *The Man Versus the State.* London: Watts, 1940.
Bought for $1.95.

SPENGLER, Oswald. *The Decline of the West.* Authorized Translation with Notes by Charles Francis Atkinson. New York: A. A. Knopf, 1946.

SPINOZA, Benedictus de. *The Living Thoughts of Spinoza, Presented by Arnold Zweig.* [3d ed.] London: Cassell, 1946. 250F.

SPOTTISWOODE, Raymond. *A Grammar of the Film: An Analysis of Film Technique.* Berkeley: University of California Press, 1950.
Galignani, Paris, sticker.

STALIN, Joseph. *Marxism and the National and Colonial Question: A Collection of Articles and Speeches.* Moscow, Leningrad: Co-operative Publishing Society of Foreign Workers in the U.S.S.R., 1935.
Autograph notation: "Wright"
"I had never read Trotsky. . . . It had been Stalin's *Marxism and the National and Colonial Question* that had captured my interest." (In Richard Crossman, ed., *The God That Failed,* p. 129).

STANISLAVSKI, Konstantin [pseud.]. *An Actor Prepares.* Translated by Elizabeth Reynolds Hapgood. New York: Theatre Arts, 1939.
Bought after 1940.
STAUFFER, Donald A., ed. *The Intent of the Critic, by Edmund Wilson, Norman Foerster, John Crowe Ransom, [and] W. H. Auden.* Princeton: Princeton University Press, 1941.
STEIN, Gertrude. *The Autobiography of Alice B. Toklas.* New York: The Literary Guild, 1933.
———. *Brewsie and Willie.* New York: Random House, 1946.
———. *Composition As Explanation.* The Hogarth Essays. Second Series, 1. London: L. & Virginia Woolf, 1926.
———. *Everybody's Autobiography.* London: W. Heinemann, 1938.
Bought on December 15, 1945.
———. *The First Reader & Three Plays.* Dublin: Fridberg. 1946.
———. *Geographical History of America; Or, The Relation of Human Nature to the Human Mind.* With an Introduction by Thornton Wilder. New York: Random House.
———. *Geography and Plays.* Boston: Four Seas Co., 1922.
Bought on May 30, 1945.
———. *How to Write.* Paris: Plain Edition, 1931.
Bought on December 15, 1945.
———. *Ida.* New York: Random House, 1941.
Bought on May 30, 1945.
———. *In Savoy; Or, Yes Is for a Very Young Man, a Play of the Resistance in France.* London: Pushkin Press, 1946.
———. *Lectures in America.* New York: Random House, 1935.
———. *Lucy Church, Amiably! A Novel of Romantic Beauty and Nature and Which Looks Like an Engraving.* Paris: Imprimerie "Union," 1930.
Bought on May 30, 1945.
———. *The Making of Americans: The Hersland Family.* Preface by Bernard Fäy. New York: Harcourt, Brace, 1934.
Bought and read in June 1945.
———. *Matisse, Picasso and Gertrude Stein, with Two Shorter Stories.* Paris: Plain Edition, 1933.
———. *Narration: Four Lectures.* With an Introduction by Thornton Wilder. Chicago: University of Chicago Press, 1935.
Wright read it on January 28, 1945, and remarked that one must live in Paris to be able to write in that way.
———. *Operas and Plays.* Paris: Plain Edition, 1932.

———. *Picasso.* London, New York: P. T. Batsford, 1948.

———. *Portraits and Prayers.* New York: Random House, 1934.

———. *Tender Buttons: Objects, Food, Rooms.* New York: C. Marie, 1914.

Bought on December 15, 1945.

———. *Three Lives.* Introduction by Carl Van Vechten. New York: Modern Library, 1933.

———. *Two: Gertrude Stein and Her Brother, and Other Early Portraits, 1908–1912.* With a Foreword by Janet Flanner. Vol. 1 of *The Yale Edition of the Unpublished Writings of Gertrude Stein.* New Haven: Yale University Press, 1951.

Galignani, Paris, sticker.

———. *Useful Knowledge.* New York: Paysen & Clarke. 1928.

———. *Wars I Have Seen.* New York: Random House, 1945.

———. *What Are Masterpieces.* Los Angeles, Calif.: The Conference Press, 1940.

———. *The World Is Round.* Pictures by Clement Hurd. New York: W. R. Scott, 1939.

Inscribed: "Merry Xmas and a Happy New Year / to Dick's little girls / Always / Gertrude Stein"

Wright started collecting Stein's books after he met her in 1946. At that time he had only read *Three Lives* (circa 1935) and reviewed *Wars I Have Seen,* which he reviewed in "Gertrude Stein's Story Is Drenched in Hitler's Horrors," *P.M. Magazine,* March 11, 1945, p. m15. He reviewed *Brewsie and Willie* the following year: "American G.I.'s Fears Worry Gertrude Stein," *P.M. Magazine,* July 26, 1946, p. m15–m16.

Wright's statements on Stein are numerous:

"He likes *Melanctha* by Gertrude Stein and said she was the first American author to treat the Negro seriously." (Interview in *N.Y. Sun & Telegraph,* March 4, 1940.)

"I had heard my grandmother speak ever since I can remember, so that I was not conscious of anything particularly distinctive in her speech. Then I read a sketch of Negro life by Gertrude Stein and suddenly it was as if I were listening to my grandmother for the first time, so fresh was the feeling it gave me." (Quoted in "Richard Wright," by Joseph Gollomb, *Book-of-the-Month Club News,* Feb. 1945, p. 8)

"I heard of Stein's *Three Lives* through reading the newspapers. I had just read a newspaper account about a very funny woman who was always talking about "a rose is a rose is a rose" and the account went on to inform me that she lived in Paris and that she smoked a rare form of dope in a pipe about three feet long while reclining on a satin couch. . . . In his condemnation of her, however, he [the author] made one exception: he said that Stein's story of a Negro girl, called 'Melanctha,' was really a good story, even though slightly screwy. . . . While turning the pages of 'Melanctha,' I suddenly began to *hear* the English *language* for the first time in my life! . . . English as Negroes spoke it: simple, melodious, tolling, rolling, rough, infectious, subjective, laughing, cutting . . ." ("Memories of My Grandmother," *Biblio.*, p. 166, U 58 Wright Misc. 473, p. 18)

"Your *Brewsie and Willie* is a speaking portrait, a portrait that speaks, and it is the most compact and incisive thing you have yet written. It was a marvel how you abstracted from all the welter of aimless GI talk and got the essence of what they felt, what worried them, what they hoped and thought and did not know. Right off I called *PM* and asked for the right to review the book. . . . You certainly in *Brewsie and Willie* went into the heart of our industrial problem in America. There are tiny sections of it that are as lovely as painting. . . . You did repeat over and over in a stabbing way what you wanted to say, and yet your repeating was never quite repeating. And the manner in which you listened so well and closely to the GI talk in Paris is a marvel. Your talk is as fresh as though you had made a trip to America." (To Gertrude Stein, March 15, 1946)

"I truly did like her *Wars I Have Seen*. It was full of good humor and some sharp observations about life and war; . . . My copy of her *Three Lives* is quite worn from use and time." (To Carl Van Vechten, May 28, 1945)

"You asked me if I had your books. I have some. Here is what I do have: *The Making of Americans, Three Lives, What Are Masterpieces, Operas and Plays, Ida, Wars I Have Seen, Geography and Plays, Useful Knowledge, The Autobiography of Alice B. Toklas, Lectures in America, Portraits and Prayers,* and *Lucy Church Amiably.* What I do not have and have not read are the following: *Tender Buttons* and *Everybody's Autobiography* and *How to Write.* I know that some of these cannot be had but I'd like any that you could send me.

I'm sending you a book called *Black Metropolis.* . . . I have marked for your attention a paragraph in the introduction; now I got the notion for that paragraph in your book, *What Are Masterpieces,* page 35, third paragraph beginning with 'And so there was the natural phenomena' and ending with '. . . and so war may be said to have advanced a general recognition of the expression of the contemporary composition by almost thirty years.'"

A Marxist read my introduction to *Black Metropolis* and said, 'Why, you are a real Marxist!' He was referring to the paragraph in question. I then go to your *What Are Masterpieces* and read that paragraph to him. He was quite stunned." (To Gertrude Stein, October 29, 1945)

"... Modernistically she has splashed some of these glaring pigments upon her canvas! *AMERICAN MEN ARE MOSTLY VIRGINS . . . PER-HAPS WE ARE NOT ISOLATIONISTS BUT ARE SIMPLY ISOLATED . . . THE LAST GENERATION WAS A LOST ONE BUT THIS GEN-ERATION IS SIMPLY A SAD ONE . . . THE ANSWER TO THE CLASS STRUGGLE IS THAT THERE IS JUST NO ANSWER . . . INDUS-TRIALIZATION MAKES A COUNTRY POOR. AS A NATION WE ARE LIVING THROUGH THE MOST DANGEROUS MOMENT IN OUR HISTORY . . . GALLUP POLLS ARE POSSIBLE ONLY IN A COUNTRY WHERE PEOPLE DO NOT THINK . . . AMERICA IS AL-READY AN OLD-FASHIONED COUNTRY. . . .* You could no more afford to miss Miss Stein's *Brewsie and Willie* than your doctor could afford not to put his stethoscope to your heart when you call him in. Reading *Brewsie and Willie* is a way of feeling and counting your own pulse, and the pulse of the nation." ("A Steinian Catechism," April 1946 blurb for Random House, reprinted in part on the dust jacket of *Brewsie and Willie*.)

"This story is the first realistic treatment of Negro life I'd seen when I was trying to learn how to write, and from my first reading of the story, I wished I had written it and I still do. For clarity, for the conveying of emotion, it is a miracle. As I've said in another place, this story made me see and accept for the first time in my life the speech of Negroes, speech that fell around me unheard." (Introduction to Gertrude Stein's "Melanctha," in Eugene J. Woods, ed., *I Wish I'd Written That*, New York, 1946, p. 234)

"The increasing modernization of life made it impossible for any sensitive artist to accept the old forms of expression. Walt Whitman broke the old molds; the French poets did the same. The reason was not sheer willfulness, it was necessity. But new forms quickly became accepted; and this made Gertrude Stein say that classics were what had been classified. I'm personally for the new free forms, forms conforming to the new experience, but I feel that such forms ought to be justified by their burden of organically felt passion rather than sheer technical ability." (Notes for a lecture in Bandung, 1955)

An interview in *L'Express,* (Oct. 18, 1955, p. 8) mentions Melanctha among Wright's favorite heroes in fiction.

Stein is alluded to in *Lawd Today,* 150; her advice to Wright about a trip to Spain is quoted in *Pagan Spain,* 12.

See APPENDIX, pp. 247–49.

S T E I N, Leopold and ALEXANDER, Martha. *Loathsome Women*. London: Weidenfield, 1959.
S T E I N B E C K, John. *Cannery Row.* New York: Bantam Books, 1947.
———. *The Grapes of Wrath*. New York: Viking, 1939.
Inscribed: "To Dick, from Sue and Kit"
———. *Of Mice and Men*. With an Introduction by Joseph Henry Jackson. New York: Modern Library, 1937.
Copy belonging to Wright's brother-in-law, M. P. Poplar, Fort Curtis [1942].
———. *The Pastures of Heaven*. New York: Penguin Books, 1942.
———. *Short Novels: Tortilla Flat, The Red Pony, Of Mice and Men, The Moon Is Down, Cannery Row, The Pearl*. With an Introduction by Joseph Henry Jackson. New York: Viking Press, 1953.
Bought after 1940.

"The ultimate test of our fiction in the future, I believe, will be the extent to which we can lift up this working-class life and show its complexity. . . . Sometimes, but not often, the pattern will be cut for us already, as the migration serves as a form for Steinbeck's *Grapes of Wrath*." (Lecture on Left-wing Literature [1940?], p. 12).

"They decided to roll the scenes together, to compound them as much as possible, to make the novel one continuous line of action involving the same characters, if possible. (In a sense one can say that *Grapes of Wrath* is one long scene, inasmuch as it deals with the same group of people against a background of migration, of open sky, of open road, etc.)" (*Ibid.* p. 15). See APPENDIX pp. 207–8.

In 1938, Wright saw the play *Of Mice and Men* with Jean Blackwell and enjoyed the anxiety in it. He visited in Mexico with Steinbeck while the latter was shooting "The Forgotten Village" with Herbert Klein in June 1940.
S T E K E L, Wilhelm. *Compulsion and Doubt (Zwang und Zweifel)*. Authorized Translation by Emil Gutheil. 2 vols. London, New York: P. Nevill, 1950.
———. *Conditions of Nervous Anxiety and Their Treatment*. With an Introduction by Samuel Lowy. London: Liveright, 1950.
———. *Frigidity in Woman in Relation to Her Love Life*. Authorized English Version by James S. Van Teslaar. 2 vols. London: Vision Press, 1953.
S T E N D H A L [Marie Henri Beyle]. *The Charterhouse of Parma;*

With a Study of M. Beyle of Honore de Balzac. Translated from the French by C. K. Scott-Moncrieff. 2 vols in 1. New York: Modern Library, 1937.
Bought after 1940.
———. *The Red and Black.* Translated by C. K. Scott-Moncrieff. New York: Modern Library, 1926?
Bought after 1940.
STERNE, Laurence. *The Life and Opinions of Tristram Shandy, Gentleman.* London, New York: Oxford University Press, 1921.
Bought after 1940.
STERNER, Richard M. *The Negro's Share: A Study of Income, Consumption, Housing, and Public Assistance.* In Collaboration with Lenore A. Epstein, Ellen Winston, and Others. New York: Harper & Bros. 1943.
STETSKY, A. See ZHDANOV, A.
STETSON, H. T. *Earth, Radio and the Stars.* New York: Whittlesey House, Mc-Graw Hill, 1934.
Bought used in Paris, 640F.
STEWART, Donald Ogden.

"Pithy and homely Donald Ogden Stewart, Hollywood humorist, epitomized the more radical spirit of the [June 1937 American Writers'] congress when he declared: 'I haven't anything very critical to say of the capitalist system except that it is a monster.'" ("The Barometer Points to Storm," *Biblio.,* p. 164, U 45, Wright Misc. 271, p. 2)

STILL, Charles E. *Styles in Crime.* Philadelphia: J. B. Lippincott, 1938.
Bought after 1940, $1.25.
STOCK, Freda. See WHITE, Moresby.
STONE, Irving. *Jack London, Sailor on Horseback: A Biographical Novel.* New York: Doubleday and Co., 1938.
Bought after 1940, $5.00.
STONEQUIST, Everett V. *The Marginal Man: A Study in Personality and Culture Conflict.* New York, Chicago: C. Scribner's, 1937.
Bought after 1940.
"I AM the marginal man."(Unpublished journal, February 13, 1945.)
Quoted in epigraph to *Black Power,* Part II, p. 49.
STORY, THE MAGAZINE OF THE SHORT STORY.
Wright only had the issue, March 1938, in which his "Fire and Cloud" novella appeared.

STOWE, Harriet Beecher. *Uncle Tom's Cabin; Or, Life Among the Lowly.* New York: Hurst & Co. [1911?]
  Bought before 1940.
  Mentioned in "Introduction" to Francoise Gourdon's *Tant qu'il y aura la peur* (Paris: Flammarion, 1961, p. 2).
STRACHEY, John. *Contemporary Capitalism.* New York: Random House, 1956.
———. *The Nature of Capitalist Crisis.* New York: Covici, Friede, 1935.
  Bought before 1940.
  On Wright and Strachey in London, see Fabre, 491, 493, 494, 495.
STREETWALKER. London: The Bodley Head, 1959.
STRINDBERG, August. *Married.* New York: Boni & Liveright, 1917.
  Bought after 1940.
———. *Plays by August Strindberg: Creditors, Pariah.* Translated from the Swedish, with Introductions by Edwin Björkman. London: Duckworth, 1913.
———. *Plays by August Strindberg; In Second Series: There Are Crimes and Crimes, Miss Julia, The Stronger, Creditors, Pariah.* Translated with Introductions by Edwin Björkman. Authorized ed. London: Duckworth, 1913.
  Bought used after 1940.
STRODE, Josephine, ed. *Social Insight Through Short Stories, An Anthology.* New York, London: Harper & Bros., 1946.
  Includes "What You Don't Know Won't Hurt You."
SUDERMANN, Hermann. *The Song of Songs.* A New Translation by Beatrice Marshall. London: John Lane, 1913.
  Gibert, Paris.
SULLIVAN, Arthur, Sir, and GILBERT, William S. *The Complete Plays of Gilbert and Sullivan.* Illustrated by W. S. Gilbert, Including Thirty-two Photographs by Jerome Robinson from Recent Performances by the D'Orly Carte Company. Garden City, N.Y.: Garden City Publishing Co., 1941.
SUSSMAN, Aaron. *The Amateur Photographer's Handbook.* Rev. by Bruce Downes. New York: T. Y. Cromwell & Co., 1948.
SUTHERLAND, Robert L. *Color, Class, and Personality.* Prepared for the American Youth Commission. Washington, D.C.: American Council on Education, 1942.

S U Z U K I, Daisetz T. *The Complete Works of D. T. Suzuki.* Edited by Christmas Humphreys. 7 vols. London: Published for the Buddhist Society by Rider & Co., 1958.

————. *Essays in Zen Buddhism.* 2d Series. London, New York: Published for the Buddhist Society by Rider, 1960.

————. *An Introduction to Zen Buddhism.* Edited by Christmas Humphreys. With a Foreword by C. G. Jung. London: Arrow Books, 1959.

S V E V O, Italo [Ettore Schmitz]. *The Confessions of Zeno.* Translated by Beryl de Ziete. With an Essay on Svevo by Renato Poggioli. New York: New Directions, 1930.
Bought after 1940.

S W E D E N B O R G, Emanuel [Emanuel Swedberg]. *Heaven and Hell.* Hammondsworth: Penguin, 1938.

S W I F T, Jonathan. *Gulliver's Travels.* London: H. Hamilton, 1947.

————. *Gulliver's Travels, the Voyages to Lilliput and Brobdingnag.* Edited by Charles Robert Gaston. New York: American Book Co., 1914.
Bought before 1940.
In an unpublished letter to the President of the United States, entitled "Let's Eat the Negroes (With Apologies to Old Jonathan)," Wright imitated Swift's satire, *A Modest Proposal,* by suggesting that eating black Americans was a way of solving the racial and economic problems (1936).

"I am aware that my proposal is not original in Christendom; in 1729 an old Englishman, Dean Swift, a man of letters and therefore given to intellectual whims of irony and bitterness, made a similar proposal in relation to the Irish to shock the wealthy people of his day to a sense of their responsibility.[2] [Note 2: Here refer to Dean Swift's 'Modest Proposal']." ("Let's Eat the Niggers," *Biblio.*, p. 168, U 65 [1936])

S W I N B U R N E, Algernon Charles. *Poems & Ballads. First Series.* London: Heinemann, 1917.
Bought used in Paris, 600F.

S Y M O N D S, John Addington. *A Problem in Greek Ethics: Being an Enquiry into the Phenomenon of Sexual Inversion; Addressed Especially to Medical Psychologists and Jurists.* London, 1901.

T

TALMON, J. L. *The Origins of Totalitarian Democracy.* London: Secker & Warburg 1952.
Galignani, Paris, stamp.

TAMBIMUTTA. See MARCH, Richard.

TAPIA ROBSON, Santiago Wealands. *The National Spanish Fiesta; Or, the Art of Bullfighting.* With the Collaboration of F. Velasco Gil. Madrid [F. Velasco Gil, 1953].

TARG, William. *The Case of Mr. Cassidy, A Mystery.* Cleveland, New York: World Pub. Co., 1939.
Inscribed: "For Mr. and Mrs. Richard Wright, / with very good wishes / from William Targ, / 5/22/1944"

TAUSSIG, Frank W. *Principles of Economics.* 3d ed. rev. New York: Macmillan, 1926.
Bought used before 1940.
Rum, Romance, and Rebellion is mentioned as background reading for *Twelve Million Black Voices.*

TAWNEY, Richard H. *Religion and the Rise of Capitalism, A Historical Study.* Hammondsworth: Penguin, 1943.

LES TEMPS MODERNES, Paris. 1, Oct. 1945 +.
Although a frequent contributor, Wright was not a regular subscriber to *Les Temps Modernes* and he only received the issues in which his own works were published in translation.

TENNYSON, Alfred Tennyson, baron. *Idylls of the King (Selections).* Edited, with Introduction and Notes by Arthur Beatty. Boston: Heath, 1904.
Bought before 1940.

———. *Tennyson's Poems, 1830–1859.* London: George Newnes, 1905.
Bought used in France.

THACKERAY, William Makepeace. *Vanity Fair.* New York: Frank & Lowell, n.d.
Bought before 1940.

THIEL, Rudolph. *And There Was Light: The Discovery of the Universe.* Translated from the German by Richard and Clara Winston. London: Andre Deutsch, 1958.

THOMAS, Dylan. *Collected Poems 1934–1952.* London: Dent, 1955.
  Quoted in epigraph to *Lawd Today,* Part I: "Sleep navigates the tides of time. . . . (6)

  "Light breaks where no sun shines;
  Where no sea runs, the waters of the heart
  Push in their tides. . . .

  . . . . . .

  Light breaks on secret lots,
  On tips of thoughts where thoughts smell in the rain;
  When logics die,
  The secret of the soil grows through the eye,
  And blood jumps in the sun. . . ."

  is quoted as epigraph to *White Man, Listen!.*

THOMAS, Frederick. See DENDRICKSON, George.

THOMAS, William H. *The American Negro: What He Was, What He Is, and What He May Become; A Critical and Practical Discussion.* New York: Macmillan & Co.; London: Macmillan & Co., 1901.
  Bought after 1940.

THOMPSON, Virginia McLean and ADLOFF, Richard. *French West Africa.* Stanford: Stanford University Press, 1958.

THOREAU, Henry David.
  "Thoreau took refuge in self-sufficiency." ("Personalism" [1935–37?], *Biblio.,* p. 167, U 62)

THORP, Margaret Farrand. See THORP, Willard.

THORP, Willard; CURTI, Merle; and BAKER, Carlos, eds. *American Issues.* 2 vols. Chicago, Philadelphia: J. B. Lippincott, 1941.
  Includes reprint of "Bright and Morning Star."

THORP, Willard and THORP, Margaret Farrand. *Modern Writing.* New York, Cincinnati: American Book Co., 1944.
  Includes an excerpt from *Twelve Million Black Voices.*

THRASHER, Frederic M. *The Gang: A Study of 1,313 Gangs in Chicago.* 2d rev. ed. Chicago: University of Chicago Press, 1947.

THUCYDIDES. *The History of the Peloponnesian War.* Translated

by Richard Crawley. London: J. M. Dent; New York: E. P. Dutton, 1936.
Bought after 1940.

T O L S O N, Melvin B. *Libretto for the Republic of Liberia.* New York: Twayne Publishers, 1953.
Author's address handwritten by Wright.

———. *Rendezvous With America.* New York: Dodd, Mead, 1944.
Inscribed: "To Dick Wright, / who pictures most powerfully / our 'rendez vous with America' / Melvin."
Wright wrote a blurb for Tolson's volume, see *Biblio.*, p. 171, U 77.
On Nov. 30, 1944, Wright suggested the following books as "important in order to know the American Negro": *An American Dilemma; Strange Fruit; The Winds of Fear; Rendezvous With America; Black Metropolis.*
Wright quoted six lines from "Dark Symphony" in "The Literature of the Negro in the United States." See *White Man, Listen!*, p. 144.

T O L S T O Y, Alexandra. *Tolstoy: A Life of My Father.* Translated from the Russian by Elizabeth Reynolds Hapgood. New York: Harper, 1953.

T O L S T O Y, Leo. *Anna Karenina.* New York: Modern Library, 1930.
Bought before 1940.
Autograph notation: "Richard Wright"

———. *The Cossacks: A Tale of the Caucasus in 1852.* Translated from the Russian by Eugene Schuyler. New York: Scribners, 1878.
Bought after 1940.

———. *Redemption and Two Other Plays.* Introduction by Arthur Hopkins. New York: Modern Library.
Bought before 1940.

———. *War and Peace, A Novel.* Translated from the Russian by Constance Garnett. New York: Modern Library.
Bought used before 1940.
Wright read *War and Peace* in Memphis, borrowing it from the public library by forging notes. (*Book-of-the-Month Club News*, Feb. 1940, p. x)
See FABRE, 176, 517.

T O O M E R, Jean.
Wright quotes "Song of the Son" in his essay on "The Literature of the Negro in the United States" to show that even when he is at

his sensually lyrical best, Jean Toomer cannot escape the horrible vision of his life. See *White Man, Listen!*, p. 139–40.

TOYNBEE, Arnold. *A Study of History.* 12 vols. London, New York: Oxford University Press, 1948–61.
   Bought in Paris, 1200F.

———. *The World and the West.* Oxford: Oxford University Press, 1949.

"Or do you consider the idea of the racial type a farce, in the sense in which Arnold Toynbee wrote in *A Study of History,* 'The so-called racial explanation of differences in human performance and achievement is either an ineptitude or a fraud.'" (Hans de Vaal, "Interview med Richard Wright," *Literair Pasport,* July-August, 1953, p. 161)

TRANSATLANTIC REVIEW. Rome, New York. 1, Summer, 1959.

TRAVEN, B. *The Death-Ship: The Story of an American Sailor.* London: Pan Books, 1950.

TREND, J. B. *The Civilization of Spain.* London, New York: Oxford University Press, 1952.
   Mistral, Paris, stamp.

TROISFONTAINES, Roger. *Existentialism and Christian Thought.* A Translation by Martin Jarrett-Kerr. Westminster [Eng.]: Dacre Press; London: A. C. Black, 1949.

TRUE DETECTIVE MAGAZINE.
   Wright was an avid reader of the tabloid. His novelette "The Man Who Lived Underground" (1944) is based on a 1940 article, "The Crime Hollywood Couldn't Believe," written by Hal Fletcher from the account, provided by Lieutenant C. W. Gains, of the Herbert C. Wright burglaries in Los Angeles in 1931–1933.
   See *World,* 93–96.

TURGENEV, Ivan. *Smoke.* Translated from the Russian by Constance Garnett. London: W. Heinemann, 1927.
   Bought in London, 3 sh. 6

———. *Virgin Soil.* London & Toronto: J. M. Dent & Sons; New York: E. P. Dutton, 1942.

TURPIN, Waters E.
   Wright wrote a review of *These Low Grounds* (1937) "Between Laughter and Tears," *New Masses,* 25 (Oct. 5, 1937), 22–25.
   See APPENDIX, pp. 250–51.

TUTUOLA, Amos. *The Palm-Wine Drinkard and His Dead Palm-Wine Tapster in the Dead's Town*. London: Faber & Faber, 1952. Wright bought *The Palm Wine Drinkard* in Accra, along with *Akan Laws and Customs* by J. B. Danquah and *Tribes of the Northern Territories of the Gold Coast* by M. Manoukian.

"I know of no African who is able to distinguish between a worldly and a sacred conception of time. The weird book by Amos Tutuola strikes by its surrealistic aspect but retains something timeless." (Interview by Jeanine Delpech, *Les Nouvelles Litteraires*, March 8, 1958. Transl. M. Fabre.)

"Now about Tutuola. . . . Yes, I read his first novel. This is a problem; you see, he is still definitely tribal and there is no direct way to his mind. What is wrong with him is that awful sense of tribal dependence. I wrote about all this in *White Man, Listen*. It is this feeling that he has to depend upon somebody else that gives him his sense of tribal life and his rich fantasy, and at the same time makes him take the dominance of the white man for granted." (To Margrit de Sabloniere, Sept. 6, 1959.).

TWAIN, Mark [Samuel Langhorne Clemens]. *The Adventures of Huckleberry Finn*. London: T. Nelson & Sons, [19—?] Galignani, Paris, sticker.
"Twain hid his conflict in satire and wept in private over the brutalities and the injustices of his civilization." ("Personalism" [1935–37?], *Biblio.*, p. 167, U 62).

"Especially did Mark Twain's *What Is Man?* intrigue me because the manner in which Twain stood outside human life and gazed at it was something that carried my mind and feelings back to the teachings and attitudes of my grandmother. I've often wondered what kind of childhood conditioning must Twain have had that made his mind run so often in such channels. Though a white American, a mocker of religion, he, too, perhaps, must have caught some inkling in his life of that tendency so widespread in the vast Mississippi Valley that made men and women stand aside and gaze with wistful and baffled eyes upon their own lives. . . . In my reading of Twain the experience of my childhood would return and reinforce what I was reading and make it *strangely familiar*. The recurring motif of the *strangely familiar* that runs through 'The Man Who Lives Underground' was based entirely upon my memories of the experiences of those years of reading and living. . . ." ("Memories of My Grandmother," *Biblio.*, p. 166, U 58, Wright Misc. 473, p. 15)

"I've always liked Mark Twain's *Innocence Abroad* [sic] and I thought that since my man stayed in the USA a reverse of that title might do. What about 'Innocence at Home?'" (To Reynolds, November 6, 1952)

"I like him; I am ashamed of him; and it is a delight to me to be where he is if he has new material on which to work his vanities where they will show him off as with a limelight. Mark Twain" ("Ideas for Celebration," p. 96)

TWO CITIES.
Wright had a complete run of this little magazine, published by Jean Fanchette in Paris. Excerpts from the original manuscript of *Pagan Spain* appeared in number 9, July 1956. Lawrence Durrell, Anaïs Nin, etc. were contributors.

TYLER, Parker. *Hollywood Hallucination.* New York: Creative Age Press, 1944.

TYRRELL, George N. *Apparitions.* [Rev. ed.] With a Preface by H. H. Price. London: Published under the Auspices of the Society for Psychical Research by G. Duckworth, 1953.
Bought in Paris, 800F.

U

UNAMUNO, Miguel de.
Wright discussed *The Tragic Sense of Life* with Ralph Ellison in 1940. See FABRE, 299.

UNDERHILL, Evelyn. *Mysticism: A Study in the Nature and Development of Man's Spiritual Consciousness.* New York: Meridian Books, 1955.
Bought in Paris, 600F.

UNDSET, Sigrid. *Kristin Lavransdattur; The Bridal Wreath; The Mistress of Husaby; The Cross.* Translated from the Norwegian by Charles Archer and J. S. Scott. New York: A. A. Knopf, 1929.
Ricour, Paris, stamp.

UNITED NATIONS PREPARATORY EDUCATIONAL, SCIENTIFIC AND CULTURAL COMMISSION. *Fundamental Education: Common Ground for All Peoples.* Paris: United Nations Educational, Scientific and Cultural Organisation, 1947.

UNRUH, Fritz von.
Wright wrote a review of his novel, *The End Is Not Yet* (1947), in "A Junker's Epic Novel on Militarism," *P.M. Magazine,* May 4, 1947, p. m3. It is quoted as a blurb on the dust jacket. See APPENDIX, pp. 251–54.

U. S. CONGRESS. SENATE. Committee on Education and Labor. *Violations of Free Speech and Rights of Labor. Hearings before a Subcommittee of the Committee on Education and Labor, United States Senate, Seventy-fourth Congress, Second Session, Pursuant to S. Res. 266. Part 8.* Washington: U.S. Government Printing Office, 1937.
Copy marked "Washington, 1937. Sol Rabkin"

U. S. COURT OF APPEALS. DISTRICT OF COLUMBIA. Julius Fisher, Appelant vs. United States, Appellee. January Term, No. 8809. *Appeal from the District Court of the United States for the District of Columbia, Grand Jury No. 29196; Criminal No. 73,393; First Degree Murder.* 1945.

The printed text was secured for Wright by Charles H. Houston, Fisher's attorney, and remained in Wright's library until his death. It was then acquired by Walter Goldwater, University Place Bookshop, New York, who allowed Michel Fabre to photostat passages underlined and pp. 24 to 83.

See *World,* pp. 108–121.

U. S. DIVISION OF PRESS INTELLIGENCE FOR THE UNITED STATES GOVERNMENT. *Magazine Abstracts,* Vol. 7 (1941). A weekly publication, reproduced from typewritten copy, "prepared for the use of government officials. . . ." Includes Wright's speech "Not My People's War."

V

VAIHINGER, Hans. *The Philosophy of 'As If': A System of the Theoretical, Practical, and Religious Fictions of Mankind.* Translated by C. K. Ogden. 2d ed. London: Routledge and K. Paul, 1935.
  Bought after 1940 for $10.00.
VALÉRY, Paul.
  "I am learning Valéry by heart . . . in order to accustom myself to speaking exceptionally fine French vocabulary." (Interview by Paul Guth, *La Gazette des Lettres,* September 14, 1946, p. 2. Transl. M. Fabre.)
VANDERCOOK, John W. *Black Majesty: The Life of Christophe, King of Haiti.* With Drawings by Mahlon Blaine. New York, London: Harper & Bros., 1928.
VAN DER POST, Laurens. *The Dark Eye in Africa.* London: The Hogarth Press, 1956.
  Mistral, Paris, 550F.
———. *Venture to the Interior.* Harmondsworth: Penguin, 1957.
VAN GUNDY, Justine. See CAMPBELL, Oscar J.
VAN LOON, Hendrik W. *The Story of Mankind.* New York: Garden City Publishing Co., 1939.
  Bought after 1940.
VAN TESLAAR, James S. *An Outline of Psychoanalysis.* New York: Modern Library, 1925.
  Bought after 1940.
VAN VECHTEN, Carl. *Peter Whiffle.* New York: Modern Library, 1922.
VAUCAIRE, Michel. *Toussaint-Louverture.* Paris: Firmin-Didot et cie, 1930.
  This copy belonged to W. A. Bradley, Paris.
VELDE, Theodoor H. van de. *Ideal Marriage: Its Physiology and Technique.* Translated by Stella Browne. Introduction by J. Johnston Abraham. New York: Random House, 1940.

VELIKOVSKY, Immanuel. *Worlds in Collision.* London: Gollancz, 1950.

VERSFELD, Marthinus. *An Essay on the Metaphysics of Descartes.* London: Methuen, 1940.
  Bought in Paris, 300F.

VIAN, Boris. *J'irai cracher sur vos tombes.* Traduit de l'Americain par Boris Vian [Vernon Sullivan]. Paris: Editions du Scorpion, 1947.

VILLON, François. *Poems, Including "The Testament" and Other Poems.* Translated in the Original Verse Forms by Norman Cameron. London: Cape, 1952.

VOLTAIRE, François Marie Aruet de. *Candide.* Introduction by Philip Littell. New York: The Modern Library, n.d.
  Bought before 1940.

———. *Candide.* With Illustrations by Samuel Adler. Introduction by Carl Van Doren. New York: World, 1947.
  Illustrated copy, no. 778 of numbered edition, signed by Carl Van Doren and Samuel Adler.

W

WAELHENS, Alphonse de. *La philosophie de Martin Heidegger.* Louvain: Editions de l'Institut Supérieur de Philosophie, 1946.
WAGENKNECHT, Edward, ed. *Murder by Gaslight: Victorian Tales.* New York: Prentice-Hall, 1948.
WAHL, Jean A. *A Short History of Existentialism.* Translated from the French by Forest Williams and Stanley Maron. New York: Philosophical Library, 1949.
WAINHOUSE, Austryn. *Hedyphagetica: A Romantic Argument after Certain Old Models, & Containing an Assortment of Heroes, Scenes of Anthropophagy & of Pathos, an Apology for Epicurism, & Many Objections Raised Against It, Together with Reflexions Upon the Bodies Politic & Individual, Their Affections, Nourishments, &c.* Paris: Olympia Press 1954.
Inscribed: "To Richard Wright,/with kindest regards,/ 14 June 1954,/Austryn Wainhouse"
WAITE, Harlow O. See BROWN, Leonard S.
WALKER, Kenneth. *The Physiology of Sex and Its Social Implications.* Harmondsworth: Penguin Books, 1940.
Bought in Paris, 200F.
WALKER, Margaret.
Wright quotes seven lines from "For My People" in "The Literature of the Negro in the United States." He states that Margaret Walker "started writing at about the age when Phillis Wheatley began writing." See *White Man, Listen!*, p. 114.
WALLACE, Henry A.
Wright did a reader's report for the Book-of-the-Month Club on Wallace's book *Sixty Million Jobs* (1945). See *Biblio.*, p. 172, U 83.
WALLACE, William. *Prolegomena to the Study of Hegel's Philosophy and Especially of His Logic.* 2d ed., rev. and augm. Oxford: The Clarendon Press, 1931.
Bought after 1940.

W A R D, Charles A. *Oracles of Nostradamus.* New York: Modern Library, 1940.

W A R D, Theodore.

Wright was closely associated with Ward in the early 1940s and tried to help with the production of his play *Our Lan'*.

"There lives in America no playwright who is better fitted for the launching of a true people's theatre for the mirroring of Negro life in America than Theodore Ward." (Introduction to the playbill for *Big White Fog,* which opened on October 22, 1940, in New York City.)

Ward adapted "Bright and Morning Star" as a "Negro Tragedy in Three Acts." See *Biblio.,* p. 214, item 6.

W A R D, Thomas H., ed. *The English Poets.* Selections with Critical Introductions by Various Writers and a General Introduction by Matthew Arnold. New York: The Macmillan Co.; London: Macmillan & Co., Ltd., 1901–1918.

Bought before 1940.

W A R D, William E. F. *A History of the Gold Coast.* London: Allen & Unwin, 1948.

———. *A Short History of the Gold Coast.* London, New York: Longmans, Green & Co., 1940.

Bought in Paris, 250F.

W A R N E R, Rex. *The Cult of Power, Essays.* London: John Lane, 1946.

W A R N E R, W. Lloyd; JUNKER, Buford H.; and ADAMS, Walter A. *Color and Human Nature: Negro Personality Development in a Northern City.* Prepared for the American Youth Commission. Washington, D.C.: American Council on Education, 1941.

W A R R E N, Robert Penn. *All the King's Men.* With a New Introduction by the Author. New York: Modern Library, 1953.

W A S H I N G T O N, Booker T. *Up from Slavery, An Autobiography.* Garden City, N.Y.: Sun Dial Press, 1937.

Bought after 1940.

The Story of the Negro (1909) is quoted among the sources for "Portrait of Harlem" in *New York Panorama* (1938).

"I would suggest that Mayor Robert R. Moton be boiled slowly, seasoned with peppers and sauces, stuffed, baked and served to the Justices of the United States Supreme Court with a red apple in his mouth. Surely he would not object greatly, for he follows the philosophy of Booker T. Washington which counsels him to be '*separate as the fingers in all things social yet one as the hand in all things essential to mutual purpose.'"* ("Repeating a Modest Proposal," *Biblio.*, p. 168, U 65, Wright Misc. 645, p. 3.)

Upon the suggestion to write the script for a life of Booker T. Washington, Wright wrote Reynolds on February 13, 1940: "I'm almost ashamed to admit that I've never read *Up from Slavery*. I shall and I must. This admission might sound doubly strange coming from me, but I escaped being educated in Negro institutions and never quite got around to reading those books everyone is supposed to have read."

W A T K I N S, Sylvestre C., ed. *An Anthology of American Negro Literature*. With an Introduction by John T. Frederick. New York: Modern Library, 1944.
  Includes "The Ethics of Living Jim Crow."
W A T E R M A N, Willoughby C. *Prostitution and Its Repression in New York City, 1900–1931*. New York: Columbia University Press; London: P.S. King & Son Ltd., 1932.
  Bought after 1940, 60¢
W E B B, Duncan. *Line-up for Crime*. London: Muller, 1956.
  Mistral, Paris, 200F.
W E B B, Mary [Gladys Meredith]. *Precious Bane*. With an Introduction by Stanley Baldwin. New York: Modern Library, 1926.
  Bought after 1940.
W E B S T E R ' S   N E W   I N T E R N A T I O N A L   D I C T I O N A R Y   O F
  T H E   E N G L I S H   L A N G U A G E. 2d ed. Unabridged. Springfield, Mass.: G. & C. Merriam Co., 1944.
  Bought in 1944.
W E E G E E [Arthur Fellig]. *Naked City*. New York: Essential Books, 1945.
———. *Weegee's People*. New York: Essential Books, Duell, Sloan & Pearce, 1946.
W E I G H T M A N, John G. *On Language and Writing*. London: Sylvan Press, 1947.
W E I N I N G E R, Otto. *Sex & Character*. Authorized Translation from the 6th German Edition. London: W. Heinemann; New York: G. P. Putnam's Sons, 1906?
  Bought after 1940.
W E I S S B E R G, Alexander. *Conspiracy of Silence*. With a Preface by Arthur Koestler. London: Hamish Hamilton, 1952.
  Galignani, Paris, sticker.
W E L C H, E. Parl. *The Philosophy of Edmund Husserl: The Origin*

and Development of His Phenomenology. New York: Columbia University Press, 1941.
Bought for $2.00.

W E L L E S, Sumner. *The Time for Decision.* New York: Harper Bros., 1944.

W E L L S, H. G. *Apropos of Dolores.* Berne: A Scribherz, 1947.
Bought in Paris, 225F.

———. *The Invisible Man.* London: Collins Clear-type Press, n.d.
Bought in Paris, 200F

———. *The Outline of History, Being a Plain History of Life and Mankind.* Garden City, N.Y.: Garden City Publishing Co., 1930.
Bought before 1940.

———. *The Secret Places of the Heart.* Leipzig: Tauchnitz, 1925.
Bought used in Paris, 150F.

———. *Tales of Space and Time.* Leipzig: B. Tauchnitz, 1900?
Ricour, Paris

———. *The Undying Fire.* New York: Macmillan, 1929.
Bought before 1940.
Wells is mentioned in *The Color Curtain,* along with Lathrop Stoddard as having predicted the rise of Third World nations.

W E L T Y, Eudora. *Delta Wedding, A Novel.* London: The Bodley Head, 1947.
Bought in London, $2.00

W E S C O T T, Glenway. *Apartment in Athens.* New York, London: Harper & Bros., 1945.
Inscribed: "For Richard Wright, / in admiration. / Glenway Wescott."
The novel was a dual Book-of-the-Month Club selection with *Black Boy.*

———. *The Grandmothers: A Family Portrait.* New York, London: Harper & Bros., 1927.
Bought used 50¢

W E S T, D. J. *Homosexuality.* With a Foreword by Hermann Mannheim. London: Duckworth, 1955.
Bought in Paris, 990F.

W E S T, Don. *Toil and Hunger, Poems.* San Benito, Texas: Hagglund Press, 1940.

W E S T, Rebecca, dame [pseud.]. *The Meaning of Treason.* 2d ed. London, New York: Macmillan, 1952.
Galignani, Paris, sticker.

———. *The Thinking Reed, A Novel.* London: Hutchinson, 1935. Gibert, Paris, 50F.

WESTERMANN, Diedrich. *The African To-day and To-morrow.* With a Foreword by the Rt. Hon. Lord Lugard. 3d ed. London, New York: Published for the International African Institute by the Oxford University Press, 1949.

WERTHAM, Frederic. *Dark Legend: A Study in Murder.* New York: Duel, Sloan & Pearce, 1941.

Inscribed: "For Dick Wright, / the study of another son. / Ella Winter."

Also signed "Frederic Wertham"

———. *Seduction of the Innocent.* New York: Rinehart, 1954.

———. *The Show of Violence.* New York: Doubleday 1949.

"Dear Dr. Wertham:

A few weeks ago I received a copy of your book, *Dark Legend,* autographed by you and Ella Winter.

I want to thank whoever is responsible—— you or Miss Winter, or you and Miss Winter—— for making it possible for me to read this highly fascinating psychological study of crime.

Needless to say, I found your book enlightening and I wish that there were many more people in public places endowed with such a gift for understanding human personality.

My reactions to Gino, his plight and his crime were so many and varied that it would be futile to attempt to set them down in a letter. It is enough to say that I think it is the most comprehensive psychological statement in relation to contemporary crime that I have come across. Indeed, it is as fascinating as any novel." (October 24, 1941)

"Dr. Frederic Wertham [is] one of the nation's leading psychiatrists. [His] attitude is that psychiatry is for everybody or none at all. He came to the conclusion that 'reform is possible only if one keeps away from the reformers.'" ("Psychiatry Comes to Harlem," *Free World,* September 1946)

On Wright's friendship and collaboration with Wertham, see Fabre, 236, 370 *passim.*

WHEATLEY, Dennis, ed. *A Century of Spy Stories.* London: Hutchinson, 1938.

Ex-libris Sylvia Beach.

WHEATLEY, Phillis.

"In 1760, a black girl, Phillis Wheatley, was brought to America from Africa. . . . she became a poet and wrote in the manner of the heroic couplets of Pope. Her *Imagination* reads:

Imagination! Who can sing thy force! . . . [The poem is quoted down to "Or with new world amaze th'unbounded soul" and the reference given as *Anthology of American Negro Literature* by V. F. Calverton, Modern Library Edition, 1929, p. 175.]
"Whatever its qualities as poetry, the above poem records the feelings of a Negro reacting not as a Negro but as a human being." (Introduction to *Black Metropolis* by St. Clair Drake and Horace Cayton, Harcourt, Brace, New York, 1945, p. xxxiii)

In "The Literature of the Negro in the United States," Wright briefly tells the story of Phillis Wheatley, an African-born slave whose poems were influenced by the heroic couplets of Pope. He quotes from her "Ode to George Washington." Wheatley was not one with her culture and can be used as a yardstick to measure the degree of integration of other Negro writers. (*White Man, Listen!*, pp. 112–15.)

W H I T E, Moresby and STOCK, Freda. *The Right Way to Write for the Films*. With an Introduction by Noel Langley. Kingswood, Surrey: A. G. Elliot; distributors: Rolls House Pub. Co., London, 1948.

W H I T E, W. L.
Wright read his *Report on the Russians* (1945) on March 24, 1945, and found the book good. (Unpublished journal).

W H I T E, Walter F. *A Man Called White: The Autobiography of Walter White*. London: V. Gollancz, 1949.
Wright is quoted in a review (*California Eagle*, March 20, 1940), considering *Native Son* as "the type of writing of *Fire in the Flint*."

W H I T E H E A D, Alfred North. *Science and the Modern World, Lowell Lectures, 1925*. London: Macmillan, 1947.

"It is A. N. Whitehead who said 'the negative perception is the triumph of consciousness.' And I believe the negative attitude of France today means that she feels more keenly than most other Western nations the agony of what is to be won or lost in political and social decisions." ("A Paris les GI ont appris à connaître et à aimer la liberté," *Samedi soir*, May 25, 1946.)

W H I T F I E L D, James.
James W. Whitfield's career is briefly recalled in "The Literature of the Negro in the United States" and ten lines of his poem "From America" are quoted:

America, it is to thee
Thou boasted land of liberty——

It is to thee that I raise my song,
Thou land of blood, and crime, and wrong,
It is to thee my native land,
From which has issued many a band
To tear the black man from his soil
And force him here to delve and toil
Chained on your blood-bemoistened sod,
Cringing beneath a tyrant's rod. . . .

Whitfield is seen as rejected by the land he loves. *See White Man, Listen!*, pp. 118–19.

WHITMAN, Albery A.
In "The Literature of the Negro in the United States," Wright quotes nine lines from *The Rape of Florida* (1884) by Albery A. Whitman. He, too, writes of wrong but there is in his verse a desire to please. See *White Man, Listen!*, p. 120.

WHITMAN, Walt. *Leaves of Grass*. Issued under the Editorial Supervision of His Literary Executors, Richard Maurice Bucke, Thomas B. Harned, and Horace L. Traubel. Garden City, N.Y.: Doubleday, Page & Co., 1917.
War Service Library copy, acquired before 1940.
————. *Leaves of Grass (1850–1881)*. With an Introduction by Stuart P. Sherman. New York, Chicago: C. Scribner & Sons, 1922.
Bought before 1940.
The titles of "I Sing the Body Electric," "Crossing Brooklyn Ferry," "Out of the Cradle Endlessly Rocking," and "Starting from Paumanok" are underlined.

"Whitman chanted of a mystical future, of a mystical renunciation of the individual and society, of a confused comradeship on an emotional plane." ("Personalism" [1935–37?], *Biblio.*, p. 162, U 62.)

"I am an American but, like Walt Whitman 'I contain contradictions . . .' I love the crude melancholy of the blues and I love the heroic melodies of Beethoven." "I am an American but. . . . ," *Biblio.*, p. 166, U 56.)

"Not until the sun excludes you do I exclude you" is quoted as epigraph to *Black Power*. Twelve lines from *Leaves of Grass* are quoted in *Black Power*, 351.

WHYTE, William H., Jr. *The Organization Man*. Garden City, N.Y.: Anchor Books, Doubleday, 1956.
WIENER, Norbert. *The Human Use of Human Beings: Cybernetics and Society*. Boston: Houghton Mifflin, 1950.

W I L D E, Oscar. *The Poems of Oscar Wilde.* Illustrated by Jean de Bosschère. New York: Boni & Liveright. 1927.
> Bought before 1940.
> "The Ballad of Reading Gaol" is quoted as epigraph to *Savage Holiday.*

W I L D E R, Thornton. *Heaven's My Destination.* New York, London: Harper & Bros., 1935.
> Bought used after 1940.

———. *Our Town: A Play in Three Acts.* New York: Pocket Book, 1941.

———. *Three Plays: Our Town, The Skin of Our Teeth, The Matchmaker.* New York: Harper, 1957.
> Inscribed: "Christmas greetings from / Mac, John Appleton, etc." A gift from the editors at Harper's.

W I L K I E, Wendell L. *One World.* New York: Simon & Schuster, 1943.

W I L K I N S, Harold T. *Flying Saucers on the Attack.* New York: Citadel Press, 1954.
> Bought in Paris, 600 F.

W I L L I A M S, Eric E.
> *Capitalism & Slavery* (1944) is quoted in *Black Power*, 9–12, and in epigraph to Part I. *White Man, Listen!* is dedicated to "My friend Eric Williams, Chief minister of the government of Trinidad and Tobago, leader of the People's National Movement."

W I L L I A M S, George Washington.
> *History of the Negro Race in America from 1619 to 1880* (1883) is quoted as a source of "Portrait of Harlem" in *New York Panorama* (1938).

W I L L I A M S, Tennessee. *A Streetcar Named Desire.* Norfolk, Conn.: New Directions, 1947.

W I L S O N, Colin. *The Age of Defeat.* London: V. Gollancz, 1959.

———. *Religion and the Rebel.* London: V. Gollancz, 1957.
> Wright wrote "Points of Criticism" on *The Age of Defeat.* See *Biblio.*, p. 172, U 84.

W I L S O N, Edmund. *Axel's Castle: A Study in the Imaginative Literature of 1870–1930.* New York: Scribner, 1945.

———. *The Boys in the Back Room: Notes on California Novelists.* San Francisco: Colt Press, 1941.
> Bought on March 30, 1945.

W I L S O N, William.

"In William E. Wilson's 'Saturday Morning' we catch echoes of the tragedy of lynching through the sensibilities of a 10-year-old white boy, son of
a sheriff, and in Carskadon's 'Nigger Schoolhouse,' we can see the germs
of race prejudice at work; in Creyke's story the cruelty of children merges
with the racial hatred of grownups." ("Foreword to *Lest We Forget*," *Biblio.*, p. 175, U 94, Wright Misc. 456 [1955])

W I R T H, Louis.
Wright possibly read *The Ghetto* (1928) as early as the 1930s.
Before writing *Twelve Million Black Voices,* he read books rec-
ommended by Professor Wirth and mentions his *Urbanism as a
Way of Life* (1938).

"In general the book [*Black Metropolis*] can be thought of in a phrase
that Louis Wirth has used to describe the lives of people who live in cities:
Urbanism as a Way of Life." (Introduction to *Black Metropolis* by St. Clair
Drake and Horace Cayton, Harcourt, Brace, New York, 1945.)

W O L F E, Thomas. *Mannerhouse, A Play in a Prologue and Three
Acts*. New York: Harper, 1948.
———. *The Web and the Rock*. New York, London: Harper & Bros.,
1939.
Bought before 1940.
———. *You Can't Go Home Again*. New York, London: Harper &
Bros., 1940.

W O O D, Clement. *The Complete Rhyming Dictionary and Poet's
Craft Book* was part of Wright's library according to Ellen Wright.

W O O D H O U S E, Bruce. *From Script to Screen*. Introduction by Sir
Alexander Korda. London: Winchester Publications, 1948.

W O O D S, Eugene J., ed. *I Wish I'd Written That: Selections Chosen
by Favorite American Authors*. London: Whittlesey House,
McGraw-Hill Book Co., 1946.
Wright comments on his choice, "Melanctha," by Gertrude
Stein.

W O O L F, Virginia. *Between the Acts*. London: The Hogarth Press,
1952.
———. *Jacob's Room*. London: The Hogarth Press, 1953.
———. *Mrs. Dalloway.* Introduction by Virginia Woolf. New York:
Modern Library. 1925.
Bought after 1940.

———. *Mrs. Dalloway.* London: The Hogarth Press, 1960.
———. *Night and Day.* New York: George H. Doran Co., 1920.
———. *Orlando, A Biography.* Leipzig: B. Tauchnitz, 1929.
Bought in France after 1940.
———. *A Room of One's Own.* London: Published by Leonard and
Virginia Woolf at the Hogarth Press, 1929.
Bought in London.
First edition, $15.
———. *To the Lighthouse.* Hamburg, Paris, Bologna: The Albatross,
1933.
Bought used after 1940.
———. *The Waves.* London: The Hogarth Press, 1950.
———. *The Years.* London: Pan Books, 1948.
WOOLLEY, Edwin C. *New Handbook of Composition: Rules and
Exercises Regarding Good English, Grammar, Sentence Structure,
Paragraphing, Manuscript Arrangement, Punctuation, Spelling,
Essay Writing, Outlining, Letter Writing, and the Making of Bibli-
ographies.* Rev. and Enl. by Franklin W. Scott. Boston, New York:
D. C. Heath & Co., 1927.
Bought used before 1940.
WRITERS' PROGRAM, Illinois. *Cavalcade of the American Ne-
gro.* Compiled by the Workers of the Writers' Program of the Work
Projects Administration, in the State of Illinois. Frontispiece by
Adrian Troy of the Illinois Art Project. Chicago: Diamond Jubilee
Exposition Authority, 1940.
WYLIE, Philip.
    In a letter to Gertrude Stein dated April 12, 1946, Wright alludes
to Philip Wylie's *A Generation of Vipers* (1942), which he finds
stronger, as a criticism of American mores and materialism, than
Henry Miller's *The Air-conditioned Nightmare:*

"It is very easy to damn America by rejecting America and it is very hard
to damn America while accepting America. . . . Miller's rejection of America seems to me the act of a weak man."

WYSCHOGROD, Michael. *Kierkegaard and Heidegger: The Ontology of Existence.* London: Routledge and Paul, 1954.

Y

YALE LAW JOURNAL.
"Passport Refusals for Political Reasons" (vol. 61, Feb. 1952).
Wright referred to this article because he was anxious about the American Embassy in Paris keeping his passport when he asked for a renewal in 1952.

YERBY, Frank.

"Frank Yerby's 'Health Card' relates a variation of the same theme, a man subjected to a sort of psychological castration, as it were, directly in front of his wife's eyes. . . . This Negro, being further from his roots, weeps tears of innocent rage." ("Foreword to *Lest We Forget*," *Biblio.*, p. 175, U 94, Wright Misc. 456 [1955])

YORDAN, Philip.
In a January 23, 1951, lecture, Wright compared Yordan's play *Anna Lucasta*, adapted by Abram Hill and Harry W. Gribble, to John Ford's *'Tis Pity She's a Whore* (1627).

A YOUNG GIRL'S DIARY. Preface with a Letter from Sigmund Freud. Translated by Eden and Cedar Paul. New York: T. Seltzer, 1921.
Bought used in Paris, 300F.

Z

ZETKIN, Clara. *Lenin on the Woman Question.* New York: International Publishers, 1936.
Bought after 1940.

ZHDANOV, A., et al. *Problems of Soviet Literature: Reports and Speeches at the First Soviet Writer's Congress by A. Zhdanov, Maxim Gorky [pseud.], N. Bukharin, K. Radek, A. Stetsky.* Edited by H. G. Scott. Moscow, Leningrad: Co-operative Publishing Society of Foreign Writers in the U.S.S.R., 1935.

ZOBEL, Joseph.
Black Boy and Wright's other books greatly influenced the author of *La Rue Cases-Nègres* (1950), who frequently visited Wright at his apartment on Rue Monsieur Le Prince. Wright knew the contents of the novel, but it was not in his library in 1968.

ZOLA, Emile. *Paris.* Translated by Ernest Alfred Vizetelly. New ed. London: Chatto & Windus, 1902.
Ricour, Paris, stamp.
When gathering information from prostitutes on American soldiers in Europe prior to the writing of "Island of Hallucinations," Wright was conscious of imitating Zola's research for *Nana* (Interview in Stockholm, Nov. 26, 1956).
Zola is mentioned in Wright's introduction to Françoise Gourdon's *Tant qu'il y aura la peur* (1960).

ZWEIG, Arnold. *The Case of Sergeant Grischa.* Translated from the German by Eric Sutton. New York: Viking Press, 1929.
49¢

ZWEIG, Stefan. *Joseph Fouché.: The Portrait of a Politician.* Translated from the German by Eden and Cedar Paul. New York: Viking Press, 1930.
Bought in Paris, 300F.

———. *Marie Antoinette, A Portrait of an Average Woman.* Translated by Eden and Cedar Paul. New York: Viking Press, 1933.
Used.

———. *Master Builders, A Typology of the Spirit.* Translated from the German by Eden and Cedar Paul. New York: Viking Press, 1939.

Appendixes

A. Blurbs, Introductions, and Reviews by Richard Wright

Horatio Alger, Jr., *Struggling Upwards and Other Works*
Nelson Algren, *Never Come Morning*
Arna Bontemps, *Black Thunder*
Gwendolyn Brooks, *A Street in Bronzeville*
Richard Brooks, *The Brick Foxhole*
Hodding Carter, *The Winds of Fear*
Erskine Caldwell, *Trouble in July*
Michel del Castillo, *The Disinherited*
Arnaud d'Usseau and James Gow, *Deep Are the Roots*
On William Faulkner
E. M. Forster, *Aspects of the Novel*
Françoise Gourdon, *Tant qu'il y aura la peur*
John Gunther, *Inside U.S.A.*
Ernest Hemingway, *To Have and Have Not,* and John Steinbeck,
    Grapes of Wrath
Chester Himes, *Lonely Crusade*
Chester Himes, *If He Hollers Let Him Go,* and Arthur Miller,
    Focus
Langston Hughes, *The Big Sea*
Langston Hughes, *The Big Sea,* and W. E. B. Du Bois, *Dusk of
    Dawn*
James Weldon Johnson, *Black Manhattan*
Harry Harrison Kroll, *I Was a Sharecropper*
George Lamming, *In the Castle of My Skin*
Carson McCullers, *The Heart Is a Lonely Hunter*
O. Mannoni, *Prospero and Caliban*
Howard Nutt, *Special Laughter*
Paul Oliver, *Blues Fell This Morning*
George Padmore, *Pan-Africanism or Communism?*
J. Saunders Redding, *No Day of Triumph*

William Rollins, Jr., *The Wall of Men*
Jean-Paul Sartre, *La Putain Respectueuse*
Morris U. Schappes, *Letters from the Tombs*
Jo Sinclair, *Wasteland*
Gertrude Stein, *Wars I Have Seen*
Edward Turpin, *These Low Grounds,* and Zora Neale Hurston,
  Their Eyes Were Watching God
Fritz von Unruh, *The End Is Not Yet*
B. Bibliography on the Negro in Chicago, 1936
C. Book Lists Compiled by Wright
D. Notes taken after reading *How to Write a Play* by Lajos Egri

A P P E N D I X   A

American Capitalism's Greatest Propagandist: Horatio Alger, Jr.

Horatio Alger, Jr., *Struggling Upwards and Other Works,* with an introduction by Russel Crouse (New York: Crown Publishers)

What motives, beyond the blatantly pecuniary, prompted the publishers to reissue in a single, 570-page volume four old boys' tales of Horatio Alger, Jr.,—*Struggling Upward, Ragged Dick, Phil the Fiddler,* and *Jed the Poorhouse Boy*—I simply and honestly don't know.

I'm no lover of the antique, and "looking back" happens not to be one of my habits or hobbies. And even though the old-fashioned, morally uplifting tales of Horatio Alger were a part of the dreams of my youth—and maybe 10,000,000 or so other youths—I failed to get a sense of rediscovery by wading through them again. Indeed, I had to drive myself through the dreary pages, feeling ashamed over the fact that I'd ever been so naive as to derive enchantment out of prose clogged with such cliches as: "sudden appearance", "eager curiosity", "mysterious stranger", "veiled contempt", "modest expenses", "an insignificant-looking man", "urgent invitation", "strikingly handsome", "a picture of perfect health", etc., etc.

The late Mr. Horatio Alger, Jr., is, was, and will forever be the most terribly bad of writers; of that, there can be no doubt. All of his sociology, psychology, politics, and insights into human nature are just so many bold lies burdening his 135 volumes and his millions of stale words.

But my report is not all negative. As I neared the end of the fourth book, entitled *Jed the Poorhouse Boy,* a glimmer of light broke through the fog. I detected in the swamp of Mr. Alger's rhetoric a meaning of which, I'm sure, he was unconscious. Mr. Alger was utterly an American artist completely claimed by his culture, and the truth of his books is the truth of the power of the wish; and the warm, Sunday-School glow that bathes his heroes is the glow of the dream and its irrational logic. Perhaps no other American writer ever took so much at their face value the popular delusions and pious moral frauds of his time. In Alger the theories of Max Weber's *Capitalism and the Spirit of the Protestant Ethic* find their most naive function and fulfillment. If you really want to know why Henry Ford and John D. Rockefeller Jr., identify their material possessions as gifts straight from God, then read Alger.

Alger was perhaps American capitalism's greatest and most effective propagandist. I do not mean, of course, that he was hired by John D. Rockefeller, Sr; and surely the Executive Committee of the Capitalist Class of 1875 did not hold an Extraordinary Plenum Session and vote to commission Alger to write books upholding the virtues of the free enterprise system. Capitalism never made any such naive mistakes; mistakes of that sort are the monopoly of our contemporary radical parties. No, Mr. Alger's word spinning was a long labor of love; incredible as it is, the man believed in what he was doing. And I'd guess that he sent more than one boy straight up to the top, to Fame and Fortune.

I'm willing to hold Mr. Alger up to the Communists, Socialists, Liberals, and labor leaders in general as a model. Instinctively, he knew something that they never seem to learn: That the masses are won to a cause not through voicing fears and threats and announcing ever-recurring dire crises, but through instilling in them the feeling that they can find the fulfillment of their lives by participating in a new movement.

And how well did Alger know this! It colored every line he wrote. It was his passion. The Algerian world teemed with kind-hearted capitalists who itched to pick up stray, starving boys—but they had to be honest and loyal in money matters:—and buy them suits, feed them, give them jobs, and put their feet on the ladder leading to Success.

Effort was not needed; thinking was not mandatory; hard work, yes, but not too much. But it was absolutely necessary to have the knack of being handy when a rich man's daughter fell off a ferry . . . You rescued her and you were rewarded. Alger's tales abound in co-incidences; indeed, his tales move by the mechanism of happy accidents, the kind of accidents that make dreams move and be. In short, his stories are the waking dreams of young men hungry to get ahead.

Here are a few Algerian concepts. (I blush to do this, but a job is a job.): The mere look of a man's face is sufficient to indicate if he is honest or not; if a man should rob you of your last penny, then when you meet him again, do him a favor; people are mean and cruel simply because they *are* mean and cruel; most all poor people are good; villainy is inevitably punished; and material success will surely crown virtue and Godliness.

Could 200,000,000 copies of 135 books carrying such slop ever have been sold in America? Yes, they have. And the next time you are puzzled over the low cultural level of our country, stop and reflect that we could be much worse off, that the mere mental digestion of 200,000,000 copies of Alger's drivel was more than enough to cripple the spirit of a nation tougher than ours, and that we are lucky today there is a mood of honesty and objectivity in some parts of our land. Not many nations of the earth have had to bear such a cultural handicap!

Published in *PM*, 16 September 1945, p. m 8 in a slightly edited form

Introduction

Nelson Algren, *Never Come Morning* (New York: Harpers, 1942)

Nelson Algren's innocent, bold, vivid, and poetic imagination—as is ex-
emplified in this novel, *Never Come Morning*—has long brooded upon the
possibility of changing the social world in which we live, has long dreamed
of the world's being different, and this preoccupation has, paradoxically, riv-
eted and directed microscopic attention upon that stratum of our society that
is historically foot-loose, unformed, malleable, restless, devoid of inner stabil-
ity, unidentified by class allegiances, yet full of hot, honest, blind striving.
Algren's centering of his observation upon the lowly and brutal strivings of a
Bruno Bicek is the product of his sound instinct and reasoning, for, strangely
enough, the Bruno Biceks of America represent those depths of life—the
realm of the irrational and the non-historical—that periodically push their
way into the arena of history in times of crisis, war, civil war, and revolution.
   It would be interesting to speculate how diverse contemporary literary tal-
ents would have handled and developed the subject matter of *Never Come
Morning*. Many competent novelists would not have considered its subject
matter as legitimate material, would have condemned this subject matter, no
doubt, as being sordid and loathsome. Others would have treated it lightly
and humorously, thereby implying that it possessed no important significance.
Still others would have assumed an aloof "social worker attitude" toward it,
prescribing "pink pills for social ills," piling up a mountain of naturalistic
detail. A militant minority, shooting straight to the mark, would have drawn
blueprints and cited chapter and page in a call for direct action. I think, however, Nelson Algren's strategy in *Never Come Morning* excels all of these by
far, inasmuch as it depicts the intensity of feeling, the tawdry but potent
dreams, the crude but forceful poetry, and the frustrated longing for human
dignity residing in the lives of the Poles of Chicago's North West Side, and
this revelation informs us all that there lies an ocean of life at our doorsteps—
an unharnessed, unchanneled and unknown ocean. And Algren does this in
prose as real, as sensory, as tactile, and as sharp as a left hook from Bruno
Bicek, his pugilistic protagonist.
   Most of us 20th Century Americans are reluctant to admit the tragically
low quality of experiences of the broad American masses; feverish radio pro-
grams, super advertisements, streamlined sky-scrapers million-dollar movies,
and mass production have somehow created the illusion in us that we are
"rich" in our emotional lives. To the greater understanding of our times,
Never Come Morning portrays what actually exists in the nerve, brain, and
blood of our boys on the street, be they black, white, native, or foreign-born.
I say this for the public record, for there will come a time in our country when
the middle class will gasp and say (as they now gasp over the present world
situation): "Why weren't we told this before? Why didn't our novelists depict

the beginnings of this terrible thing that has come upon us?" Well, Mr. and Mrs. American Reader, you are being told: The reality of the depths of our lives is being depicted. Algren's *Never Come Morning* vies with the war for your attention, and vies in terms of literary realism as hard-hitting as any to be found in American prose.

A Tale of Folk Courage

Arna Bontemps, *Black Thunder* (New York: Macmillan)

In that limited and almost barren field known as the Negro novel, Arna Bontemps's *Black Thunder* fills a yawning gap and fills it competently. Covering all those skimpy reaches of Negro letters I know, this is the only novel dealing forthrightly with the historical and revolutionary traditions of the Negro people.

Black Thunder is the true story of a slave insurrection that failed. But in his telling of the story of that failure Bontemps manages to reveal and dramatize through the character of his protagonist, Gabriel, a quality of folk courage unparalleled in the proletarian literature of this country. Gabriel is a young slave, who, hearing of the struggles of the French proletariat and the exploits of L'Ouverture, decides to avenge the murder of a fellow-slave by leading the Negroes of Richmond, Virginia, against the landowners. On the night when the attack is to take place, Gabriel's ragged slave-host, armed with cutlasses, pikes, and a "peck of bullets," hides in the woods near Richmond, waiting for the call to advance and capture the arsenal. At the crucial moment, a terrific rainstorm sweeps down, flooding the fields and bogging the roads. This, coupled with the treachery of two members of his band, makes the uprising impossible. Gabriel's army deserts him. The next three weeks are times of wild terror, for everywhere the white plantation owners are asking one another, "What Negro can you point to and say definitely he is not involved?"

From that juncture onward, *Black Thunder* is mainly the story of Gabriel, who believes in the eventual triumph of his destiny in spite of all the forces which conspire against it. He is convinced that God and the universe are on his side. He believes he must and will lead the Negro people to freedom. He seems to have no personal fear and no personal courage. He thinks, dreams, and feels wholly in terms of Negro liberation. His mind is a confused mixture of superstition, naive cunning, idealism, and a high courage born partly of his deep ignorance and partly of an amazing ability to forget his personal safety. He contemptuously refuses to run to the mountains to save himself and decides to stay near the scene of the insurrection "to get in two-three mo' good licks fo' my time comes." When considering Gabriel solely as an isolated individual, he seems sustained by an extremely foolish belief in himself; but

when one remembers his slave state, when one realizes the extent to which he
has made the wrongs of his people his wrongs, and the degree in which he has
submerged his hopes in their hopes—when one remembers this, he appears
logically and gloriously invincible.

The plan for the uprising is so simple and daring that when it is disclosed
and tracked to its source, the fear-ridden whites can scarcely believe it. But
Gabriel believes, he believes even when he is caught; even when the black cowl
is capped about his head, even when the ax swings, he believes. Why?

For me the cardinal value of Bontemps's book, besides the fact that it is a
thumping story well told, lies in the answer to that question. Perhaps I am
straying further afield than the author did in search for an answer. If I do, it
is because I believe we have in *Black Thunder* a revelation of the very origin
and source of folk values in literature.

Even though Gabriel's character is revealed in terms of personal action and
dialogue, I feel there is in him much more than mere personal dignity and
personal courage. There is in his attitude something which transcends the
limits of immediate consciousness. He is buoyed in his hope and courage by
an optimism which takes no account of the appalling difficulties confronting
him. He hopes when there are no objective reasons or grounds for hope; he
fights when his fellow-slaves scamper for their lives. In doing so, he takes his
place in that gallery of fictitious characters who exist on the plane of the
ridiculous and the sublime. Bontemps endows Gabriel with a myth-like and
deathless quality. And it is in this sense, I believe, that *Black Thunder* sounds
a new note in Negro fiction, thereby definitely extending the boundaries and
ideology of the Negro novel.

Partisan Review and Anvil, No. 3, April 1936, p. 31

Letter to Mr. Edward C. Aswell, Harper & Brothers

Gwendolyn Brooks, *A Street in Bronzeville* (New York and London: Harper
& Bros.)

September 18, 1944

Mr. Edward C. Aswell
Harper & Brothers
49 East 33 Street
New York, N.Y.

Dear Ed:

Thanks for letting me read Gwendolyn Brooks' poems. They are hard and
real, right out of the central core of Black Belt Negro life in urban areas. I
hope she can keep on saying what she is saying in many more poems.

There is no self-pity here, nor a striving for effects. She takes hold of reality as it is and renders it faithfully. There is not so much an exhibiting of Negro life to whites in these poems as there is an honest human reaction to the pain that lurks so colorfully in the Black Belt. A quiet but hidden malice runs through most of them. She easily catches the pathos of petty destinies; the whimper of the wounded; the tiny accidents that plague the lives of the desperately poor, and the problem of color prejudice among Negroes. There are times when open scorn leers through. Only one who has actually lived and suffered in a kitchenette could render the feeling of lonely frustration as well as she does:—of how dreams are drowned out by the noises, smells, and the frantic desire to grab one's chance to get a bath when the bathroom is empty. Miss Brooks is real and so are her poems.

Now for observations: I don't feel that there are enough poems here to make the kind of book that she wants. And I don't feel that the poems need any artist to make them more vivid. Indeed, drawings would detract from them, I think.

Miss Brooks handles the ballads, the blues, and tiny images of lost people well. Yet there is lacking, in my opinion, a personal note. What I'm trying to say is this: poems like "When You Have Forgotten Sunday", "Negro Hero", "Obituary for a Living Lady", give the book real poetic substance. Most volumes of poems usually have one real long fine poem around which shorter ones are added or grouped. I'm not saying that Miss Brooks' book ought to be like that; but there either ought to be almost twice as many poems of the kind she has, or she ought to give us one real long good one, one that strikes a personal note and carries a good burden of personal feeling. Then I think she would have a book of poems. What do you think?

The only poem of Miss Brooks that I did not really like was "The Mother". Maybe I'm just simply prejudiced, but I don't think that poems can be made about abortions; or perhaps the poet has not yet been born who can lift abortions to the poetic plane.

But she is a real poet; she knows what to say and how to say it. I'd say that she ought to be helped at all costs. America needs a voice like hers and anything that can be done to help her to bring out a good volume should be done.

Sincerely,
Richard Wright

Ellen Wright's papers

Blurb

Richard Brooks, *The Brick Foxhole* (New York: The Sundial Press)

What a lucky thing it is that popular moral compunctions do not solely dictate the creation of our literature! Of late there has been a lot of shouting about how the writers of the 20's and 30's "sold the country down the river" by trying to tell the truth as they saw it and felt it. Archibald MacLeish and Bernard DeVoto have claimed that the moral health of the nation has been undermined by realistic novels, and they have called upon writers to give "constructive" pictures of our lives.

The call for novels is being answered, but it is doubtful as to how "constructive" are the novels that are being delivered. Richard Brooks' *The Brick Foxhole* starts off the critical realism that is bound to prevail in the post-war world at a level of hard-hitting truth-telling that makes the literary revolt of the 20's seem puny and timid. Before the last shot of the war is fired, before we have had a chance to dance in the streets to celebrate our victory, while our soldiers are still in action (—and the characters in *The Brick Foxhole* are soldiers!—) Richard Brooks uses simple words and keen ears and sharp eyes to recreate the tissue and texture of our contemporary experiences. The picture he paints is moving, but certainly not flattering.

Can truth and patriotism be partners? If you tell the truth, you "seem" to hurt your country. If you lie, you "seem" to help it. So goes popular thinking. There will be many people who will read *The Brick Foxhole* and exclaim: "How can the oppressed people of the earth think of us as liberators when Brooks paints us like this? And how can we think of ourselves as God's own chosen people when we are reminded that we act like this?"

If considerations of this sort had concerned Mr. Brooks exclusively, *The Brick Foxhole* could not have been written. But I feel that the author of this slashing, shocking, and photographically exact novel is serving his country as an artist-soldier and serving it well; he wears the uniform, don't forget that as you read! His is the harder battle, for it is to reveal—while living with it!—the greed, the blindness, the racial hatred, the stupidity, the emotional confusion, the easy thinking and shallow feeling that govern so wide an area of our existence. *The Brick Foxhole* is a call to realism, to seeing honestly again, to standing again with our feet on the earth. It reminds us that the function of literature is to extend our vision, to sensitize our personalities, to heighten our consciousness, to enable us to see the form and color of our world and to come to conclusions about the nature of our experience in that world. Mr. Brooks accomplishes his task with such devastating ease, with so sure an aim, that I'm willing to swear that we will hear from him again and again and again. He writes in a muscular, straight-from-the-shoulder style out of the

American tradition of those who would tell us how we live in our Brave New World.

Beinecke Rare Book and Manuscript Library, Yale University

Review

Richard Brooks, *The Brick Foxhole*

Why do some authors hunch over their typewriters feeling that they must, figuratively, raid society—that they must point a gun at their neighbors as though their neighbors were enemies; must raise the black flag and write in the spirit of pirates brandishing swords. I don't know the answer to this question but now and then comes a writer who puts down words in a straight, functional, fit-for-action style, who feels a driving necessity to tell the truth, come hell and high water.

Richard Brooks, a Philadelphia newspaperman now serving with the Marines, is such a writer, and his novel, *The Brick Foxhole*, is his first public excursion into fierce truth-telling. Jeff, the protagonist or victim, is a white-collar boy drafted into the Army and assigned the boring task of drawing maps in an office (the brick foxhole). The terror of waiting and not knowing what he is waiting for fills his mind with thoughts of killing.

"I'll kill somebody, he thought . . . The thought made his blood pound . . . It was a feeling that made him forget Mary [his wife]. . . . That was the solution. It was simple. Easy. Merely kill somebody . . . But who? The girl in uniform walking through the office? He could call her over to his desk and kill her off easy. And everybody would look at him with wonder and awe and even fear."

Jeff's knowledge of war is derived from barrack rumors and newspapers. He is lonely and frantically hungry for his wife. Brooding upon his cot one day, he overhears a description of the favors given by a married woman who lives in his home town, and he becomes obsessed with the notion that the woman is his wife.

His swollen anxiety demands release. He attends a gory prize-fight, but the brutality cannot make him forget. Neither can whisky, though he drinks himself into a stupor. Finally he joins the weekly trek to Washington (the largest city near his camp) and goes to the whorehouse.

We follow Jeff into the seltzer-water frenzy of wartime America on a moral holiday; the fetid rooms of crowded hotels, the poker and crap games in reeking latrines, the apartments of men who like to pick up lonely soldiers, the bars where men who have made their pile of profits from war contracts spew hate against the world, especially against Jews, Negroes and organized labor.

In sentences that are mockingly bare and terse, Brooks depicts Jeff's emotional reactions. He shows us hurried, fumbling love-scenes between soldiers and their girls and tells us what a sensitive, emotionally starved man searches for, and cannot find, in a prostitute.

Jeff winds up with a fake murder charge placed against him by an ex-Chicago cop, a 100-per-cent patriot. When Mary arrives, he finds that he cannot reveal his alibi, for he was with a whore when the murder was committed. Sweating and blundering, this caricature of a hero finally stammers out the truth and wins back his wife.

All this is rendered in prose that seems to have been lifted directly out of the thought processes of people we all know. The result is an uneasy acceptance by the reader of a repellent and truly awful environment, peopled by convincing, but strangely incomprehensible, human beings.

An implicit, though unobtrusive, idealism prompts Brooks to lash out in this manner at the noble citizens who inhabit this great arsenal of democracy. He is a man on fire, and, though he knows that he cannot set our disjointed times aright, he seems to have sworn to let the world know how he feels about it. He does—with stinging, photographic realism.

Published in *PM*, 24 June 1945, p. m 16

Lynching Bee

Erskine Caldwell, *Trouble in July* (New York: Duell, Sloan and Pearce)

This time Erskine Caldwell's theme is lynching, that haunting symbol of America's desire to right "wrongs" with adolescent violence. In language as simple, melodious and disarming as the drawl of his outlandish characters, Caldwell depicts the bucolic tenderness and almost genial brutality that overtakes a Southern community when a white woman has been "raped." Hovering grimly in the background of the lynching is King Cotton, an inanimate character whose influence is as fatal as that of any living being, and whose rise and fall on the commodity market sets the narrow channel through which the political, social and even personal destinies of the other characters flow.

The character in the foreground, Sheriff McCurtain, turns out to be a damp rag in the face of a whirlwind. Caldwell accounts for his sheriff and the subsequent lynch panic in wider terms of social and political reference than he has heretofore used in his fiction, and the result is a picture of an unheroic man who is pitiably human. With a political boss to order him about; with two hundred pounds of fat to tote around at ninety in the shade; with a desire to "keep this lynching politically clean"; with a political opponent seeking to send all Negroes back to Africa; a bitter hatred of swamp mosquitoes; and a sentimental love for "niggers" who commit petty wrongs—with all this against him the sheriff tries to follow his wife's advice to go fishing until the lynching "blows over." In his blundering generosities and naive sense of fitness, Sheriff Jeff makes us understand why lynchings are possible.

Katy Barlow, Aryan and oversexed, is surprised by Narcissa Calhoun, an aspiring political spinster, as she solicits a Negro boy on a Georgia road. The boy, Sonny Clark, runs away because he is not only mortally afraid of her, but is a virgin. Narcissa persuades Katy to give the traditional alarm of "rape"; a mob forms under the leadership of Katy's father and terrorizes the Negro quarters. Just as small boys pour salt on snails to watch their agonized convulsions, so the mobsters casually pour turpentine on the bodies of Negro women to see them writhe and tear their flesh with their nails.

Fear is the pivot of the story: plantation owners are afraid that their fields will be ruined by the mob; Katy is afraid that her claim of rape will be revealed as a falsehood; her father is afraid of what neighbors will think if he does not avenge his daughter; the sheriff is afraid that if Sonny Clark is *not* lynched his political enemies will drum up enough racial panic to make him lose the impending election; the political boss, Judge Allen, is afraid that something will happen *one* way or the *other;* Sonny Clark is really more afraid of leaving home than of facing the mob, since he has never been away from his grandmother before. The most poignant fear of all is that of Glenn, the cotton farmer, who, discovering Sonny Clark hiding out in the woods, is afraid to help him escape for fear of being called a "nigger-lover." Some of the most laughable, human and terrifying pages Caldwell has ever written deal with Sonny trotting with doglike obedience at the heels of Glenn, who is trying to decide what to do with him. When the perplexed boy learns that he is to be given over the mob, he pleads for Glenn to shoot him, and Glenn, choking with pity because "the niggers has always to put up with it," answers, "I ain't got a gun to do it with."

Katy basks in the glory of her martyrdom until the taunts of her fiancé prod her to hysteria. Then, shamed and fearful, she screams out the Negro boy's innocence when she sees him swinging from a tree. "It ought to put an end to lynching the colored for all time," the disconsolate sheriff mutters as he stumbles away from Katy's body. She had been stoned to death by the mob when it learned that she had lied.

P.S. Do not accept as good Caldwellian fun Narcissa Calhoun's idea of shipping the Negroes back to Africa. Caldwell was serious, no matter how fantastic it sounds, for such notions are being aired in the halls of Congress today.

Letter to Mr. Philip Wylie, Farrar & Rinehart

Hodding Carter, *The Winds of Fear* (New York: Farrar & Rinehart)

On *The Winds of Fear,* by Hodding Carter

Oct. 10, 1944
89 Lefferts Place
Apartment C-23
Brooklyn, NY

Mr. Philip Wylie
Farrar & Rinehart
New York, NY

Dear Mr. Wylie:

Please find enclosed a short statement on Carter's novel, *The Winds of Fear.* You are free to use all of this, or part of it, or none of it; if you think it will help the book, use your discretion.

I liked the novel a lot, and I'm glad that more white people of the South are finding the strength and courage to accept race relations as the subject matter of expression. I feel that out of this trend must come an extension, no matter how slight, of understanding of what is at stake in this matter for both white and black.

What I liked about Carter's book, even more than the story, was the contained and concealed indignation that ran beneath it. This is good; it is American; it is healthy. One wonders again and again why one does not hear it more often. Moral rejection of wrong is one of the most natural traits of our country, but there are today in our country so many forces—educational, industrial, etc.—that militate against its expression.

While speaking of moral indignation, let me tell you how much I admired your blasts in *Generation of Vipers!* (I'm assuming that you are the same Philip Wylie who wrote that book.) God knows, we need more of that kind of feeling from everybody everywhere. Why have so many Americans lost the capacity to react in that way? Why is it no longer regarded as "nice" to be real and react honestly? After all, it is the feeling that wrongs can be righted that makes us Americans what we are, that makes us different from most of the other people of the earth, that gives us our national character. Then why have we grown ashamed of embracing what we are? It was a belief in the capacity of the common man that gave birth to this nation; and an American, I believe, is at his best, his traditional and historical best, when he acts and lives out of such motives. But our culture, it seems, is, gradually excluding and denying that feeling.

Speaking of culture: When the mailman arrived with Carter's novel, I was busy rereading an old favorite novel of mine, D. H. Lawrence's *Sons and Lovers.* The transition was terrific! What a comedown! (I'm not panning Carter's book; I like and admire it for what it is.) But what a difference between two first novels! Lawrence cuts deeper into human feeling, and there does not exist in him the slightest hesitancy in revealing everything. Indeed, one could say that his passion was simply to do that to the best of his strength. Again I say that this is not directed against Carter; what I'm saying is leveled against our culture as a whole. We, both white and black, have so much to learn in our country. And I feel that an honest grappling with the Negro problem is one of the ways in which a therapeutic and loosening process could enter our culture, our feelings, and allow us to react freely.

The truth of the matter is this: In the South the fear created by the presence of the Negro has stunted the entire section of that life! It has blighted their art, science, government, and almost everything.

But, enough . . . Anyway, thank you for giving me the chance to read Carter's book and here's hoping that he comes back, like his hero Alan, and writes more of them.

Sincerely yours,
Richard Wright

Ellen Wright's papers

Ill-Paid Were the Players of the Communist Drama: The Voiceless Ones

Michel del Castillo, *The Disinherited,* trans. Humphrey Hare (New York: Knopf)

From Dostoevsky's "The Possessed" to Arthur Koestler's "Darkness at Noon," a Niagara of serious fiction has depicted man's outliving the mythological symbols of Christendom and his agonized groping for some new faith. In no area of contemporary life has this dilemma assumed so intense a form as in the reality of the rise and meaning of world Communism. Hitherto this dramatic Communist reality has been almost exclusively treated in the literature produced by bourgeois philosophical novelists who repeatedly posed the question of Communism in terms of: If there is a God, then Communism is an aberration, a sin, a spawn of intellectual pride; but, if there is no God, then Communism is the logical consequence of a God-less universe; anything is possible; man becomes God; the floodgates to criminality are open; etc., etc.

Yet I, an ex-Communist who spent ten years under Party discipline, never met a single functioning Communist whose actions were informed by such absurd and abstract notions. The Communists I knew were victims of a society, men and women and children whose personalities bore the festering wounds of the Church and State, repressive organs of power wielded by acquisitive and exploitive social classes; at times they were victims of racial or economic conditions; at other times they were double victims, victims of their own backward society and that of distant colonial powers. And not once did I ever hear a victim say, "If there is a God, then what is happening to me is right and I accept it." Indeed, the contrary was most often true; the more stoutly Christian the victim, the more inclined was he toward rebellion and eventual Communism.

It was, then, with a sense of relief that I turned the gripping pages of Michel del Castillo's second novel, "The Disinherited," which tells the story of the making of a Communist in terms of how I saw and lived that process. I do not exclude other processes; perhaps Dostoevsky's and Koestler's mentally tormented heroes really do exist, but they surely would (and this applies as much to Marx as to Lenin and Stalin) have had no human raw material to organize and catapult into tragic action if the conditions of poverty and degradation, as so graphically depicted by Castillo, had not thrown up hordes of violently exasperated men eager to embrace any philosophy that even hinted at redemption or liberation.

How is it that so many of the portraits of Communists presented to us have been pale-visaged high-brows thrashing about in the throes of metaphysics— high-brows whose presence or absence would not have mattered much, as history has so amply demonstrated? Hundreds of thousands of intellectual Communists, as Khrushchev has testified, have been slain for jaywalking in the path of the revolution and that revolution has roared relentlessly on. How was that possible? Who has been trying to fool us? Was it their fault that the voiceless ones who bore the brunt of the revolution could not tell their side of the story? Why did not the Communist or ex-Communist intellectuals recount the experience of those voiceless ones instead of extolling and celebrating the state of their own tired and frayed nerves?

In "The Disinherited," Castillo has done this. Olny, his hero (if such calloused and determined men can be imagined in that genre), embittered and hard, simple in action but confoundingly complex in reaction, springing out of a quarantined slum on the outskirts of Madrid just prior to Franco's onslaught on Spanish freedom, is a truly terrifying man whose existence calls into account our responsibility, for our society produces Olnys with the same skilled efficiency that River Rouge produces Fords. Not even Gorky ever drew such pictures of human brutality and suffering. Beneath the Spanish Church and State, today as then, is a subworld where there is more death than bread, where curses have superseded caresses, where murder is a casual joke, where sadism is entertainment, where prostitution is almost respectable, where all human joy has been put on deposit in the cathedrals to be withdrawn in a life beyond the grave. And with what terse power Castillo delineates the volatile, sodden, drunken, and dreamy denizens of this slum!

Here is that human motor power that the Bolsheviks called the "locomotive of history," a motor power which they alone seem to be able, no matter what their motives, to weigh in terms of its dynamic potentials, a motor power without which no single Communist intellectual, no matter how genius-ridden, would ever dream of going into revolutionary action. Without history's generations of Olnys there would have been no energy to move Spain toward republican government or to sustain its self-sacrificial struggle against Fascism; there would have been no wild human tide to drag the Russian October-train down its bloody rails; there would have been no élan to spur China upon its long arduous march; no fire to set ablaze the hearts of Africa's black millions.

Castillo, artist that he is, reaches no hard conclusions in his dramatic recital of degradation, sacrifice, and death; instead, he concentrates with white-hot heat on showing his chief characters becoming entangled in a web of insoluble contradictions. The brooding Santiago, impelled, like so many before him, toward Communism out of Christian love, finds himself a traitor lurching between the exploiters and the exploited and is slain by his Communist comrades; led by Santiago into the Party and freed of poverty and hunger, Olny is frozen with horror at the tragic price he pays, a symbolical and biological emasculation. Carlos, a dry, arrogant, crippled intellectual, discovers that he can't fight Franco's dictatorship and approve proletarian dictatorship at the same time, and he reaches that point of despair that makes him give his life for a revolution in which he no longer believes; Loto, the fifteen-year-old boy who swears continually to keep up his courage and prefers to die in battle than live in a slum; a kindhearted and weary priest who, about to die before a Communist firing squad, stands bewildered at complexities of life never hinted at in the Scriptures—all these brave and trembling men slide down the grim Greek route to defeat, without glimpsing why they are fighting or what they are dying for, shipwrecked upon the shoals of their own illusions, yet somehow managing to cling until the end to their dream of a world of peace for all mankind.

Out of this welter of negation, the sheer fierceness of despair tints the horizon of feeling with the afterglow of hope. Only the proud and bitter Spanish women—Olny's mother and wife (Consuelo and Marianita) emerge with some tattered dignity in Castillo's laconic narrative, but theirs is a dignity born more of biological functioning than of clear-eyed hope.

Castillo restates the Communist drama in a manner that reminds us that its strength is in each hungry body, in each outraged sense of human dignity, in each alienated personality, in each thwarted dream of comradeship and love, a challenging reality that is not all new and that predates the appearance of proletarian political parties. Anti-Communist, anti-Fascist, Castillo writes with blazing fury about men thrown into conflict by forces in themselves they but dimly perceive. His is a new voice whose accent is on the wordless words of the heart. Religion seems to be no answer to the needs of these deeply troubled men; indeed, as is evident in Asia and Africa today, religion all too often awakens the initial impulse to rebellion that leads to Communism.

What then is the answer? Castillo does not tell us, but his suffering-wrought book rouses us to speculation. May it not ultimately develop that this sense of being disinherited is not mainly political at all, that politics serves it as a temporary vessel, that Marxist ideology in particular is but a transitory makeshift pending a more accurate diagnosis, that Communism may be but a painful compromise containing a definition of man by sheer default?

If any of the foregoing speculations are but remotely true, then I believe that the present Cold War, and all the contemporary schemes for the "containment" of Communism, are beside the point, and Communism, deriving its nuclear energy from mankind's global awakening out of traditional and tribal slumber, might well turn out to be an even greater problem to the Communists themselves than to their strident enemies.

The Saturday Review, vol. 43, 16 April 1960, pp. 20–21

Review of 1945 New York production

Arnaud d'Usseau and James Gow, *Deep Are the Roots*

While Congress and Army brasshats stagger under the pressure of millions of U.S. parents demanding that their GI sons be demobilized and sent home at once, there are millions of white Americans who dread to see dark-skinned GI's who have been eating and sleeping with foreign whites return to America. The white South, in particular, knows that its black boys who have served in France, England, and Italy have tasted the fruits of a kind of racial freedom that does not exist in Dixie.

White America, both North and South, has been traditionally used to keeping its Negroes on a short political and social chain, educating them to accept an inferior place in the nation's life, and penalizing them when they resisted. Along comes a war and the Negroes are needed in industry, in the army, and navy; and for the duration of the war the Negroes are educated, along with their white brother, to read and write, to operate machines, to make decisions, and to kill . . . Jerked out of their debased positions by the vicissitudes of war, hundreds of thousands of them are transported to Melbourne, London, Naples, Paris, Rome, Le Havre where for the first time in their lives they consort with whites who do not possess the American white supremacy complex. Naturally the coming of peace and demobilization will bring trouble along America's far-flung Color Line. How Negroes, who have "got out of hand" with the sanction of society during a national emergency, can be put back in their "places" is the theme of Broadway's newest racial drama, *Deep Are the Roots*, by Arnaud D'Usseau and James Gow.

After World War I, white supremacy Southerners and Negroes who had been stimulated by war promises, drifted like sleep-walkers into racial conflict in a dozen or more U.S. cities. Authors D'Usseau and Gow, who shocked Broadway two years ago with their anti-Nazi play, *Tomorrow the World*, have anticipated the racial reactions that will follow in the wake of World War II and have set them forth in their much too talky, foggily resolved but highly dramatic *Deep Are the Roots*. For those whites who still cling to their irrational ideas about race, *Deep Are the Roots* is a public analysis of their attitudes toward Negroes. For an hour and a half they can lean back in an airconditioned theatre and watch a sharp-edged dramatization of their medieval racial emotions.

Deep Are the Roots is a drama of racial pathology depicted in terms of stock characters, white and black, of the present-day South. There is aged, reactionary Senator Ellsworth Langdon (Charles Waldron), who dreams of the nobility of an ante-bellum South that never existed save in legend, and who laments King Learishly over the drift of his daughters away from his stern philosophy of "keeping the niggers down". There is Alice (Carol Goodner), the Senator's older daughter, who tries to perform the miracle of treating Negroes right without changing the South's pattern of white supremacy. There is Alice's younger sister, Genevra (Barbara Bel Geddes), who is intimidated by the cruelty around her and who emotionally rejects the white South and yearns toward a Negro boy with whom, in her childhood, she has had her only moments of joy and friendship. There is Roy Maxwell (Harold Vermilyea), cousin of the family who is scornfully regarded by the Senator and who represents the conscience of an uncertain and divided New South. And there is Howard Merritt (Lloyd Gough), Yankee novelist and fiance of Alice, who spouts bewildered goodwill toward Negroes.

On the black side the characters are no less pat and familiar. There is Brett Charles (Gordon Heath), who has, with the help of Alice, emancipated himself from the morass of fear and ignorance which claim so many southern Negroes. Brett's mother, Bella (Evelyn Ellis), is the typical, loyal, religious Negro mammy who nurses Senator Langdon and functions as a kind of mother in the home. Honey (Helen Martin), is a grinning, hysterical Negro servant girl who in her fear does more harm than she is able to grasp.

The play's basic situation is simple and could perhaps be duplicated today in a million southern homes where whites try to unburden their heritage of guilt by showering petty favors upon dependent Negroes who are counted as "members of the family". Alice assumes the education of Brett, grooming him to become a leader of his people. She is successful until Brett is snatched from her cautious hands by the draft. The Army makes Brett an officer, "a gentle-man by act of Congress", and he is sent overseas. In England Brett finds a warm friendship in an English family, a friendship that is so free of reserva-tions that it makes the patronizing charity of Alice seem hypocritical. Brett returns to America with medals attesting his bravery and with a new sense of manhood; he is received by the Langdons with some trepidation. He startles his benefactors by refusing to accept their plans to further his education in a northern college and announces his intentions of remaining in the South and fighting to make the "war promises" come true for his people, a statement which Senator Langdon brands as revolutionary. Brett asks Alice to help him become the principal of a Negro school. Frightened at Brett's independence but striving to remain a liberal, Alice consents. She wants mightily to help Brett to be a man, but she is afraid of him when he acts like one. The dilemma of the southern white liberal, who claims that he wants to help Negroes, but who is determined to keep white supremacy in the South, is laid mockingly bare. Hard-bitten Senator Langdon knows that liberalism and white suprem-acy do not mix; he has fearful recollections of black senators and congress-men after the Civil War, and he itches to call upon the white trash to don sheets and pillow-cases and ride again. He knows that some 750,000 black GI's are about to return to civilian life and he senses that they will not fit humbly again into their niches of inferiority. He warns his daughters that Brett's "soul has changed", that this "nigra boy has been sleeping with white women and has been ripping his bayonet into white flesh".

To northerners the trivial wheels upon which most the drama turns may seem inadequate, but to those who know the South there can be no surprise when death threatens at the loss of a dime or a penknife or a watch; and it is a missing watch that creates the opportunity for the Senator to brand Brett a thief. Then both white and black go crazy. The Civil War is re-enacted in miniature, with Yankee novelist Merritt siding sentimentally with the Ne-groes. Normal values are turned upside down. Wisdom turns into hysteria. Nobility reveals itself as craven fear. Honor degenerates into bald lying. Sin-cerity becomes madness. Virtue tends toward murder. Hospitality descends into brutality. White supremacy assumes the guise of tragedy. And the mag-nolias and honeysuckles of Dixie begin to stink . . .

Matters are not helped when Brett confesses his love to Genevra. But Brett's mother, Bella, fearing whites more than she loves them, slaps her son and warns him that he will be killed if he keeps trying to cross the race line. The two lovers are seen as they rashly walk at night down by the river. An anon-ymous letter discloses Genevra's romance to Alice, who, schizoid-like, hides the dreadful secret from her father, but collaborates with him in trying to get Brett lynched, presumably because of the stolen watch, but really because of her sister's love for him. She phones the sheriff. Brett is trapped, slugged, and carted off to jail and held without charge. Cousin Maxwell, congressional aspirant, shocks the audience no less than he does Senator Langdon when he throws his lot in with the doomed Negro boy and wins his freedom. A pending lynching is averted only by the pleading of Alice's fiance who has accidentally wormed the truth out of the half-witted Negro servant girl, Honey, who had been bribed by the Senator to accuse Brett of theft.

Acts I and II of *Deep Are the Roots* are strict realism. But when the curtain lifts on Act III, we see Brett, now freed from jail and given a railroad ticket to the North, returning foolishly to Senator Langdon's mansion (no southern Negro ever made a mistake like that!) to plead his innocence before Alice. From that point on an infantile moralism creeps into the play and eventually swallows it. There are recantations; characters begin to switch sides without sufficient motive. Genevra offers herself nobly in marriage to Brett because he "has been so much hurt by whites"; but Brett rejects her, feeling that intermarriage is no solution. Under the tongue-lashings of Merritt, Alice recants her deathwishes against Genevra and Brett. And the Yankee novelist, displaying more hope than common sense, decides to remain in the South. Even the fire-eating Senator fails at the supreme test; when he learns of the love affair between Brett and his daughter, he simply mutters a pious oath instead of shooting the Negro boy on the spot as would all good 100% southern white gentlemen who have sworn to uphold what they quaintly call the "sexual chastity" of their women.

Having left the plane of realism, *Deep Are the Roots* plunges vaguely into the realm of attempted solutions of the race problem, ending with Senator Langdon's rushing from his mansion to raise a mob. Genevra leaves home to live and learn in some far, strange city. Alice and Brett form an alliance, as unconvincing as it is unreal, to work for a better world. *Deep Are the Roots* raises more issues than it solves.

In one beautifully enacted scene with Merritt, Genevra spills the beans about the psychological causes of race hate; she explains how, before she had the power to reason for herself, her sister had attempted to instill race hate into her, had forbade her to play with Brett when she was twelve years of age, hinting darkly of awful, unmentionable consequences. Genevra's inoculation of race hate did not take, but that does not mean that the vast majority of southern whites are immune to it. In most cases it takes fatally, lasting for life, becoming a part of their personal culture, their morality. To treat a Negro as an equal human being is as impossible with the average southern white as incest or atheism, and is about as reprehensible. To withhold from Negroes treatment such as is accorded other human beings is taught in the home, in church, at school and finds powerful sanction throughout the social structure of the South: in jobs, politics, education . . . *Deep Are the Roots* treats not so much of the Negro Problem as of the White.

Superb acting by an expert cast carries the play over many a stretch of limping script. The play will not solve the race problem in the minds of many whites or blacks, but most certainly it projects vividly upon the stage what is happening in race relations in our post-war world. Topical and engrossing, *Deep Are the Roots* handles America's Number One minority problem with the same dramatic intensity that characterized the authors' previous play, *Tomorrow the World.*

Unpublished review written for *Time,* 29 September 1945

Beinecke Rare Book and Manuscript Library, Yale University

"L'Homme du Sud"

[Since the first page is missing from the English original in the Wright papers, it is translated here from the French by Michel Fabre.]

It has taken a long time for Americans suddenly confronted with the outstanding reputation which Faulkner was enjoying in Europe to separate the astonishing genius of the man from the teeming jungle he had created from one novel to the next.

Only through reasoning were many Americans able to discover that the greatness of Faulkner lay precisely in his ability to transpose the American scene as it exists in the Southern States, to filter it through his sensibilities and finally to define it in words.

A Frenchman remarked one day that American writers write in the same fashion as artists paint; in other terms, that American literature is lacking in ideas and perspective. Such criticism may be founded or not, but there is in Faulkner's work an element that reminds [*The following text is Wright's original*] often of the painter more than the writer *per se;* and that is the purity of the artistic intention. I doubt seriously if Faulkner has ever written one line of what could be called propaganda. In fact I doubt if he would even know how. Simply to represent, in terms of form, color, movement, light, mood, and atmosphere has been the most notable hallmark of every Faulkner book from *Sartoris* to *Intruder in the Dust.*

The achievement of Faulkner is all the more arresting in that he is a southern white man, the product of a section of America which has withstood and nursed the stings of a Civil War defeat which it could never accept, and misinterpreted that defeat in the most infantile and emotional manner. The literature of the white South, as well as its public life, has been for almost a century under a pressure as intense and cruel as that under which the Negro was forced to live; and it would be a grave mistake to feel that the Negro was the only victim of the white South's proud neurosis. The almost atavistic clinging to the "aristocracy of the skin", the reduction of all life's values to the protection of "white supremacy", crippled not only the Negro but the entire culture of the whites themselves. That is why there was never a symphony orchestra in the South until 1928; the tardy development of the social sciences in America can be traced to the South's abysmal fear of all facts relating to human relationships; and it was from the background of the fears of the South that sprang the fantastic behavior of the southern senators in the nation's capitol.

In the realm of artistic expression, the pressure to ensure conformity was almost as fierce as that which Russian Communists bring to bear upon their artists. Southern American art fell under the interdiction of "protecting the South's reputation," and no man save the hardiest dared challenge this standard. Talented and sensitive southerners fled the section, and those who remained brooded and accepted a scale of values which killed their souls.

But the south could not remain isolated forever; wars and convulsions of social change were bound to engulf it; industrialization induced such impersonal social relations that controls loosened and allowed a certain degree of negative freedom, and it was in this transition period of confusion that the genius of Faulkner leaped through and presented itself to a startled world.

The main burden of Faulkner's work is moral confusion and social decay and it presents these themes in terms of stories of violence enacted by fantastic characters. If Popeye, of *Sanctuary,* seems unreal and mechanical, it is because Faulkner cast him into a symbol of the rising tide of the soulless and industrial men who are beginning to swarm over the southern scene. If Joe Christmas, of *Light in August,* seems like a villain beyond redemption, it is because Joe Christmas represents the violence of the southern Negro reacting against social pressures too strong for him. And if other Faulkner characters exert frenzied efforts that lead to no end, as of the characters in *As I Lay Dying, Absalom, Absalom!,* and *The Unvanquished,* it is because so much of the south's energies, both of the blacks and whites, is spent fighting ghosts.

But, like all great art, the work of Faulkner cannot be restricted to merely the South when one attempts to unravel its implications. Southern American fear is basically no different from fear anywhere; and the obsessive compulsion to violence of the South obtains wherever men are men. Through that dialectical leap in meaning which art possesses, Faulkner, in showing the degradation of the South, affirmed its essential humanity for America and for the world. Happily, a Bilbo's hate-charged racist utterances will be forgotten, but Faulkner's gallery of characters will live as long as men feel the need to know themselves, as long as confused souls, needing repose and reflection, repair to books which form a reservoir of a nation's emotional experiences.

It was fitting that a recognition of Faulkner's labors should have been crowned with the Nobel Prize for Literature for 1950.

France-Etats-Unis, December 1950, p. 2 in French

English original at Beinecke Rare Book and Manuscript Library, Yale University

E. M. Forster Anatomizes the Novel

E. M. Forster, *Aspects of the Novel* (New York: Harcourt, Brace and Co.)

When first requested to review E. M. Forster's *Aspects of the Novel,* a series of Cambridge lectures now reissued after being out of print for 20 years, I demurred because I had not read any of Forster's novels, *A Passage to India, Howard's End* and so on. Finally I felt that this was, perhaps, precisely the kind of reaction most needed: a review that would take the book for simply what it was, a book about the novel and not a book mainly by Forster, the novelist.

Let me say at once that the publishers have rendered American writers and readers alike a service by reissuing this volume, for Forster writes with a wise and subtle mind. His supple, conversational prose cuts deep and dredges up important facts.

The heart of what Forster has to say can be quickly revealed by our imagining that, in the year 3947, Atomic Citizen Xc-34-66y is reading a 20th-century manuscript found in the ruins of the Empire State Building, and this Atomic Citizen is amazed to learn—from, say, Hemingway's *The Sun Also Rises*—that we spent our waking hours making love and cultivating human relationships: we rarely ate, slept or worked. Now, you and I know that, though many of our novelists depict our lives in this manner, we do not live like that.

Forster contends that the novel must distort life, for it is, at bottom, not so much a picture of life as a reflection of the concerns and temperaments of the novelists themselves. Insofar as Forster is right about this, and I believe that he is, he underscores Nietzsche's argument that art is fundamentally a sublimated will to power, a frenzy, a state of intoxicated vitality, an overloaded and swollen will trying to contagiously communicate.

To Forster the backbone of the novel is the crude and simple story, and he sadly admits: "Yes—oh, dear, yes—the novel tells a story."

And a story is a narrative of events arranged in sequence, in Time, and this tyranny has enslaved the worst and the best of novelists from Scott to James Joyce. No matter how fiercely Proust or Gertrude Stein may rebel against it, Time still makes one damn thing happen after another.

How, then, was the novel, with such a primitive foundation, made into so sensitive an instrument? Forster exhibits the means by which modern writers have introduced other values into the novel: plot, character, fantasy, rhythm. He leads us from the loosely constructed plot-novels of Scott to the looming character of Moll in Defoe's *Moll Flanders*—from the celebration of Time in Arnold Bennett's *The Old Wives' Tale* to Tolstoy's triumph over Time in *War and Peace*—from Emily Bronte's attempt to make passion swell until it excludes Time to Stein, who actually throws away the clock and jumbles her sentences until normal communication breaks down.

In describing the sensitization of the novel, Forster discusses "flat" and "round" characters. He finds the characters of Dickens "flat" and those of Defoe "round." The test, according to Forster, as to whether a character is "flat" or "round," is the ability of that character to surprise us in a convincing way. "Flat" characters cannot surprise without stepping out of their roles and spoiling the story, whereas a Lord Jim or a Raskolnikov, psychologically "rounded" and complex, can convincingly surprise.

Forster does not mean that Jane Austen, Dickens and H. G. Wells are not great novelists, for he finds that many writers can make "flat" characters, which are mostly representatives of ideas, seem to live by "shaking" them. "Flat" characters sum up the difference between a Dickens and a Conrad, a Wells and a Melville, and they indicate a lack of passion on the part of the artist.

Forster introduces plot and knits it, as another value, into the novel:

"Plot is . . . a narrative of events, the emphasis falling upon causality . . . *The king died, and then the queen died,* is a story . . . *The king died, and then the queen died of grief,* is a plot . . . *The queen died, no one knew why, until it was discovered that it was through grief at the death of the king,* is a plot with a mystery in it. . . ."

Story *plus* plot *plus* character *equal* novel, but what about *Tristram Shandy* and *Moby Dick?* Forster had to add more values to his definition of the novel, for who would bar Melville and Sterne? If you take what Forster calls the "fantastic-prophetical axis" from Virginia Woolf, D. H. Lawrence, and Joyce, practically nothing would be left. To account aesthetically for many modern novelists, Forster finds himself at odds with Aristotle, who declared: "All human happiness and misery take the form of action."

Forster maintains the opposite: "It [the modern novel] seeks means of expression other than through plot."

And Forster is never so rigid as to exclude overtones or undertones. After analyzing *Moby Dick* for its many meanings, he confesses (Americans can be proud that he pays Melville the highest tribute to be found in his book):

"Nothing can be stated about *Moby Dick* except that it is a contest. The rest is song . . . Melville—after the initial roughness of his realism—reaches straight back into the universal, to a blackness and sadness so transcending our own that they are undistinguishable from glory."

The weakest part of this admirable volume is the section which Forster devotes to pattern and rhythm. He compares Anatole France's *Thaïs* to an hour-glass and Percy Lubbock's *Roman Pictures* to a grand chain. This is far-fetched. He could have found sounder definitions, I feel, had he sought for psychological, rather than physical, ones. Indeed, Forster explains the more recondite phases of the novel much better than he does the obvious.

He honors Henry James for his brilliant technical achievements, but he does not overlook the hollow content of the Jamesian novel.

Forster realizes that James deliberately pruned his subject-matter in the interests of pattern and cohesion. Beauty floats on the surface of a James novel, but as a tyrant and at too great a cost, and, instead of the Jamesian novel conveying the exuberance of the novelist's sensibility, it resolves into something pale, oblique and evasive. His parting shot at James is, in our modern slang, a killer: "Put Tom Jones or Emma . . . into a James book, and the book will burn to ashes."

After dissecting a score of novels, Forster states that the novel, even when it is as sophisticated and sensitive as André Gide's *The Counterfeiters*, still is not a free and open art form, still misses much of the truth of life. The novel, with its primitive spine of story, has served some of the greatest minds in art as an instrument for the expression of intense reality, but Forster feels that its limitations constitute a challenge:

"When the symphony is over we feel that the notes and tunes composing it have been liberated. . . . Cannot the novel be like that? . . . History develops, art stands still. The novelist of the future will have to pass all the new facts through the old, if variable, mechanism of the creative mind."

Is there any chance for the novel to alter, to become bigger, different, freer, more open? Not unless we learn to see ourselves in a new light, can we see others differently, and, of course, the possibility of that takes us beyond the realm of the novel.

Aspects of the Novel is richly rewarding in insights, and it contains some of the best criticism in contemporary literature. It is a book not only for writers, but for readers as well.

"Book Review Section," *PM*, 16 March 1947, p. 3

Introduction

Françoise Gourdon, *Tant qu'il y aura la peur* (Paris: Flammarion)

The protesting voice of the oppressed rings loud in the history of literature, whether it be a Greek voice bewailing an implacable fuss, or a Jewish voice lamenting bondage, or a Negro voice declaiming against slavery, or a Protestant voice defiantly asserting the right to free conscience, or a woman's voice pleading for the consideration of her personality, or an adolescent voice registering dismay at a world it never made,—the voice of protest embodies some of the most moving and familiar cadences in mankind's literature.

Allied with and/or akin to, or perhaps deriving from, that voice of protest is another voice more powerfully persuasive and penetrating, a voice that rolls through the hearts of men when the gods (Jesus), or a member of the oppressor's race or class (Karl Marx), or a literary artist fired by a sense of injustice (Emile Zola and Harriet Beecher Stowe), come forward and voluntarily shoulder the moral burden of the oppressed and speak for them; then that voice of protest, until then exceptional, or rejected, or but dimly heard, becomes universal, speaking all tongues, widening the horizons of men, recreating a new sense of human solidarity.

In America the only contemporary white novelist I know of who has performed this singular feat in regard to the sufferings of the American Negro is Lillian Smith in her "Strange Fruit"; now, from a totally unexpected direction, from clear across the stormy Atlantic whose misty bosom bore the slave trade, comes a white French writer, Mlle. Francoise Gourdon, who has voluntarily assumed the exasperated emotional state of the beleaguered American Negro and has given it a new kind of interpretation and has endowed those engaged in fighting racial prejudice with an extension of moral sanction. Mlle. Gourdon's "Tant qu'il y aura la peur" is the vivid, poetic record of a white girl's descent into the maelstrom of America's Negro problem. Psychologically anchored on that hot borderline where the American white world touches the American black world, the sensitive scenes of her novel evoke the reality of that inexplicable fear of the white world for the black world, and the black for the white.

As an American Negro writer who has lived both in the American North and the American South, I unhesitatingly declare Mlle. Gourdon's novel as "corroborative evidence," as the legal phrase has it, emotionally conceived, imaginatively fashioned, and artistically projected, of the racial reality of America today, not only of the South, but also of the North, where her story is laid.

Julia, her French heroine, a medical student, coming from an old, rich culture rooted in a traditionally structured society whose members enjoy a genre of social security unknown to the new, raw industrial American world, seeks to adjust herself to a mid-western college town ridden with racial strife induced by the problem of school integration. Julia's humanist conditioning sustains shock after shock as she attempts to attain the admission of a black girl to a campus club, and Julia's stubborn courage serves to delineate, with slow-burning acid strokes, the racial distances enveloping all aspects of life from housing to sex, existing in this well-bred and literate American community.

The heart of this novel deals with fear,—fear of love, fear of the "unknown," fear of friendship, fear of one race for another, fear of declaring one's feelings, fear of one's neighbors, and, in the end, the fear of fear itself. Perhaps no one but an outsider could have captured, as was the case with Gunnar Myrdal in his "An American Dilemma," with such deft admirableness the nuances of racial tension of American whites struggling vainly to reconcile their democratic pretensions with their racial practices.

In quick succession, Mlle. Gourdon shows us Miriam, the tense, proud black girl who sacrifices herself as a kind of guinea pig to enter a hostile white world is an example of her race; Philip Tiptou, a sweet-tempered white mystic who fights to make the dream of Christian brotherhood come true; Hill, a dignified, dedicated young black preacher striving against inner psychological odds to reconcile his memories of racial segregation and lynch terror with Gentle Jesus' gospel of love he preaches to his black flock each Sunday; and, above all, Mlle. Gourdon spins with great skill the poignant story of the love between Julia and Bill, a love that floats like a lost echo in the darkness and finally fades out to silence and nostalgic recollection in an environment of hate and fear where no such love can exist.

Mlle. Gourdon depicts her racial drama against a background of an American mid-western winter whose arctic winds are as freezing as the choked fear and the inhibited love in the hearts of her characters, a winter whose snow is as blinding as the passions of men who flee their homes at the mere approach of a race speaking their own tongue and sharing their own culture and religion, but with a different color of skin.

Mlle. Gourdon's frame of reference is never political or ideological; her engrossing story is sifted to us through a temperament welded to humanist ideals. She makes no attempt to solve the American racial problem; she is content, artist that she is, to weigh and measure the manner in which irrational passions inevitably defeat themselves. Above all, she has that magic narrative power that sweeps the reader with her into realms of nightmarish racial anxieties, thereby enlarging our capacity to understand. Here is a vital talent handling vital material that has the power of lifting us out of our petty world and transporting us into that sphere of feeling where we are aware of the earth beneath our feet and the stars above our heads. She writes from a heart that has reasons that reason does not know, and a great portion of her narrative power derives from her specializing in the close-up scene whose hallucinatory intensity conveys the illusion of reality with stunning force; for example, white Julia and black Bill kissing clandestinely on the dingy threshold of the church rectory in the summer dusk; the elegant sorority meeting where stylishly dressed American white girls nibble teacakes and sip Coca-Cola and think of "race" but never permit themselves to speak of it; the brash young South African student who pours out his bitter racial hate upon the colored races of the world; Julia's frightened and frantic search for Bill through the sordid warrens of Chicago's South-Side Negro ghetto.

The reader is bound to ask himself: How did a French white girl manage to dig so deeply into the black life of America and throw into relief basic attitudes and feelings that even Negroes themselves are compelled to admit as true? How could she, a stranger, seize so firmly upon those racial realities that even American whites, native born, claim are utterly beyond them? I do not know. But she most surely did it. Was it sympathy? Empathy? Psychological techniques? Religious emotion? Or just good old-fashioned fellow feeling? Well, whatever it was that led Mlle. Gourdon to such valid insights, the world today, and particularly America, could use much more of it.

There is about this novel a haunting ambiguity that leaves you wondering ... And what is the aim of art, if it is not to make us wonder?

Published in French. English original at Beinecke Rare Book and Manuscript Library, Yale University

Review

John Gunther, *Inside U.S.A.* (New York: Harper & Bros.)

When I heard that Gunther was writing on *Inside USA*, I felt that it was all right for an American journalist to write objectively about Europe, Asia, and Latin America but that it was quite another thing for him to write objectively about America. Well, I was wrong. Gunther looks at his own country with alien but sympathetic eyes; he is one of those rare Americans who have not subscribed to the racial mores and folklore of his time. Proof of this is found in that chapter in his book dealing with the Negro's relationship to the American scene.

Now, a wise-guy journalist would have avoided that problem altogether, but Gunther's honesty ruled that approach out. Gunther found that one phase of what is known as the American problem is the Negro problem, which is an indirect way of saying that there is no Negro problem but a white problem.

Though Gunther omits to deal in detail with the exploitation of Negroes he does stress the shameful gap between what America preaches and what she practices. In describing the plight of the Negro, Gunther is not afraid to call to mind the treatment of Jews under Hitler and India's caste system. Gunther knows that you cannot educate Negroes and keep them submerged; he states America's choice boldly: either stop educating Negroes or admit them to the equality of democracy . . .

Gunther could have sounded a warning in his chapter on the Negro, and that warning is this: it is as distinctly possible for this nation to be split and destroyed on the question of the Negro as it was possible for Hitler to split and ruin Europe on the question of the Jew. In her treatment of the Negro, America has created her most serious domestic and international problem . . .

Unpublished, Yale, JWJ, Wright Misc 686–687

Review

Ernest Hemingway, *To Have and Have Not* (New York: Grosset & Dunlap)
John Steinbeck, *Grapes of Wrath* (New York: Viking Press)

It is within these limits that the best writers of today are approaching the life of the working class. Two books, Hemingway's *To Have and Have Not*, and Steinbeck's *Grapes of Wrath* can give us a measure of their worth and weaknesses as methods of putting working-class life upon paper in the form of fiction. When one begins to examine these books, and they are very good books, one finds that they have structural flaws in common at the precise moment when they begin to interpret the lives of workers. Hemingway never deserted the character-in-the-foreground method until he drew the character of Harry Morgan; and Steinbeck never spoke over the heads of his characters to the reader until he came to the family of the Joads.

With Hemingway the case is clear. Hemingway wanted to tell the American people that an individual alone had no chance. So he depicted Harry Morgan, showing the futility of his struggles and the meaninglessness of his death. Then, when the life of Harry Morgan was over and when, keeping the technical principle of Hemingway's books in mind, one thought the novel was over, Hemingway wrote on, began to tell the reader what he *really* wanted to say. The novel broke in two; Hemingway's technique carried him along the old road, but when he wanted to write of the meaning of the workers' life, he threw it overboard and began to talk.

The same is true, though in a different way, with Steinbeck and his *Grapes of Wrath*. One hundred and seven pages out of six hundred and fourteen are used to tell the reader what to think of his material and his characters, leaving five hundred and seven pages of straight story (Again, I hasten to add that this is not a condemnation of either Hemingway or Steinbeck but to show how the most eminent writers of our time found their own trusted tools inadequate to work the ground of working-class life). . . . There is a still more surprising observation to make . . . on the exercise of imagination in both books. Those interlarded passages in Steinbeck and the final section of *To Have and Have Not* contain some of the finest imaginative writing both men have done; but it was not done in terms of character and action. It seemed that as soon as they wanted to tell of the most important things in working-class life they swept their characters aside with a gesture of impatience and told us straight out. Why? The most obvious answer is that the working-class characters did not possess the intelligence to allow the writers to remain faithful to their old method and do so. . . . Why don't they use more intelligent characters? . . . These characters, Harry Morgan, the Joads, constitute types which are true to the American scene; further, they might answer that they do not want to falsify. An intellectual Harry Morgan discussing the obscure causes of individual loneliness and isolation in America would simply not ring true; and a Joad who understood the complex stream of forces that shunted him from his farm land would not be believed in. . . . Bolder, more intricate character types must be conceived in order to take the novel into new fields and at the same time retain what is best in the technical achievements of the old fiction. . . . For example, all of that portion of *Grapes of Wrath* which describes the country-side, which tells the reader of the vast forces at work, will have to reside in some character; and, likewise, that part of *To Have and Have Not* which describes the lives of the lazy wealthy who go to Florida to live will have to be fused organically into the action and body of the story.

From a lecture on left wing literature, 1940, pp. 15–18

Beinecke Rare Book and Manuscript Library, Yale University

Blurb

Chester Himes, *Lonely Crusade* (New York: A. A. Knopf)

Chester Himes' *Lonely Crusade* chalks up another significant victory for Negro prose expression in America. His hard, biting style reveals the truth of a marital situation never before depicted in novels about Negro life. Lee Gordon's tragic search for integrity cuts deeper into our consciousness than piles of academic volumes of sociology and psychology. Himes stands in the front ranks of the truth-tellers in our nation. Long Live Chester Himes.

Beinecke Rare Book and Manuscript Library, Yale University

Introduction to the French Edition

Chester Himes, *Lonely Crusade* (Paris: Corréa)

In 1944, Gunnar Myrdal, the Swedish savant, published a huge sociological work on race relations in the United States. This work, entitled *An American Dilemma*, totalling some 1000 pages, dramatically contrasted American democratic pretensions with American daily practices. In the fields of sociology and academic thought, *An American Dilemma* cut a path that was awesome and caustic; it evoked high praise and violent condemnation. At the time of the appearance of *An American Dilemma*, I recall saying to myself, "This is good indeed. What we need now is a novel which will contrast, in terms of rich images and sensual prose, the schism existing between America's ideals and her practices."

In 1947 this wish of mine was fulfilled when Alfred A. Knopf published Chester Himes' powerful novel, *Lonely Crusade*. But let me say at once that this *Lonely Crusade*, as a novel, is much, much more than a contrast between America's preaching and practice. It is a scathing criticism of the Negro, the Communist Party, trade unionism, and the anti-Negro feelings of white American workers.

Lee Gordon, the novel's protagonist, is an honest, idealistic young Negro who finds himself thrown against his will into the role of a labor organizer. Lee thinks that labor unions and revolutionary movements are honest endeavors led by honest men, but he is soon bitterly disillusioned and swept into Machiavellian political currents that test him beyond his capacity and finally thrust him into a position where he feels that his honor as a human being is at stake. To redeem himself, he ruins his home, betrays his friends, becomes involved in murder, and finally is shot by the police as he seeks to prove his worthiness to men who despise him.

Dramatically the novel shows the corroding effects of race consciousness by depicting how Gordon fails as a husband, fails as a union organizer, fails in the end to even understand that he is a Negro in white America. The prose of Himes searches into the most hidden aspects of Negro existence in the United States and reveals how race consciousness conditions religion, sex, personal relations, and political movements.

There is an ancient rubric which says, "Seek the truth and the truth shall make you free." What this rubric does not tell us who live in the 20th century Western Civilization is that besides making you free, truth can hurt, wound, and even kill, as Himes' hero, Lee Gordon, learned at so great a cost.

Like most contemporary American novels, *Lonely Crusade* is strict realism, stating issues acidly, offering no apologies and granting no concessions. And I declare that in these pages we have for the first time a truthful and realistic picture of the American Negro's relationship to Communism and the American trade union movement. To French readers the anti-Negro attitude of American labor will come as something of a shock, but I must remind you that American trade unionists are simply Americans, sharing the faults and the virtues of a young, crude, violent, confused nation which as yet does not fully know itself and which, in many respects, can hardly be called a nation at all, so divided and vast are its social, racial, and geographical realities. In *Lonely Crusade* America is reported to you not by a paid official propagandist, not by a man who feels that God has asked him to speak, but simply by a young Negro artist whose sole passion is to tell the truth as he sees and feels it. This book is not anti- or pro-American, not anti- or pro-Communist, not anti- or pro-Negro, not anti- or pro-Capitalist; it is simply human. I commend it highly to French readers who want to know the truth of a phase of American life.

English original at Beinecke Rare Book and Manuscript Library, Yale University

Two Novels of the Crushing of Men, One White, One Black

Chester B. Himes, *If He Hollers Let Him Go* (New York: Doubleday, Doran & Co.)
Arthur Miller, *Focus* (New York: Reynal & Hitchcock)

When, sweeping aside what Karl Marx called the "immense accumulation of commodities" that gluts our nation, one probes into the naked consciousness of our citizens, one is almost always impressed by the discovery that, somehow, our American environment fails to sustain the individual, fails to relate him effectively to his fellow man.

Even amidst our lush plenty, there is always a gnawing tension, stemming from our relationship to an industrial world that seems to have mastered us before we have had a chance to master it—that seems to have corrupted the springs of our consciousness, robbing us of the capacity of knowing what it is we really want.

This emotional confusion holds true for black and white, Jew and Gentile, rich and poor, employed and unemployed, for those who make high wages as well as for those whose wages are low. Take away his easy grin, discount his hard-boiled vernacular—and invariably you find that an American is possessed by demons of uncertainty.

Two fairly competently executed novels, Chester B. Himes's *If He Hollers Let Him Go* and Arthur Miller's *Focus* implicitly depict this conflict and the fateful consequences flowing from it. The protagonists of these novels, one white, one black, are engaged in a defensive war with an environment that gives them food and shelter. But insofar as their relationship to their fellow men is concerned, that environment teases, taunts, and finally crushes them.

Cleverer than it is profound and more coincidentally contrived than passionately felt, *Focus* portrays the plight of a middle aged, middle class American, Lawrence Newman, who because of his eyeglasses is mistaken for a Jew.

Newman, whose ancestors came from England, had a good job, a nice home, and a comfortable bachelor life. Then, suddenly, he was accused of being what he probably hated most in all the world: a Jew. For his definition of a Jew was a popular one: loud clothes, gesturing, lying, cheating, and concealing one's racial identity. He once thought he had detected these qualities in a girl applying for a job in his office, and he rejected her application.

The first day Newman wears his eyeglasses to work, his boss decides his appearance is too Jewish and suggests that he should work out of sight of the public. Insulted, Newman quits.

His joblessness coincides with the high tide of an "invasion" of Jews into his neighborhood, and when his nextdoor neighbor, a Christian Fronter, urges him to join in the crusade to "clean up" the block, he is too confused and frightened to act. Then, when he marries the girl whom he had once rejected for a job because she looked too Jewish, it is taken for granted by his neighbors that not only is *he* a Jew but his loudly-dressed wife is one also.

There are some penetrating passages of psychological analysis that show how Newman gradually takes on the feelings of an outcast, how he becomes sensitized to every nuance of social disparagement, how he finally embraces what he previously hated.

His wife pleads with him to join the Christian Front, declare his non-Jewish origin and make peace. But neither her pleadings nor the threats of his neighbors move him.

In the end a blurred streak of decency saves Newman's integrity. Assaulted by a gang of Christian Fronters (during which episode his wife runs away), he sides openly with a Jewish storekeeper, named Finkelstein, and stands shoulder to shoulder with him, cracking Christian Front skulls with a baseball bat. More, he takes the Jew home and treats his wounds. The climax is reached when Newman turns his back upon his wife and neighbors and goes naively to the police to register a complaint against the Christian Front. At police headquarters he is interviewed by what is indubitably an Irish Christian Front cop.

The policeman studied the edge of the desk, formulating his questions. Newman watched his broad, Irish face. "How many of you people are there on that street?" the policeman began, trying to make a plea.

"What's that?" Newman whispered faintly.

"On that street," the policeman said once more. "How many of you people live there?"

"Well," said Newman, wetting his lips, . . . and stopped. "There are just the Finkelsteins on the corner . . ."

"Just them and yourself?" the policeman asked.

The policeman had assumed that he was Jewish and Newman accepted the assumption.

The point at which Miller's hero resolves to fight is the beginning of Himes's novel. When you leave the reasonable, intellectual pleas of *Focus* to read *If He Hollers Let Him Go,* you are plunged into a sea of prose so blindingly intense that it all but hurts your eyes to read it.

Miller writes out of his head; Himes writes out of his guts. Miller has space into which to maneuver; Himes uses words like a soldier shooting at you from a foxhole; Miller paints his characters in light and shadow; Himes lights up race relations among shipyard workers in a neon glare.

Himes pits an educated northern Negro against poor southern whites in a West Coast shipyard, and the results are violent and shocking. The author's stripped and functional prose style, developed in the slick magazines, takes on a new quality when it describes, in psychological terms, the contrast between a Negro believing in democracy and the brutal realities of our industrial system. In the end, Robert Jones, the hero, is crucified on a cross of chromium and steel.

The story is simple. Bob Jones's authority as a straw boss on a ship construction gang is not recognized by his white workers. When a Texas blonde, Madge, refuses to work with what she calls "niggers," Jones calls her a slut. She informs the supervisor. Jones is demoted and his chances of going to law school at night and marrying his upperclass Negro girl, Alice, go up in smoke.

He finds the best way to repay Madge is to violate the symbol of her superiority, her white body. She is frightened at first but finally yields, telling him to hurry up or she'll tell that he is raping her. The word rape unnerves Jones and he flees.

Racially humiliated, he seeks to wound the feelings of Alice for he has to hurt somebody to redeem his manhood. He takes her—he is dark and she is light enough to pass—to a white hotel for dinner where she is deeply wounded by the white snubs she receives. Since Jones has hurt her, she hurls a hurt at him by revealing that she has had Lesbian experiences. Feeling now that they are even with each other, they become reconciled. Jones promises to apologize to Madge, beg his job back and be a "good nigger."

Next day he stumbles upon Madge sleeping in an empty cabin on the ship. The situation reverses itself. Madge now wants him, but he does not want her. While they argue in a locked room that has but one door, they are surprized by a ship inspector. To save herself, Madge screams out the traditional words: "Help! I'm being raped!"

Jones is slugged and cast into jail. But, for the sake of national unity, the judge lets him go with:

"Suppose I give you a break, boy. If I let you jin the armed forces—any branch you want—will you give me your word of honor you'll stay way from white women and keep out of trouble?"

The book concludes with a single sentence: "Two hours later I was in the Army."

I wonder how many white readers will catch the irony of sending a man rendered incapable of discipline by personal conflicts into the most highly-disciplined organization in the world!

Jerky in pace, *If He Hollers Let Him Go* has been compared with the novels of James M. Cain, but there is more honest passion in 20 pages of Himes than in the whole of Cain. Tough-minded Himes has no illusions: I doubt if he ever had any. He sees too clearly to be fooled by the symbolic guises in which Negro behavior tries to hide, and he traces the transformation by which sex is expressed in equations of race pride, murder in the language of personal redemption, and love in terms of hate.

To read Himes conventionally is to miss the significance of the (to coin a phrase) bio-social level of his writing. Bob Jones is so charged with elementary passion that he ceases to be a personality, and becomes a man reacting only with nerves, blood and motor responses.

Ironically, the several dreams that head each chapter do not really come off. Indeed, Himes's brutal prose is more authentically dreamlike than his consciously contrived dreams. And that is as it should be. In this, his first novel, Himes establishes himself not as what has been quaintly called a New Negro but as a new kind of writing man.

Published in *PM*, 25 November 1945, p. m7–m8

Forerunner and Ambassador

Langston Hughes, *The Big Sea: An Autobiography* (New York: Alfred A. Knopf)

The double role that Langston Hughes has played in the rise of a realistic literature among the Negro people resembles in one phase the role that Theodore Dreiser played in freeing American literary expression from the restrictions of Puritanism. Not that Negro literature was ever Puritanical, but it was timid and vaguely lyrical and folkish. Hughes's early poems, "The Weary Blues" and "Fine Clothes to the Jew," full of irony and urban imagery, were greeted by a large section of the Negro reading public with suspicion and shock when they first appeared in the middle twenties. Since then the realistic position assumed by Hughes has become the dominant outlook of all those Negro writers who have something to say.

The other phase of Hughes's role has been, for the lack of a better term, that of a cultural ambassador. Performing this task quietly and almost casually, he has represented the Negroes' case, in his poems, plays, short stories and novels, at the court of world opinion. On the other hand he has brought the experiences of other nations within the orbit of the Negro writer by his translations from the French, Russian and Spanish.

How Hughes became this forerunner and ambassador can best be understood in the cameo sequences of his own life that he gives us in his sixth and latest book, "The Big Sea." Out of his experiences as a seaman, cook, laundry worker, farm helper, bus boy, doorman, unemployed worker, have come his writings dealing with black gals who wore red stockings and black men who sang the blues all night and slept like rocks all day.

Unlike the sons and daughters of Negro "society," Hughes was not ashamed of those of his race who had to scuffle for their bread. The jerky transitions of his own life did not admit of his remaining in one place long enough to become a slave of prevailing Negro middle-class prejudices. So beneficial does this ceaseless movement seem to Hughes that he has made it one of his life principles; six months in one place, he says, is long enough to make one's life complicated. The result has been a range of artistic interest and expression possessed by no other Negro writer of his time.

Born in Joplin, Missouri, in 1902, Hughes lived in half a dozen Midwestern towns until he entered high school in Cleveland, Ohio, where he began to write poetry. His father, succumbing to that fit of disgust which overtakes so many self-willed Negroes in the face of American restrictions, went off to Mexico to make money and proceeded to treat the Mexicans just as the whites in America had treated him. The father yearned to educate Hughes and establish him in business. His favorite phrase was "hurry up," and it irritated Hughes so much that he fled his father's home.

Later he entered Columbia University, only to find it dull. He got a job on a merchant ship, threw his books into the sea and sailed for Africa. But for all his work, he arrived home with only a monkey and a few dollars, much to his mother's bewilderment. Again he sailed, this time for Rotterdam, where he left the ship and made his way to Paris. After an interval of hunger he found a job as a doorman, then as second cook in a night club, which closed later because of bad business. He went to Italy to visit friends and had his passport stolen. Jobless in an alien land, he became a beachcomber until he found a ship on which he could work his way back to New York.

The poems he had written off and on had attracted the attention of some of his relatives in Washington and, at their invitation, he went to live with them. What Hughes has to say about Negro "society" in Washington, relatives and hunger are bitter poems in themselves. While living in Washington, he won his first poetry prize; shortly afterwards Carl Van Vechten submitted a batch of his poems to a publisher.

The rest of "The Big Sea" is literary history, most of it dealing with the Negro Renaissance, that astonishing period of prolific productivity among Negro artists that coincided with America's "golden age" of prosperity. Hughes writes of it with humor, urbanity and objectivity; one has the feeling that never for a moment was his sense of solidarity with those who had known hunger shaken by it. Even when a Park Avenue patron was having him driven about the streets of New York in her town car, he "felt bad because he could not share his new-found comfort with his mother and relatives." When the bubble burst in 1929, Hughes returned to the mood that seems to fit him best. He wrote of the opening of the Waldorf-Astoria:

Now, won't that be charming when the last flophouse has turned you down this winter?

Hughes is tough; he bends but he never breaks, and he has carried on a manly tradition in literary expression when many of his fellow writers have gone to sleep at their posts.

The New Republic, 103, 24 October 1940, p. 600

As Richard Wright Sees Autobiographies of Langston Hughes and W. E. B. Du Bois

Langston Hughes, *The Big Sea: An Autobiography* (New York: Alfred A. Knopf)
W. E. B. Du Bois, *Dusk of Dawn: An Essay toward an Autobiography of a Race Concept* (New York: Harcourt, Brace)

These two Negro autobiographies stand as signposts of two ways of Negro life in contemporary America.

Langston Hughes, author of "The Big Sea," and W. E. B. Du Bois, author of "Dusk at Dawn," have lived lives that are deeply symbolic of what the Negro has done in America and what he is likely to do and feel in the days to come. Both books are lyrical and poetic and in an ideological sense they reflect class divisions within the area of Negro experience. Du Bois, born in 1868, stands as an exemplar of the "old school," the conservative outlook stemming from a belief in the capacities of men to respond to reason and through this response to alter the conditions of life. Despite the fact that Du Bois' ideas have undergone a series of evolutions over a long period of years, he still clings to the hope of a "talented tenth" leading and guiding the masses of the Negro people.

Hughes, born in 1902, the product of a much different set of social forces, looks to the masses of the people for hope and guidance. He feels that they are best fitted to protect and extend the basic values of our civilization and he has cast his hope with them in their struggles toward enlightenment and organization.

In a larger sense, the world-view of these two men reflect the titanic forces struggling for mastery on a world scale.

Hughes' life zigzagged between a half dozen Midwestern towns until he entered high school in Cleveland, Ohio, where he began to write poetry. Hughes' father longed to educate him and establish him in business, but Hughes would have none of it. Instead, he quit school, grabbed a job on a merchant ship, threw his books into the sea and sailed for Africa, then again he sailed for Rotterdam, where he left the ship and made his way to Paris. After an interval of hunger he got a job as doorman, then as a second cook in a night club. He went to Italy to visit friends and had his passport stolen. Jobless in an alien land, he became a beachcomber until he found a ship upon which he could work his way back to New York.

In contrast, DuBois comes from a Puritan New England background, a product of French, Dutch and African blood. His boyhood resembles that of millions of whites. While still young he lived in the South as a student and schoolteacher. Later he received a degree of Doctor of Philosophy from Harvard; he spent two years at the universities of Paris and Berlin. For 14 years he was professor of economics and history at Atlanta University. As a result of a tilt with Booker T. Washington and his school, he abandoned pedagogy and spent 31 years as director of publicity and research for the National Association for the Advancement of Colored People and as editor of *The Crisis*.

The goal of these two men, as it emerges from the story of their lives, was identical, but the means for its realization varied so widely as to build up two camps of leadership within the Negro people.

The two books are recommended highly for those anxious to examine at close range the tissue and texture of contemporary Negro life. But I think the average reader will finish them with a hunger for something more, with a feeling that something is lacking. What is lacking in the lives of these two men is an effective rationale of action or program. May not the future of the Negro consist of a fusion, a synthesis of the principles of both Hughes and Du Bois, that is, an alliance between the educated Negro and the masses of workers?

Chicago News, 4 December 1940, p. 10

Richard Wright Reviews James Weldon Johnson's Classic, *Black Manhattan*

James Weldon Johnson, *Black Manhattan* (New York: Alfred A. Knopf)

With the European war as a lurid backdrop, James Weldon Johnson's *Black Manhattan* (reissued after 10 years; it was first published in 1930) should afford for those concerned with the destiny of the American Negro an opportunity for study. Because the history of the Negro in New York so closely parallels the history of the Negro nationally, this book can be taken as a foreshortened drama of black America.

Excluding the depression, of which the book does not treat, this record of struggle and achievement will enable a balance sheet to be struck in terms of the Negroes' progress and, if the reader is enterprising, he can surmise what is to come. On the basis of Johnson's record, one is struck by the fact that most of the epochs of advance or defeat came to the Negro in times of war or domestic upheaval. This holds true from the beginning of the Negroes' entry into New Amsterdam in 1626, through the slave rebellions, through the Civil War, through the draft riots, through the post-Civil War unrest, up to and including the first World War.

An interpretation of *Black Manhattan* shows that the Negro advanced or retreated not in accordance with his abilities but in direct proportion to the tolerant or intolerant pressure of his environment. Hence his story is not one that runs in a straight line, but it zigzags, teeters, totters and in times of stress seems almost to stop, only to spurt forward again under the stimulus of a sudden wave of national prosperity.

In a style at once both firm and easy Johnson depicts the growth of slavery, the rise of the Negro abolitionists and the maintenance of the underground railroads, the Negro as a soldier, the Negro as cook and cake-walker, as race track jockey and prize fighter, as actor and song writer, down to the death of peerless Florence Mills in 1927. As the story unfolds the variety of Negro personalities is astounding. Rebellious slaves who saw mystic visions give way to tragedians of the Ira Aldridge type, who are replaced by banjo strumming, black-faced comedians, who in turn are supplanted by Jack Johnson, who makes way for the puzzling and nationalistic Marcus Garvey, who gives way to blues-writing black poets and Negro riot victims of the post-World War period.

Johnson tells how, during the World War, the United States Army issued copies of an order entitled: "Secret Information Concerning Black American Troops." This military information urged French officers not to display too much friendliness to the black officers of the A. E. F., for fear of wounding the sensibilities of white American officers and soldiers. As incredible as it sounds, the French military authorities were even cautioned by the heads of the A. E. F. not to "commend too highly the black American troops" for acts of bravery, particularly in the presence of (white) Americans. After the Armistice many Negroes wearing the United States Army regulation uniform were lynched in many parts of the United States.

There is increasing danger that we might participate in the fight to stop Hitler, and if we do, will such orders be issued again? If we fight, and if the Jim Crow tactics of the last war are applied to Negro troops in the field, will there not follow tense periods of racial unrest, just as followed after the Armistice?

Of all the incidents which Johnson relates, this is the most poignant because it symbolizes the story of the Negro in America, an unbelievable story of three centuries of courageous fighting for liberty and justice within the boundaries of the "democratic" United States!

Chicago News, 22 May 1940, p. 10

A Sharecropper's Story

Harry Harrison Kroll, *I Was a Sharecropper* (Indianapolis: The Bobbs-
Merrill Company)

I Was a Sharecropper made me grit my teeth. Its author is a white Southerner and I, the reviewer, am a black Southerner. His people and my people
have glared and cursed at each other for more than three centuries over a gulf
of falsehood. My people called his kind "po' white trash"; and his people
called my kind "niggers." But despite this, as I turned the pages I was assailed
time and again with nostalgic love and recognition for a multitude of familiar
events, for black and white life in Dixie is swathed in the same daily reality.
Kroll's mother, father, brother and sister are types that can be found a million
times in white and black families throughout the South.

    Drenched in authentic agrarian detail, and sparing neither the simple glory
nor the repelling sordidness, Kroll's autobiography traces his growth in the
West Tennessee backlands from childhood to adolescence, from a vagabond
photographer to school teacher, and finally to his status as the author of a
best-seller, "The Cabin in the Cotton." Kroll's astonishing story is as indubitably American in its flavor as is the fact of Lincoln's rise from log cabin to
the White House. With a candor that is at times both refreshing and embar-
rassing, he tells of hunger, superstition, queer herb remedies, incest, lynching,
death from sheer neglect; of his amazing and vital mother and his wistful,
futile father. He relates how his illiterate family, under the spur of conditions
for which poverty is no adequate name, tried to write best-selling novels, tried
to invent a hair-straightener for Negroes, tried to make a new kind of ice
cream, tried to manufacture synthetic diamonds and, last, tried to establish a
motion-picture industry in the hills of West Tennessee. Indeed, Kroll's own
escape from this Sargasso Sea of ignorance is as unbelievable as are the fantastic aspirations of his child-minded parents.

    As I turned page after page I hoped that some experience would enable
Kroll to see beyond the "white fog" of his hungry days; out of all the dreams
he dreamed I longed for just *one* dream of what the South *could* be if white
and Negro sharecroppers could stop hating long enough to find common
ground for hope. But Kroll's hope is couched in these terms: "black niggers,"
"black sons of bitches," "nigger bucks," "fry the lard out of that black bas-
tard," etc. To Kroll Negro "inferiority" is immutably fixed in the very moral
structure of the universe. His philosophy, for all of his courageous striving, is
one which perpetuates the hated system from which he escaped. He says: "I
did it by lifting up one foot and putting it down, through the hours, the days
and years . . . all the problems of life can be solved as simply and easily as
that."

    As a social type the sharecropper has become an interesting object of popular curiosity. The public, however, has had to depend for its information mainly upon research workers and specialists. But in the case of Kroll the usual procedure is reversed; the object of curiosity turns the tables by reporting ably the life of his own people. In doing so the incredible facts of "Tobacco Road" and "God's Little Acre" assume a new value, inasmuch as they are for the first time strained through the imagination of one who has actually lived the life he depicts. Yet I hope he does not become a prototype that the masses of white sharecroppers of the South will want to follow.

The New Republic, vol. 93, 1 December 1937, p. 109

Introduction

George Lamming, *In the Castle of My Skin* (New York: McGraw-Hill)

Accounting for one of the aspects of the complex social and political drama in which most of the subject people of our time are caught, I once wrote: ". . . to a greater or less degree, almost all of human life on earth today *can* be described as moving away from traditional, agrarian, simple handicraft ways of living toward modern industrialization."

These words deal with vast, cold, impersonal social forces which are somewhat difficult to grasp unless one has had the dubious fortune of having had one's own life shaped by the reality of those forces. The act of ripping the sensitive human personality from one culture and the planting of that personality in another culture is a tortured, convoluted process that must, before it can appeal to peoples' hearts, be projected either in terms of vivid drama or highly sensual poetry.

It has been through the medium of the latter—a charged and poetic prose—that George Lamming, a young West Indian Negro of Barbados, has presented his autobiographical summation of a tropical island childhood that, though steeped in the luminous images of sea, earth, sky, and wind, drifts slowly toward the edge of the realms of political and industrial strife. Notwithstanding the fact that the Lamming's story, as such, is his own, it is, at the same time, a symbolic repetition of the story of millions of simple folk who, sprawled over half of the world's surface and involving more than half the human race, are today being catapulted out of their peaceful, indigenously earthy lives and into the turbulence and anxiety of the twentieth century.

I, too, have been long crying these stern tidings; and, when I catch the echo of yet another voice declaiming in alien accents a description of this same reality, I react with pride and excitement, and I want to urge others to listen to that voice. One feels not so much alone when, from a distant witness, supporting evidence comes to buttress one's own testimony. And the voice that I now bid you hear is sounding in Lamming's "In the Castle of My Skin." What, then, is this story that Lamming tells?

Without adequate preparation, the Negro of the Western world lives, in *one* life, *many* lifetimes. Most whites' lives are couched in norms more or less traditional; born of stable family groups, a white boy emerges from adolescence, enters high school, finishes college, studies a profession, marries, builds a home, raises children, etc . . . The Negro, though born in the Western world, is not quite of it; due to policies of racial exclusion, his is the story of *two* cultures: the dying culture in which he happens to be born, and the culture into which he is trying to enter—a culture which has, for him, not quite yet come into being; and it is up the shaky ladder of all the intervening stages between these two cultures that Negro life must climb. Such a story is, above all, a record of shifting, troubled feelings groping their way toward a future that frightens as much as it beckons.

Lamming's quietly melodious prose is faithful not only to social detail, but renders with fidelity the myth-content of folk minds; paints lovingly the personalities of boyhood friends; sketches authentically the characters of schoolmasters and village merchants; and depicts the moods of an adolescent boy in an adolescent society . . . Lamming rehearses the rituals of matriarchal families so common to people upon whom the strident blessings of an industrial world are falling—families whose men have been either killed, carted off to war, or hired to work in distant lands, leaving behind nervous mothers to rule with anxious hysteria over a brood of children who grow up restless, rebellious, and disdainful of authority.

Lamming recounts, in terms of anecdote, the sex mores of his people, their religious attitudes, their drinking habits, their brawls in the sunlit marketplaces, the fear of the little people for the over-seers, and the fear of the overseers for the big white boss in the far-away house on the hill. (Unlike the population ratio in the United States, the English in these tiny islands comprise a minority surrounded by a majority of blacks; hence, that chronic, grinding, racial hatred and fear, which have so long been the hallmark of both white and black attitudes in our own Southland, are largely absent from these pages.)

Lamming objectifies the conscience of his village in those superbly drawn character portraits of Pa and Ma, those folk Negroes of yesteryear whose personalities, bearing the contours of Old Testament, Biblical heroes, have left their stamp upon so many young Lammings of the Western world. I feel that Lamming, in accounting for himself and his generation, was particularly fortunate in creating this device of a symbolic Pa and Ma whose lineaments evoke in our minds images of simple, peasant parents musing uncomprehendingly upon the social changes that disrupt their lives and threaten the destinies of their children . . .

The clash of this dying culture with the emerging new world is not without its humor, both ribald and pathetic: the impact of the concept of marriage upon the naïve, paganlike minds is amusingly related by Lamming in his story of Bots, Bambi, and Bambina. The superstitions of his boyhood friends are laid engagingly before us. And there's a kind of poetry suggested even in the outlandish names of his boyhood playmates; Trumper, Boy Blue, Big Bam, Cutsie, Botsie, Knucker Hand, Po King, Puss-in-Boots, and Suck Me Toe. . .

Just as young Lamming is ready to leave Barbados Island for Trinidad, Trumper, who has gone to America and has been influenced by mass racial and political agitation, returns and, in a garbled manner, tells of the frenzied gospel of racial self-assertion—that strange soul-food of the rootless outsiders of the twentieth century. The magnetic symbol of Paul Robeson (shown here purely in racial and *not* political terms!) attracts as much as disturbs young Lamming as he hears Robeson sing over a tiny recording device: Let My People Go!

Even before Lamming leaves his island home, that home is already dying in his heart; and what happens to Lamming after that is something that we all know, for we have but to lift our eyes and look into the streets and we see countless young, dark-skinned Lammings of the soil marching in picket lines, attending political rallies, impulsively, frantically seeking a new identity . . .

Filtered through a poetic temperament like Lamming's, this story of change from folk life to the borders of the industrial world adds a new and poignant dimension to a reality that is already global in its meaning.

Lamming's is a true gift; as an artist, he possesses a quiet and stubborn courage; and in him a new writer takes his place in the literary world.

Inner Landscape

Carson McCullers, *The Heart Is a Lonely Hunter* (Boston: Houghton Mifflin Company)

Out of the tradition of Gertrude Stein's experiments in style and the clipped, stout prose of Sherwood Anderson and Ernest Hemingway comes Carson McCullers' *The Heart Is a Lonely Hunter*. With the depression as a murky backdrop, this first novel depicts the bleak landscape of the American consciousness below the Mason-Dixon line. Miss McCullers' picture of loneliness, death, accident, insanity, fear, mob violence and terror is perhaps the most desolate that has so far come from the South. Her quality of despair is unique and individual; and it seems to me more natural and authentic than that of Faulkner. Her groping characters live in a world more completely lost than any Sherwood Anderson ever dreamed of. And she recounts incidents of death and attitudes of stoicism in sentences whose neutrality makes Hemingway's terse prose seem warm and partisan by comparison. Hovering mockingly over her story of loneliness in a small town are primitive religion, adolescent hope, the silence of deaf mutes—and all of these give the violent colors of the life she depicts a sheen of weird tenderness.

It is impossible to read the book and not wonder about the person who wrote it, the literary antecedents of her style and the origins of such a confounding vision of life. The jacket of the book tells us with great reserve that she is twenty-two years old. Because the novel treats of life in the South, we assume that she is Southern born and reared. A recent news story says she is married and now lives in New York. And that is all.

I don't know what the book is about; the nearest I can come to indicating its theme is to refer to the Catholic confessional or the private office of the psychoanalyst. The characters, Negro and white, are "naturals," and are seen from a point of view that endows them with a mythlike quality. The core of the book is the varied relationships of these characters to Singer, a lonely deaf mute. There are Mick Kelly, a sensitive, adolescent white girl; aged Dr. Copeland, the hurt and frustrated Negro; Jake Blount, a nervous and unbalanced whiskey-head; and Biff Brannon, whose consciousness is one mass of timid bewilderment. All these characters and many more feel that the deaf mute alone understands them; they assail his deaf ears with their troubles and hopes, thereby revealing their intense loneliness and denied capacity for living.

When the deaf mute's friend dies in an insane asylum, he commits suicide, an act which deprives the confessional of its priest. The lives of Miss McCullers' characters are resolved thus: Mick Kelly is doomed to a life of wage slavery in a five-and-ten-cent store; Dr. Copeland is beaten by a mob of whites when he protests against the injustices meted out to his race; Jake Blount stumbles off alone, wistfully, to seek a place in the South where he can take hold of reality through Marxism; and Biff Brannon steels himself to live a life of emptiness.

The naturalistic incidents of which the book is compounded seem to be of no importance; one has the feeling that any string of typical actions would have served the author's purpose as well, for the value of such writing lies not so much in what is said as in the angle of vision from which life is seen. There are times when Miss McCullers deliberately suppresses the naturally dramatic in order to linger over and accentuate the more obscure, oblique and elusive emotions.

To me the most impressive aspect of *The Heart Is a Lonely Hunter* is the astonishing humanity that enables a white writer, for the first time in Southern fiction, to handle Negro characters with as much ease and justice as those of her own race. This cannot be accounted for stylistically or politically; it seems to stem from an attitude toward life which enables Miss McCullers to rise above the pressures of her environment and embrace white and black humanity in one sweep of apprehension and tenderness.

In the conventional sense, this is not so much a novel as a projected mood, a state of mind poetically objectified in words, an attitude externalized in naturalistic detail. Whether you will want to read the book depends upon the extent to which you value the experience of discovering the stale and familiar terms of everyday life bathed in a rich and strange meaning, devoid of pettiness and sentimentality.

The New Republic, vol. 103, 5 August 1940, p. 195

White Faces: Agents Provocateurs of Mankind

O. Mannoni, *Prospero and Caliban: The Psychology of Colonization* (New York: Frederick A. Praeger)

As the tide of white domination of Asia and Africa recedes, there lies exposed to view a procession of shattered cultures, disintegrated societies, and a writhing sweep of more aggressive religion than the world has known for centuries. And, as scientific research, free of the blight of colonial control, advances, we are witnessing the rise of a new genre of academic literature dealing with colonial and post-colonial facts from a wider angle of vision than was ever possible before. The personality distortions of hundreds of millions of black, brown, yellow, and *white* people that are being revealed by this literature is confounding and will necessitate drastic alterations in our past evaluations of colonial rule.

O. Mannoni's *Prospero and Caliban* (first published in Paris in 1950 under the title: *Psychologie de la Colonisation*) is a prime model of this new literature which is destined to modify the attitude of white men toward themselves. (See Hannah Arendt's *The Burden of Our Time*, and Gunnar Myrdal's *An International Economy*.) In Mannoni's terse, academic pages one enters a universe of menacing shadows where disparate images coalesce,—white turning into black, the dead coming to life, the top becoming the bottom, and you think you are seeing Biblical beasts with seven heads and ten horns rising out of the sea . . . Imperialism is turning out to have been a much more morally foul bit of business than even Marx and Lenin imagined!

Utilizing psychoanalytic concepts and restricting his study to the last fifty years of French rule in Madagascar, Mannoni deliberately ignores the economic and political aspects the more to concentrate upon that fateful subjective emotional relationship of Frenchmen and Madagascar natives, showing how the colonial and his victim emotionally complement each other until, out of mutual frustration, political violence, nationalism, and revolution resulted. Deep psychological compulsions drove the Europeans toward the native, and equally deep psychological compulsions prompted temporary native compliance.

What is the gist of Mannoni's concept? Well, let's imagine a mammoth flying saucer from Mars landing, say, in a Swiss peasant village and debouching swarms of fierce looking men whose skins are blue and whose red eyes flash lightning bolts that deal instant death. The inhabitants are all the more terrified because the arrival of these men had been predicted. (The Second Coming of Christ, the Last Judgment, etc.) Hence, they feel that all real opposition is useless. Yet these blue strangers are casually kind as long as they are obeyed and served.

Is this a fragment of paperback science fiction? No; it's more prosaic than that. The religious myths of the Western world have conditioned us for just such an improbable event. Similarly, the legends and religions of Asia and Africa and the New World Indians had prepared hundreds of millions for the arrival of the white man. (Recall the Cortes-Montezuma drama among others . . .)

But what of the attitude of the arriving stranger, be he blue or white? Why has he come? Does he want gold, women, power? It's here that Mannoni's volume can help us, for he contends that the 15th and 16th century neurotic, restless Europeans, sick of their thwarted instincts, were looking not only for spices and gold and slaves when they set out, but for a world peopled by shadow men that would permit free play for their repressed instincts. Stripped of tradition, these misfits, adventurers, indentured servants, convicts and freebooters were the most advanced individualists of their time. Buttressed by the influence of the ideas of Hume and Descartes, they had been rendered emotionally independent and could doff cloying ties of family. The Asian-African native, anchored in family dependence-systems of life, could not imagine why these men left their homelands, could not conceive of what was sustaining them . . .

Living in a waking dream, generations of emotionally impoverished colonial European whites wallowed in the quick gratification of greed, reveled in the cheap superiority of racial dominance, slaked their sensual thirst in illicit sexuality, draining off their dammed up and condemned libido . . . Asia and Africa thus became a neurotic habit that Europeans could forego only at a cost of a powerful psyche wound, for this emotionally crippled Europe had, through the centuries, grown used to leaning upon this crutch of black, brown, and yellow people.

The colonial, Mannoni says, is not born, but made; he states:

> He would not in the first place feel the urge to go to the colonies, but even should he find himself there by chance, he would not taste those emotional satisfactions which, whether consciously or unconsciously, so powerfully attract the predestined colonial.

But what of the impact of these neurotic white faces upon the personalities of the native? Steeped in dependence and anchored in ancestor-worshiping religion, the native is prone to identify those powerful white faces falling athwart his life with the potency of his dead father who had sustained him in the past. Accepting the invasion, he transfers his loyalties to those faces, but, because of the psychological, racial, and economic luxury derived from white domination, those faces keep aloof. An agony is induced in the native heart, rotting and pulverizing it as it tries to live under a white domination that mocks it. The more Westernized that native heart becomes, the more anti-Western it has to be, for that heart is now weighing and judging itself in terms of (white) Western values that make it feel degraded. Vainly attempting to embrace the world of white faces that rejects it, it recoils and seeks refuge in the ruins of moldering tradition. But it's too late; it finds haven in neither . . . This is the psychological stance of the populations of present-day Asia and Africa; this is the revolution that the white man cast into the world and it is before this revolution (a large part of which the Communists have already successfully captured) that he stands paralyzed with fear . . . Mannoni ought to know whereof he speaks, for he is a former colonial administrator . . .

Mannoni's important book is biased, and that, perhaps, is as it had to be. Two-thirds of this volume, devoted to the personality of the Madagascar native, creates the impression that Mannoni is convinced that those natives are somehow the White Man's Burden. Well, maybe the other side of the coin will someday be described by black, brown, and yellow men who are psychologically free enough of the mangling processes of imperialism to account for how that emotionally disturbing white face roused them and sent them hurtling toward emotional horizons as yet distant and dim.

Original text of the review which appeared in *The Nation,* No. 183, 20 October 1956, pp. 330–31 under the title "Neurosis of Conquest"

Beinecke Rare Book and Manuscript Library, Yale University

Introduction

Howard Nutt, *Special Laughter* (Prairie City, Ill.: Press of James Decker)

Dear Howard,
I was tremendously excited when word reached me that a volume of your poems was to be published, for I remembered the many times during the past few years when I'd picked up a magazine and found your irreverent, satirical, and laughing images. Because we'd been friends for so long, because I'd watched these poems multiply and appear in print, and, above all, because I'd

felt that your poems, woven out of the common perceptions of our lives, had conferred upon my sensibilities a new dimension, I was rash enough to ask you to let me tell others what these poems meant to me. I am glad that you consented.

Frankly, I asked this privilege because I felt that one of the best ways to introduce a book to a reader is to let that reader know what that book means to someone, what that book has done to someone. So I'm going to try to tell some of the experiences I've had reading your lines, and I hope that many, many others may overhear and become as infected with the contagion of your vision as I have been.

Let me tell this as though we were sitting quietly in a tavern on State Street in Chicago, indulging in one of our interminable talks about life, literature, politics, and that acute consciousness which our generation has inherited from the anonymous millions who (as you so aptly phrase it) live and die ". . . without benefit of dignity."

I prefer to talk about your book in this way because I've felt that your poems were a kind of terrifying conversation, slyly draping in the guise of humor an awful secret which our generation shares in common, a secret which makes us chronically aware of a class that does not know that

> Anticipation
> Of disaster
> Has its own sort
> Of special laughter.

Yes, Howard, I'm afraid many are going to suspect that you do not regard that species of human life which vegetates in the great Mississippi River Valley as being beautiful. They're going to wonder if you have forsaken the homes and heritage of your forefathers. They're going to be shocked to find you probing and poking with rebellious fingers into the moldy fabric of their daily experience only to tell them that they live ". . . So far apart together," until for them life becomes merely this:

> And death comes on in ignominious ways!

Of all the poems in this volume, I like MOTHER GOOSE best. It is our poem, an American poem, as American as strawberry shortcake or lynching! MOTHER GOOSE captured me completely, and I refer to it in my thoughts as a kind of ghoulish tap dance, exquisite as skillfully played castanets, executed by a vaudeville comedian dancing and grinning atop an empty coffin, with hollow reverberations echoing the memories of childhood! The opening line, "LITTLE BOY BLUE, COME, BLOW YOUR HORN!" assumes a sinister meaning compounded of a paradoxical mixture of tenderness and leering irony.

Like the pioneers who made their lives out of what was nearest at hand, you take words from the street and tavern and endow them with significant meaning and form, as in PORTRAIT IN A GLASS DOOR KNOB, or when you invent speech to snare the ludicrous and pathetic, as in ANTICLIMAX— FOR THOSE WHO LIVE IN A SUITCASE, or when you, detached, simply point your finger amusingly at a daily incident, as in METROPOLIS PIL-GRIM. I anticipate that there will be those who will say that your laughter is bitter ONLY. If any do, let them remember those images of yours that tell poignantly of specks of beauty discerned in the Midwestern murk, as when you say,

> . . . While at his feet the darkness licks
> The almost liquid light from yellow bricks.

If I were to try to think of a word that would describe how these poems of yours strike me, I'd pronounce: Yankee! Yankee poetry, but the poems of a Yankee grown wary, conscious, and knowing, yet still casual, loitering, terse of speech, and, like a Mark Twain of the Twentieth Century, retaining the traditional manly reticence by camouflaging the horrible truth. I feel, how-ever, that the implied hope out of which you write is in some degree fulfilled in the manner in which you have created, for us all, the pulse of contempo-raneousness in the beat and measure of your lines . . .

So, Howard, I know why you, being a poet yourself, yank your thumb in contempt at the young poet in SLOPING CEILINGS. But there is one thing I'm sure of, and it's this: These poems will aid in the conquering of our death-ridden environment by fostering among us, not pity, nor naïve hope, nor that brand of cultivated liberal gentleness we've grown so sick of—but FELLOW-SHIP, fellowship of a kind that breeds a special and knowing laughter!

As ever,

Foreword

Paul Oliver, *Blues Fell This Morning* (London: Horizon Press)

Millions in this our twentieth century have danced with abandonment and sensuous joy to jigs that had their birth in suffering; I'm alluding to those tunes and lyrics known under the rubric of the blues, those starkly brutal, haunting folk songs created by millions of nameless and illiterate American Negroes in their confused wanderings over the American Southland and in their intrusion into the Northern American industrial cities.

The blues are fantastically paradoxical and, by all logical and historical odds, they ought not to have come into being. I'm absolutely certain that no one predicted their advent. If I may indulge in an imaginative flight, I can hear a White Christian Virginia planter, say, in 1623, debating thus with his conscience while examining a batch of the first slaves brought from Africa:

"Now, these black animals have human form, but they are not really human, for God would not have made men to look like that. So, I'm free to buy them and work them on my tobacco plantation without incurring the wrath of God. Moreover, these odd black creatures will die early in our harsh climate and will leave no record behind of any possible sufferings that they might undergo. Yes, I'll buy five of these to be used as slaves . . ."

But that mythical Virginia planter would have been tragically deluded. Not only did those blacks, torn from their tribal moorings in Africa, transported across the Atlantic, survive under hostile conditions of life, but they left a vivid record of their sufferings and longings in those astounding religious songs known as the spirituals, and their descendants, freed and cast upon their own in an alien culture, created the blues, a form of exuberantly melancholy folk songs that has circled the globe. In Buenos Aires, Stockholm, Copenhagen, London, Berlin, Paris, Rome, in fact, in every large city of the earth where lonely, disinherited men congregate for pleasure or amusement, the orgiastic wail of the blues, and their strident offspring, jazz, can be heard.

How was that possible? I stated above that the possibility of those shackled, transplanted blacks ever leaving behind a record of their feelings about their experiences in the New World ran smack against historical odds. What were some of those odds?

First, those blacks were illiterate and it was not until some three centuries later that their illiteracy diminished to any appreciable degree.

Second, how could tribal men, whose values differed drastically from those of the Puritan Christian environment into which they were injected as slaves, ever arrive at an estimate or judgment of their experiences? How could they determine whether their lives were better or worse in America than in Africa?

Third, upon being sold into slavery, many tribes were deliberately separated one from another, so that the possibility of tribal intercommunication would be nullified, and, thus, the likelihood of revolt eliminated.

Fourth, not only were slaves bought and sold, employed as commodity-mediums of exchange, but they were intentionally bred as livestock, thereby augmenting the wealth of the planters.

Fifth, the spur to obtain the slaves' labour was brutality; the effort of the slave to learn merited punishment; self-assertion on the slaves' part met with rebuff; the penalty of escape, death.

How could such men, then, speak of what they underwent? Yet they did. In a vocabulary terser than Basic English, shorn of all hyperbole, purged of metaphysical implications, wedded to a frankly atheistic vision of life, and excluding almost all references to nature and her various moods, they sang:

Whistle keeps on blowin' an' I got my debts to pay.
I've got a mind to leave my baby an' I've got a mind to stay.

This volume contains three hundred and fifty fragments (a fraction of the material extant) of the blues, and I believe that this is the first time that so many blues, differing in mood, range, theme, and approach have been gathered together. We thus have here a chance to cast a bird's-eye view upon the meaning and implication of the blues. Certain salient characteristics of the blues present themselves at once.

The most striking feature of these songs is that a submerged theme of guilt, psychological in nature, seems to run through them. Could this guilt have stemmed from the burden of renounced rebellious impulses?

There is a certain degree of passivity, almost masochistic in quality and seemingly allied to sex in origin, that appears as part of the meaning of the blues. Could this emotional stance have been derived from a protracted inability to act, of a fear of acting?

The theme of spirituality, of other-worldliness is banned. Was this consciously done? Did it imply reflection upon the reigning American religious values?

Though constant reference is made to loved ones, little or no mention is made of the family as such. Was this because family life was impossible under slavery? (Family life among American Negroes has remained relatively weak until the present day!)

The locale of these songs shifts continuously and very seldom is a home site hymned or celebrated. Instead, the environmental items extolled are saw-mills, cotton-gins, lumber-camps, levee-banks, floods, swamps, jails, highways, trains, buses, tools, depressed states of mind, voyages, accidents, and various forms of violence.

Yet the most astonishing aspect of the blues is that, though replete with a sense of defeat and down-heartedness, they are not intrinsically pessimistic; their burden of woe and melancholy is dialectically redeemed through sheer force of sensuality, into an almost exultant affirmation of life, of love, of sex, of movement, of hope. No matter how repressive was the American environment, the Negro never lost faith in or doubted his deeply endemic capacity to live. All blues are a lusty, lyrical realism charged with taut sensibility. (Was this hope that sprang always Phoenix-like from the ashes of frustration something that the Negro absorbed from the oppressive yet optimistic American environment in which he lived and had his being?)

All American Negroes do not sing the blues. These songs are not the expression of the Negro people in America as a whole. I'd surmise that the spirituals, so dearly beloved of the Southern American Whites, came from those slaves who were closest to the Big Houses of the plantations where they caught vestiges of Christianity whiffed to them from the Southern Whites' cruder forms of Baptist or Methodist religions. If the plantations' house slaves were somewhat remote from Christianity, the field slaves were almost completely beyond the pale. And it was from them and their descendants that the devil songs called the blues came—that confounding triptych of the convict, the migrant, the rambler, the steel driver, the ditch digger, the roustabout, the pimp, the prostitute, the urban or rural illiterate outsider.

This volume is the first history of those devil songs; it tells how fortuitously they came to be preserved, how their influence spread magically among America's black population, and what their probable emotional and psychological meaning is. It would be very appropriate to recount that an American Negro was the first person to attempt a history of the blues and their meaning. But, like the blues themselves, this volume is paradoxical in its origin. It was written neither by a Negro nor an American nor by a man who had ever seen America and her teeming Black Belts.

Paul Oliver, the author of this interpretation of the blues, an interpretation that cuts across such categories as anthropology, economics, and sociology, first heard the Negro's devil songs on phonograph records when he was a child living in London. Those songs haunted that English boy. They spoke to him and he was resolved to understand them. For twenty years, as a student, a teacher, a lecturer, Paul Oliver studied the blues, collected records, pored over the literature relating to the Negro and created by the Negro, interviewed blues singers and jazz players, and has finally presented us with this interesting and challenging documentary volume.

As a Southern-born American Negro, I can testify that Paul Oliver is drenched in his subject; his frame of reference is as accurate and concrete as though he himself had been born in the environment of the blues. Can an alien, who has never visited the "milieu" from which a family of songs has sprung, write about them? In the instance of such a highly charged realm as the blues, I answer a categoric and emphatic Yes. Indeed, I see certain psychological advantages in an outsider examining these songs and their meaning: his passionate interest in these songs is proof that the songs spoke to him across racial and cultural distances; he is geographically far enough from the broiling scene of America's racial strife to seize upon that which he, conditioned by British culture, feels to be abiding in them; and, in turn, whatever he finds enduring in those songs he can, and with easy conscience, relate to that in his culture which he feels to be humanly valid. In short, to the meaning of the blues, Paul Oliver brings, in the fullest human sense, what courts of law term "corroborative evidence."

I'm aware of certain possible difficulties. The Cold War climate in which this non-political book will appear might well militate in some quarters against its being received in the same warm, impartial, and generous spirit in which the author conceived and wrote it. Much of the material, factual and authenticated, and drawn from official sources, upon which Paul Oliver floats his interpretations of the blues, no longer "officially" exists: that is, American Negro middle-class writers as well as some American Whites with psychological vested interests might not only decry the material, but may seek to cast doubt upon its validity. If such were the case, it would be tragic indeed that material relating to aesthetics should come under the racial or political hammer.

Yet the contents of the 1954 Supreme Court decision regarding the integration of black and white children in American schools ought, at least, to open our minds a bit on this subject, and Paul Oliver's book, directly and indirectly, deals with that psychological area of tension and depression consequent upon social exclusion, documenting it, illustrating it.

Recently, when commenting upon the death of Big Bill Broonzy, a well-known Negro blues singer, a powerful and popular American Negro magazine announced the "death of the blues." But can anyone or anything hand down an edict stating when the blues will or should be dead? Ought not the contraction or enlargement of the environment in which the blues were cradled be the calendar by which the death of the blues can be predicted?

The American environment which produced the blues is still with us, though we call labour to render it progressively smaller. The total elimination of that area might take longer than we now suspect, hence it is well that we examine the meaning of the blues while they are still falling upon us.

Foreword

George Padmore, *Pan-Africanism or Communism?* (London: Dobson)

Concerning George Padmore I am biased, for he is my friend. Yet, despite a personal relationship, I think that I can be objective about him. My admiration for him is evoked not only by his undeniable qualities, but by the objective position which he occupies in the minds of black people throughout the world.

George is, in my opinion, the greatest living authority on the fervent nationalist movements sweeping Black Africa today. Not only does he know those movements intimately, not only does he understand them in terms of their leaders, aims, structures, and ideologies, but George and his life *are those movements, aims and ideologies.* His activity has, for more than twenty-five years, helped to shape and mould those movements in all of their bewildering complexity. George has ranged from the Kremlin to the African bush, from that asylum for ex-slaves called Freetown (Sierra Leone) to the multi-racial societies of the West Indies, from the lonely black men lost in the white London fogs to the store front churches in the Black Belts of America. Indeed, George is the veritable ideological father of many of the nationalist movements in Black Africa, having been the mentor of scores of African nationalist leaders who now hold or will soon hold power. By his background, his training, and his experience, he possesses a wealth of knowledge which he has selflessly poured into the minds of his black brothers.

George lives in a small apartment near Mornington Crescent in London and I have often been a guest in his home. I have seen him labour day in and day out, to the exclusion of all other interests, upon the one thing that really matters to him: freedom for black people. The kitchen in that apartment is George's office and workroom and through that kitchen have trooped almost all of the present day leaders of Black Africa. They came seeking information, encouragement, and help, and George gave of his days and hours to expounding the intricacies of politics to nationalists like Wallace Johnson, Nkrumah, Kenyatta, Azikiwe, Joe Appiah, Musazi, Mayanja, and the Sudanese leaders, Abdulla Khalil, Mahgoub, Osman, etc. George is an ascetic, loving ideas more than public display, valuing scrupulously political facts and social processes.

The present volume represents the ripe wisdom of a great and tireless fighter. Mellowed, balanced, conversant with the ideologies and personalities of colonial struggles, he now feels that he can point out the road to freedom for Black Africa and indicate how that road should be travelled.

This book is uniquely valuable in that it relates, for the first time, the history of black nationalist movements from the establishment of the first Negro settlement in Sierra Leone in 1787 up to and including the period (1920–56) of the abortive attempts of the Communist International to capture those movements. (It may surprise many people to learn that Black Nationalism is far older than International Communism!) This book also contains an account of why and how black nationalists feel that Western imperialists sought to capture those movements . . . What? Negroes view both Communists and Imperialists as having an element in common?

At long, long last it may be possible to spell out something to European and American readers and to the men in the Kremlin about how black people feel . . . Black people primarily regard Russian Communists as *white* men. Black people primarily regard American, British and French anti-Communists as *white* people . . . Is that surprising? It ought not to be. If this comes as a shock to those interested in this problem, it simply means that they have never understood the Colour Problem. The black man's is a strange situation; it is a perspective, an angle of vision held by oppressed people; it is an outlook of people looking upward from below. It is what Nietzsche once called a 'frog's perspective'. Oppression oppresses, and this is the consciousness of black men who have been oppressed for centuries,—oppressed for so long that their oppression has become a tradition, in fact, a kind of culture. This elementary fact has baffled white men, Communist and non-Communist alike, for more than fifty years. The Negro's outlook is basically determined by his economic and social position, by his colour, and racial oppression. The Negro did not create the issue of colour, or race, or the condition in which he lives, but he has been moulded and influenced by them. The Negro's fundamental loyalty is, therefore, to *himself*. His situation makes this inevitable. [Am I letting awful secrets out of the bag? I'm sorry. The time has come for this problem to be stated clearly so that there is no possibility of further misunderstanding or confusion. The Negro, even when embracing Communism or Western Democracy, is not supporting ideologies; he is seeking to use *instruments* (instruments owned and controlled by men of other races!) for his own ends. He stands outside of those instruments and ideologies; he has to do so, for he is not allowed to blend with them in a natural, organic and healthy manner.]

There will be Negroes who will rush indignantly forward to decry what I have just said. The higher their position of trust in France, England or America, the more vehemently they will deny what I am saying, for they will be ashamed to !et their white neighbours or friends know how they really feel. It is most amazing that society can induce in people basic feelings which those people are ashamed to own!

In these pages George gives us a graphic exposition of the relationship of International Communism to African, West Indian and American Negro mass movements, and I can say flatly that no man living is better qualified to write that exposition than George Padmore, for, from the Comintern itself, he helped to shape much of the later phases of that relationship. But, when George discovered that, beyond doubt, Stalin and his satraps looked upon black men as political pawns of Soviet power politics, to be manoeuvred in Russian interests alone, he broke completely with the Kremlin. BUT HIS BREAKING DID NOT MEAN THAT HE THEN AUTOMATICALLY SUPPORTED THE ENEMIES OF THE SOVIET UNION. AND HIS REFUSAL TO SUPPORT THE ENEMIES OF THE SOVIET UNION WAS NOT DICTATED BY ANY LOVE FOR STALIN. NO! HE CONTINUED HIS WORK ALONE, STRIVING TO ACHIEVE THROUGH HIS OWN IN-STRUMENTALITIES THAT WHICH HE HAD WORKED FOR WHEN HE WAS IN THE COMINTERN HIERARCHY. THAT IS, FREEDOM FOR BLACK PEOPLE. I have laboured this point, for there is a great danger that any struggle conducted by Negroes will be branded as Red-inspired, and people must open their minds and understand the historic background of Negro struggle, or, truly, tragedy will engulf Africa.

That the Africans, West Indians and American Negroes have flirted with Communism is undeniably true, but just as true is the sad fact that in almost every instance the black victim discovered that he was not serving his own interests when he was caught in the Stalinist coils. Today nobody is more immune to the call of Communism than black men who found, to their bitter sorrow, that they were being used for ends that were not theirs.

This book recounts the great saga of the rise of black people from slavery to freedom on an intercontinental scale and brings us to the crucial cross-roads—a hopeful resolution for black freedom and a partnership of races purged of terror, lynching and colour lines, etc., or a continental mass struggle conducted by Africans in Africa, a struggle that will duplicate the tragic upheavals in Asia. It is not up to black men to say how this issue will be resolved; but make no mistake: the black man will cling tenaciously to his dream of freedom!

If my words carry any weight, I can commend this volume for close study to the white governmental officials of the Western world, to white churchmen, Catholic and Protestant alike, and equally to the dour and brooding white rulers in the Kremlin. I would urge them to read it and get a true, human perspective of the hopes, fears, struggles and hard-bought progress of the Negro in the modern world.

I, for one, salute and congratulate George Padmore for his having kept the faith and fought the good fight.

Original at Beinecke Rare Book and Manuscript Library, Yale University

Introduction

J. Saunders Redding, *No Day of Triumph* (New York: Harpers)

It has long been my conviction that the next quarter of a century will disclose a tremendous struggle *among* the Negro people for self-expression, self-possession, self-consciousness, individuality, new values, new loyalties, and, above all, for a new leadership. My reading of Redding's *No Day of Triumph* has confirmed and strengthened this conviction, for his book contains honesty, integrity, courage, grownup thinking and feeling, all rendered in terms of vivid prose. *No Day of Triumph* is another hallmark in the coming-of-age of the modern Negro; it is yet another signal in the turn of the tide from sloppy faith and cheap cynicism to fruitful seeking and passionate questioning.

Redding is the first middle-class Negro to break with the ideology of the "Talented Tenth" in a complete and final manner. Some may feel that he tears down more than he builds, but that is beside the point. Redding's main task is to expose, exhibit, declare, and he does this job in a dramatic and unforgettable manner, offering his own life as evidence. His narrative moves on a high, sensitive plane, and he depicts how one man, surrounded with falsehood and confusion, groped toward truth and dignity and understanding.

For a long time this book cried out to be written. I predict that it will rock the Negro middle class back on its heels; I forecast that it will set the "Talented Tenth" on fire with its anger; I prophesy that it will be as acid poured in the veins of the smug Negro teachers in Negro colleges. *No Day of Triumph* is a manifesto to the Negro and a challenge to America.

Adventure and Love in Loyalist Spain

William Rollins, Jr., *The Wall of Men* (New York: Modern Age Books, Inc.)

William Rollins' *The Wall of Men* is the first romance to be written about Loyalist Spain since Franco started his ill-fated drive on Madrid more than a year ago. Against the background of the present civil war, Rollins depicts how the typical village of Morino, in the Basque country, under the leadership of two young communists, José Aldez and Dolores Garcia, shook off the deceptions and provocations of the Catholic Church and the fascists and prepared to defend itself against Franco's Moors, Italians and Germans.

Told in a racy, dramatic style, the story opens on the Magdalene's feast day when Father Mario secretly plots with fascists to burn a church as a signal to turn public opinion against José. Father Pedro, a priest sympathetic to the people's cause overhears the plot and is slugged and thrown into a dungeon because he is considered too dangerous. Lured to the church just before the fire starts by a note to which is attached the forged signature of his fiancée, José is cast into prison amid a Reichstag fire atmosphere. Escaping with the aid of his comrades, José makes his way to the Communist lines and is wounded in action. He seeks refuge in San Sebastian, at the home of his cousin, who in turn attempts to betray him to the invaders. Trapped in his cousin's home, José shoots his cousin and assumes his cousin's identity in time to deceive the fascist military officials. He poses as an intelligence agent of the fascist high command and is given work to do in the military headquarters, where he is all but betrayed by Rafael Aznar, a young acquaintance of fascist sympathies, who knew him in Morino. Through sheer bluff, José convinces the officials that Rafael is jealous and is trying to betray him because of Dolorés. As a result José is granted freedom but is placed under surveillance.

Contacting local communists, José hears that Morino his village, is about to be attacked. His comrades arrange for him to run the gauntlet of the fascist lines and warn the people. Necessary credentials are obtained by a daring ruse; to distract the attention of a fascist guard while José is sacking a desk at headquarters, Vicente, an old loyalist deliberately places himself in a position to be killed so that the authorities are thrown off the trial long enough for José to escape during the excitement.

José returns to his village disguised as a fascist, makes certain of the expected attack, and rescues Father Pedro, who explains to the villagers who their real enemies are. The attack on the village is temporarily repulsed but that is only the beginning of a long and bitter war. Dolores is at the side of José when he declares that "We Spaniards are a wall of men standing against the attacks of all the forces of darkness!" The story closes with the appearance of the first members of the International Brigade—Americans, Englishmen, Frenchmen, Germans—and the drone of the planes of Hitler and Mussolini.

This is a new kind of revolutionary fiction, a fiction which retains the popular figures of hero and heroine, but places them against a fictional background which is serious and meaningful. All the hairbreadth escapes, love scenes, spies, wild midnight rides, dungeons, kidnappings, the villain and the beautiful girl, etc. are here; added is that element of truthfulness which makes them more than entertainment. THE WALL OF MEN may be the beginning of popular mass pulp fiction in America, a brand which can be read with pleasure by workers, without the danger of their becoming doped or misled.

New Masses, 8 March 1938, pp. 25–26

Introductory Note to The Respectful Prostitute

Jean-Paul Sartre, *La Putain Respectueuse* (London: H. Hamilton)

Jean-Paul Sartre, principal exponent of French Existentialism, has brought his keen and philosophical temperament to bear upon the problem of race relations in America, and the result, *La Putain Respectueuse,* is a calculated challenge to those who feel that America is a finished democracy. Though this drama might well seem strange and fantastic to American eyes, it deals with a reality which is all-too-familiar to the citizens of a nation living under the banner of White Supremacy.

One might wonder why Sartre, in writing a play about American race relations, omitted the traditional Negro protagonist in the foreground. But Sartre, with his insight for the truth of situations, deliberately suppressed the obvious, unnatural method of placing the moral blame of the Negro problem upon the Negro himself—as it is all too often done—and sought to reverse the manner of stating the issue. Sartre knows that the so-called Negro problem in America is not really a Negro problem at all, but a white problem, a phase of the general American problem.

The jocular, almost flippant tone of *La Putain Respectueuse* is not without its logic. The French mind—and especially French minds of the Sartre level—is rigorously logical; and when that mind examines a problem which (despite all the "scientific books" written about it!) is couched in terms of economics as well as folklore, something startling will be revealed.

In *La Putain Respectueuse*, Sartre views America's White Problem in terms of farce. It is not that Sartre wants to make light of our great racial issue, but that the intellectual position he elects to occupy automatically reveals the moral comedy of the white American character.

The dismally lowered tone of popular personality expression in America seems ludicrous to the mind of a man who, above all modern writers, is seeking and preaching the integrity of action. Hence, Sartre is unable to see tragedy in his white characters; he is unable to make a satire out of his play; he is unable to take the tirades of self-justification poured out by his characters seriously. The people with whom he had to deal simply did not lend themselves to depth interpretations of such a nature.

I witnessed the performance of *La Putain Respectueuse* in Paris last autumn, and the keynote of the reaction of the white Americans in the audience was: "That's not fair; we don't act like that . . ." But this naturally defensive reaction was not justified in fact or theory, and the quickest refutation of such an attitude can be achieved by referring to the celebrated Scottsboro Case.

While reading this play, keep in mind Victoria Price and Ruby Bates, those two pathetic symbols of white America's ambiguous morality where things racial are concerned. Feeling the human claim of nine black boys who approached them on a freight train one night, the girls surrendered themselves; and a few hours later they surrendered themselves again and with equal sincerity to a group of white boys who sought release in their bodies. A few days later they saw, with equal clearness and conviction, the claim of the southern white sheriff who told them that they had been raped by the "nigger boys."

Lacking inwardness, deep-set convictions, these two girls responded when the International Labor Defense came to defend the nine black boys who had been put on trial for their lives, charged with rape. Then these wonderful girls, when the case had become internationally famous, agreed with the governor that White Supremacy should be upheld and changed their minds. But, later, they altered their minds once more when the American Communist Party recruited them and made them realize the utter monstrousness of what they had done. From the beginning to the end, these girls were respectful of authority and humanity and power, no matter in what various guises they were presented to their incredibly naïve minds.

This is the theme of *La Putain Respectueuse*. Let us be honest. Seen from Sartre's philosophical point of view, this is farce. It took a "foreign mind" to see that the spirit of virgins could exist in the personalities of whores; that it was misplaced respect that created an injustice that agitated a nation; that we are Americans, even when we want to "do the right thing", do not always know what the right thing is and do not always know how to do the right thing when we know what it is . . .

Let us then be thankful for the eyes and mind of Jean-Paul Sartre who, in *La Putain Respectueuse*, is helping us to see ourselves, for we native born are too swamped by our own myths and folklore to see race issues objectively.

And if you are inclined to feel that Sartre is in any way inhospitable, then remember that he has said even harsher things about his own country. Finally, remember that the artist is, in the last analysis, a judge, and that it is the business of this judge to render judgments.

ART *and* ACTION. New York: Twice A Year Press, 1948, pp. 14–16

Reactions to the Script of *La Putain Respectueuse*

Jean-Paul Sartre, *La Putain Respectueuse*

In general the sequence of events move toward their end very well with an economy of movement except for the middle part. The characters are well-drawn and the overall atmosphere in the USA is very well caught. There are, of course, several minor mistakes which are natural when a Frenchman tries to depict the US scene, but these are minor. My overall reservations concern the dramatic structure of the script, especially if the script ought to begin with the fight in the train or in some other way. Beyond that my most definite reservation concerns that of the manner in which Sidney is made to go to the home of Lizzie; this simply would not happen in the United States, and, therefore, some other method of having Sidney go to Lizzie's must be devised. Another reservation is that concerning that of the "closed nature" of the script; I feel that though an attempt has been made to broaden out the action compared with the action of the stage play, it is not broad enough and when it does become broad it includes what I feel to be the wrong elements. What I mean is this: I'd not place so much emphasis upon the action of the mobs hunting Negroes, which has been done again and again in both the movies and the novel. I'd concentrate hard upon the consequences of the killing of the Negro upon the political life of the senator and upon the personal life of Sidney. My notes that follow demonstrate how I feel that this should be done. Further, I feel that such a reconstruction would follow more closely the sense and purpose of Sartre's original idea. I'd leave, except for the personal destiny of Sidney, the Negroes out of the script; and I'd make what brutality the whites do to Negroes and Sidney almost an accidental by-product. These structural changes call for alteration in the script; it means that the role of Sidney, instead of being merely a chase, ought to be shown in his relation to his family. I'd suggest giving Sidney a profession, maybe that of a rural school-teacher and a family. Hence, Sidney has to choose between running away, which makes him automatically guilty, and remaining to carry on his work and continuing the head of his family. The method of his going to Lizzie ought to be shown through whites whom Sidney knows. In this way the real tragedy of the Negro will be clearly shown. The mobs can run and rule the streets, but I'd keep them definitely in the background. The middle of the script bogs down; much too much time is given over to Fred's pursuit of Lizzie and not enough time to why he is doing it. I suggest the introduction of a public relations man for the senator; this character would pull the strings, make the analysis as to why it is absolutely necessary for Lizzie to sign the paper saying that she was violated. It is essential for the reelection of Senator Clarke. On the other hand I'd have Sidney have a white liberal friend and a Negro woman friend who would help him to get in touch with Lizzie; this white friend could be a liberal journalist who is anxious to help Sidney because it would help defeat Senator Clarke; I'd also have a conflict between the liberal journalist and his wife because his wife does not want him to meddle in something dangerous. I'd also have a row between Sidney and his family; they want him to flee and he wants to remain and carry on his work. In this way the real harm done by the murder in a wide sense can be brought out, and all of these repercussions can be built into the middle of the script.

The following are all the above suggestions given as they occur in the script. (The letters below refer to the letters which I marked in my script.)

1. A. Page 3: It is absolutely necessary to make sure that it is indicated that toilets are sexually separated and that they are marked: FOR WHITE WOMEN, FOR WHITE MEN, FOR COLORED MEN, FOR COLORED WOMEN, etc. In fact, this fact ought to be observed in the whole script, in the railroad station and other public places.

2. B. Page 4: Though I told Mr. Bost that there are times when whites by mistake do sit in the coaches reserved for Negroes in the South, I'd not at that time read the script and my remarks to him were quite out of context. Now that the script is before me I can say that it is highly unlikely that Lizzie would sit or be allowed to sit, in a voyage from New York to, say, Atlanta, in a half empty coach with Negroes, and surely not alone! This incident must be reconstructed so as to fit without question into the present day patterns of Southern race relations. I feel that the same effect could be obtained if two Negroes, Sidney and his friend, are in the act of passing and Teddy, miffed for having dropped Lizzie's suitcase, takes sharp offense at being joustled by Sidney's friend on the fastly moving train. He starts a fight. Or, Lizzie, disgusted at the drunken manner of Teddy, could ask Sidney and his friend who are passing through the coach, to pick up her suitcase. Sidney's friend could bend forward to do it and Teddy could tell him no, to leave it; Lizzie could say, no, give it to me. And then the Negro could innocently be caught between the two of them. He tries to pick up the suitcase for Lizzie and Teddy strikes him with the bat and the fight is on. Teddy's motive for hitting Sidney's friend would be that the Negro disobeyed him, a white man. Or, again, Teddy can accost Lizzie in a half empty coach and begin making passes at her, blocking the aisle while doing so. At that moment Sidney and his friend enter and cannot pass

and must stand and witness the drunken attempt of Teddy to molest Lizzie. This last, I feel, is the most natural; the two Negroes are trying to regain the coach reserved for blacks and their stumbling upon the attempt of Teddy to molest Lizzie is quite accidental. But is must be recalled that Lizzie cannot be found sitting alone in the coach reserved for Negroes. IT IS AGAINST THE LAW FOR HER TO BE THERE: SHE MIGHT ENTER MISTAKENLY AND RIDE THERE FOR A HOUR OR SO, BUT SURELY THE CONDUCTOR WOULD HAVE TOLD HER TO MOVE ALONG BEFORE THIS!

3. C: In any case, whatever incident is chosen to show the fight and killing of the Negro, it is necessary to have a few hot words bandied to and fro between the whites and Negroes. As it now stands, the conflict arrives much too suddenly.

4. D. Page 13: In evidence would be signs, FOR WHITE, FOR COLORED. And you would see two separate crowds on the station platform, one white and the other colored. In entering the station, these signs designating racial distinctions, would be in evidence. Inside of the office of the police station would be also manners and attitudes which indicate race.

5. E. Page 15: In the Deep South where this action takes place, the whites would not be seen carrying a Negro's body. In fact, at the moment the police would not allow anyone to touch the body. The body would still be under guard in the train with one or two policemen standing guard over it. This can be solved, I think, by having the coach containing the body, unhitched from the rest of the train and left standing in front of the railroad station platform.

6. F Page 16: Some other solution must be found for this whole incident. I'd suggest, as I did above, that all this action take place directly on the station platform or in the coach where the dead man is lying with a crowd about, both whites and blacks looking on and with the police yelling for them to break it up and move on.

7. G Page 18: The inspector's first question would be natural, "What was this nigger doing?" This attitude would set and color the whole tone of the subsequent questioning. It would be assumed that the white man was right and that the Negro was wrong. The start of the drama is right here; there must be an attempt to clear the white man, and when they see that they must hold him, then the police, I feel, in the South, would act in concert with Fred and his father. The charge of attempted rape must be brought up at once, or the motive for the killing is not clear.

8. H. Page 19: I'm positive that Willy would not tell the truth here; he would attempt at once to defend his friend, a white man, against a Negro. This would fit into the mentality of the white South. FROM THE BEGIN-NING THE CHARGE OF RAPE MUST ENTER AND FIGURE BIGLY, OR THERE IS NO CAUSE FOR FURTHER ACTION HERE. If the charge of rape is leveled, then Sidney can be let go; but if there is any vagueness here, then Sidney himself will be held.

9. H. Page 20: Here again, when the police talk to Fred, I'd make clear that the police, even though they are holding Teddy, expect to get Teddy clear. The policeman would tell Fred to get in touch with his father at once for the charge is grave, Teddy is drunk and is babbling, etc. Here, as elsewhere, I'd have an atmosphere of complicity between the police and Fred.

10. I. Page 21. The treatment of Sidney would differ here, I feel. He would not be treated roughly, but surely no one would ask him to sit down! In fact, I'd suggest that he be questioned alone with the police; the whites would only enter the room to identify him and then the police would question him alone. He would not be spoken to in a familiar way. It may be, of course, that they do not want Sidney now, feeling that he might be an adverse witness.

11. K. Page 25: Sidney would be standing—It is here that I make my suggestion for a major change. I do not "get" Sidney in this role. Why just a poor truck driver? I'd suggest making him a poor school teacher who is on his way from an educational conference. He has a family; he has charge of an elementary school. This at once places him in a position which can evoke empathy for him and it also slowly introduces the right to show later on people who are on his side and who help him to get in touch with Lizzie. I'm suggesting this to lift the whole plane of action to a new level. So far, with but minor reservations, the action has gone on fairly well, but it is here that a basis for new action should be laid. Furthermore, if the police felt at that moment that Sidney was a known truck driver, but sometime schoolteacher, with a reputation for respectability, they would be more inclined to accept his word that he saw nothing. It is only later that they will discover their mistake and want to find him. I'd identify the Negro who was killed as a truck driver.

12. L. Pages 27 to 41: It is here that the line of action bogs down hopelessly. It is here that basic reconstruction must take place. It is not interesting that Fred follows Lizzie in this manner. Fred ought to be at the home of his father talking to his father's right hand man, telling him that Teddy has killed a "nigger" and that the opposition might get hold of it and make trouble in the coming elections. The new character ought to represent a phase of the young, educated South, a man versed in public relations, with no deep-seated race hate but simply following the line of tradition. This new character, let's call him Greenwell, at once takes charge of this new situation; his aim is to clear Teddy, of course; but he is baffled as to how to act. Teddy has committed a clear case of murder and to get him out is not easy. Greenwell feels that this is a matter which must at once be brought to the attention of the Senator who is secluded in his office. Fred accompanies Greenwell and the two of them see the Senator who is busy with many affairs. He finally hears the story and explodes and demands why something drastic has not been done. He upbraids Greenwell as a whippersnapper, not a son of the old South. He says that when he was a young man and was faced with issues like that he knew at once what to do. He claims that the racial instincts of Greenwell are weak and that

though Greenwell is educated he is lost when he comes to defending the white South. The girl was raped, of course she was, he says. He phones the police and finds that Sidney has been released and he demands that he be picked up to face the charge of rape. What in hell is wrong with you guys? he demands, to let a nigger guilty as hell go free on his own word. He is told that the girl says that no one molested her and the senator storms and says that the damn girl does not know what has happened to her, and they must move heaven and earth to get that girl to sign a complaint against Sidney. The senator claims that both Sidney and the other Negro were certainly in on it. Chastened, Greenwell agrees. Sweating, he and Fred retire to discuss how to get Lizzie to sign a statement to the effect that both Negroes attempted rape upon her. This is the method the senator wants to use to get Teddy free. Fred and Greenwell get into a car and shoot to the "Blue Bell" and enter. Lizzie is pointed out to them. They are struck dumb by her beauty and youth. (I'd not have Fred see Lizzie at the station and his surprise at seeing her in the nightclub will be all the stronger!) Greenwell says, "Well, there's your work, son." Fred is a little ashamed, doubtful; he says, "But can I get her to sign?" Greenwell says, "Make love to her if necessary, but get her moniker on that paper. Don't leave unless you have it. Life and death depends upon it." Fred approaches Lizzie at once and starts in. No long delay is necessary, for Lizzie is there to meet and talk to men. Fred flashes money and that is enough to make Lizzie notice him. But she is more struck by his clothes and manner than his money. This last trait ought to be made empathic, for this is the beginning of her spiritual prostitution.

13. M. Pages 27 to 51: Meanwhile Sidney runs to his friend Rex, who owns a small laundry and a truck; Rex has gone to bed; Sidney awakens him and breathlessly tells his story, adjuring him not to let his wife know of his whereabouts. Rex urges Sidney to flee; Sidney protests, saying that his work, his family, and even himself will be lost if he flees. Sidney has a white friend, a fellow school teacher whom he has known since childhood and who has told him that if he ever is in trouble he would help him. But Rex trusts no white persons and says, "Run, man, while you got the time!" Sidney persuades Rex to put him in the back of the laundry truck and the two of them go to Ashley's house and pull into the driveway. Rex rouses the Ashleys and tells them what has happened. Mrs. Ashley is against doing anything. Ashley, however goes out to the truck and listens to Sidney's story; Mrs. Ashley hovers listening in the background. Ashley says that the point of the story is to get Lizzie to sign a paper saying that she was not raped. Mrs. Ashley is afraid of trouble. "Leave it alone," she says. But Ashley feels a duty and responsibility and he asks: "What harm is there in trying to get the girl to sign a paper saying what she told the police? It'll free Sidney . . ." Sidney feels that Mrs. Ashley is scared and he gives Ashley a way out by saying, "You don't have to do it, Mr. Ashley. "You don't have to help me 'less you want to." "But you told me to come to

you if I ever got into trouble, so here I am," he begs. Ashley says he'll try. He and his wife go into the house; his wife takes his arms and leads him to the bedroom of their two sleeping children and with tears she says, "Be careful for their sake, Jim." Ashley promises he will, puts on his hat and coat and takes Sidney into his car and they head for the "Blue Bell." He asks the doormen where Lizzie lives, gives him $5, and heads for the address and waits for Lizzie to show up. Meanwhile Fred has won the attention of Lizzie who is dazzled by him. Lizzie agrees to admit him to her apartment at midnight. Fred reports to Greenwell that he will see Lizzie later and get the paper signed. Greenwell suspects that he likes the girl and warns him not to let anything stand in the way of his getting the paper signed. Fred swears that he will be successful. Ashley sees Lizzie enter her apartment building and he and Sidney creep forward to the door. Ashley knocks and Lizzie opens and is startled by his strange face. Sidney waits in the shadows behind Ashley and Ashley asks to speak to Lizzie who thinks he is a cop. Ashley explains the case and says that Lizzie ought to sign and clear Sidney. Lizzie says she does not give a damn, she wants none of it. She readily admits that she was not raped, but that it is not her business to meddle further. Ashley calls Sidney into the room and Sidney falls on his knees and begs for his life, saying that if she does not sign the paper, he is a dead man; Lizzie says run away. Ashley asks why must he run and leave his family and his work? If he runs away, Ashley says, it means that Sidney admits a guilt that is not his. If Sidney stays, they surely will frame something on him to free Teddy. Ashley reminds her that he is only asking her to sign a paper saying what she told the police. He produces the paper and she signs. Sidney leaves with Ashley, both relieved and happy. They head for the police station. As their car disappears, Fred arrives in his car. He rushes into the apartment of Lizzie and embraces her. He finds her trembling and frightened. She says that she is glad he has come, that she is alone and a stranger. He tells her that she need not be afraid for he is there. She tells him that she has something to tell him, but Fred kisses her and says it can wait. He goes to bed with her, rushing her off her feet. Meanwhile Ashley arrives at the police station, leaves Sidney hiding in the rear of his car, enters and shows the signed paper to the chief of police. They take the paper from Ashley, tear it up, slap him and tell him to go home and go to bed and not meddle. Ashley is supremely humiliated, goes back beaten to his car and drives off. Sidney smiles in the back. The car stops. Sidney lifts his head and sees Ashley weeping. He wants to know what happened. And Ashley tells him. "You are on your own now, Sid," Ashley says. "I've done all I can. It's you and God now." Shattered, Sidney is left standing on the street in the night. He hears the rousing voice of a mob in the distance. He runs, hugging close the houses and shadows. We do not know where he is going . . .

14. L. Page 55:59: I'd open again with Fred and Lizzie. Fred, after sleeping with Lizzie as in the script, now tries to wheedle her toward signing the paper

he has brought from Greenwell. Lizzie is furious as she guesses his game. She now dares not tell him what she wanted to tell him that evening, but she is scared. I'd keep the line of action as it stands more or less in the script until we are in the home of the Senator. Here, for the first time, Lizzie realizes what the whole game has been. Overcome by the words of the Senator, she signs as in the script, but also tells them that she has already signed for Ashley. They are stunned, and refuse to give her money, toss her out. From here on, the script seems to follow the line of action very well and the resolution is good.

Unpublished remarks made by Wright to Sartre concerning the (un)likelihood of certain "American" details.
Original at Beinecke Rare Book and Manuscript Library, Yale University

Foreword

Morris U. Schappes, *Letters from the Tombs* (New York: Schappes Defense Committee)

The spirit of the letters in this little book is as old as Western civilization. Indeed, these letters were written under the conditions that gave birth to the most noble thought and sentiment we possess, the most selfless utterances in our culture.

In reading them you cannot but ask yourself: "How on earth can such as this happen over and over again? What kind of bacillus is it that infects the blood of the keepers of the law that makes them immune to understanding?"

When the same unjust event occurs time and again throughout history, you get the eerie feeling that history is a nightmare and that the men who hold the reins of authority are under some malevolent spell that compels them to act as they do. Pontius Pilate was the first judge to render an unjust decision with an uneasy conscience, and it has been happening ever since. . . .

I do not know law, but I do not feel that knowledge of law is important in forming a judgment about the Case of Morris U. Schappes. All one's mind must do in forming a judgment about the charges against Morris U. Schappes is to remember the countless thousands of men and women who have been imprisoned over the centuries because of their beliefs and at once one recalls that those beliefs were never killed in that way, that no Society ever saved itself in such a manner, that no State ever survived by the use of such methods, that no Government ever made itself strong through such practices.

Such were my feelings when reading the letters written by Morris U. Schappes to his wife and friends from the Tombs. Change the contemporary frame of reference, and the letters could have been written by Sacco and Vanzetti, Debs, and so on. . . .

When will the class that rules learn that it cannot kill the generous motives of the human heart through legal indictments? When will a judge learn that he cannot impose a court sentence upon the impulses that move a man towards what he feels to be right and just? When will jailors learn that thoughts cannot be locked in a prison cell?

Many of our officials in America today believe that they are protecting their civilization when they imprison a man for thinking in "a certain way"; but they are not protecting their civilization. Instead, they are destroying its very foundations.

Read these letters with an honest heart and your heart will tell you that the society that seeks to imprison Morris U. Schappes is wrong. If sending a man to jail for his beliefs is not wrong, then nothing is wrong.

Wasteland Uses Psychoanalysis Deftly

Jo Sinclair, *Wasteland* (New York: Harper and Bros.)

Out of the flood of books tumbling from our heaving presses, we can count ourselves lucky if, now and then, there falls a novel that surprises us with its insight and courage. Such books are rare at any time, and especially so in our anxiety-ridden, postwar-America, where the novel that *pays* is often more entertaining than emotionally moving, more grimly optimistic than revealing, more cheaply moral than truthful.

Jo Sinclair's prize-winning novel, *Wasteland* (don't doubt for the moment the quality of this book just because it won Harper's $10,000 prize for 1946. Times are changing!), lifts itself easily above the current pious hopes and delusions that claim so much of our fiction. Miss Sinclair is skeptical toward the family and toward morality: she suspects that they are not what they pretend to be. In spite of conventions—and there are no more fiercely-held conventions than those held by orthodox Jews—she seems to have said to herself: "I will not accept the ready-made explanations for the reality I see. Something is wrong with immigrant-Jewish family life, and I want to know what it is."

And since Miss Sinclair has a passion for truth, *Wasteland* is full of the excitement of discovery, and what it reveals about the Jewish family challenges our assumptions and compels us to accept a reality which we have been all too prone to reject or misinterpret.

But this is not "a novel with a story," for, in her refusal to be bound by the traditional lumber of novel-building, Miss Sinclair has demonstrated her independence as an artist. In general, *Wasteland* is akin, in form and approach, though not in obscurity, to Stein's *The Making of Americans*, Proust's *Remembrance of Things Past* and Joyce's *Finnegan's Wake*, insofar as it is concerned with being and consciousness rather than with action and plot.

The mechanics of the book are simple and direct. Jake, a neurotic photographer on a metropolitan newspaper, has reached a point of despair that interferes with his ability to function, and for some time, he has been using alcohol as a crutch for his crippled emotions. When his Lesbian sister, Debby, whom he both loves and hates, urges him to go to her analyst, he finds that he cannot talk to the analyst unless he is half drunk. He is determined, however, to end his suffering by laying bare his life before the analyst and, consequently, as he gropes, stammers, weeps and sweats out his confessions, the story of his entire family is overheard by the reader. As Jake conquers shame and forgetfulness, and as his anxieties are drained off, he grows less dependent upon alcohol. Slowly the reader comes to know why Jake is so devoid of love, why he hates his family, why he denies his Jewishness and why he is ashamed of his Lesbian sister.

The inner movement in *Wasteland* is a tremendous effort to understand something which is considered alien and objectionable. The landscape of Jewish family life thus revealed is not beautiful, and doubtless some Jews will rise and declare that *Wasteland* is not true. But Miss Sinclair's nervous prose carries the kind of conviction that will confound carping critics, for it contains a quality of reality that simply could not have been imagined or contrived. It is too circumstantial, too filled with the stamp of things seen and heard, to be sincerely doubted.

Out of the dialogue between Jake and his analyst there rises before us a gallery of mean, closemouthed, hateful, stingy and hysterical people. But before you have read a third of the book, you have learned so much about them that they no longer repel, and your sympathy and pity are engaged, instead. We learn why these people act as they do, not as Jews but as people.

Miss Sinclair's use of psychoanalysis is done with great deftness. Many writers are led astray by thinking that they can use the seemingly easy device of the psychoanalyst in novelistic structure. Most of those who fail do so because they naively take the device as they find it and apply it to the novel, plowing up the unconscious as they write. And I confess that I was filled with foreboding when I read this opening paragraph in *Wasteland*:

"Even in the secrecy of his mind Jake called him 'the doctor.' He hated the word *psychiatrist*. He hated it even if Debby did say it was a beautiful word."

But I had not read far before I knew that the psychoanalytic device was being handled with discernment, that, in Miss Sinclair's skilled hands, it was no longer a psychoanalytic device but a literary technique applied with slow and burning power, saying what she wanted it to say, revealing character and destiny at each step of the narrative and thereby vindicating her appropriation of it.

Wasteland depends, for much of its effect, upon subtle repetitions. The psychoanalytic technique aids the author as she returns, time and again, to a description of the Seder, the Jewish Passover ceremony, and to Jake's agonizing relationship to it and his final acceptance of Jewish historical traditions as a guide to living. But each time we see Jake participating in the Seder, we see a different situation, one which reflects a slightly changed attitude in Jake. Miss Sinclair's adroit use of psychoanalysis blends with a sound literary principle: Repetition that never quite repeats.

I am anxious about the reception of so nakedly honest a novel, for it can be said that if *Wasteland* fails to win an appreciative audience, that will indicate a failure in our reading public rather than the failure of the novel itself. If Miss Sinclair can build upon the talent revealed in *Wasteland*, she will go far.

PM Magazine, 17 February 1946, p. m8

Gertrude Stein's Story Is Drenched in Hitler's Horrors

Gertrude Stein, *Wars I Have Seen* (New York: Random House)

Gertrude Stein has laid the 19th century by its heels. For years she has been chasing that proud, stubborn century, mocking it, lying in ambush for it, trying to kill it. Well, at last she has done it. And now she trumpets forth that hope, idealism, aspiration, the sense of the future, high-blown metaphysics and all the big, vague, emotional words of our time have gone down the drain of World War II.

But, you might ask, why do I, a Negro, read the allegedly unreadable books of Gertrude Stein? It's all very simple, innocent even. Years ago, I stumbled upon her books without the guidance of those critics who hint darkly of "the shock of recognition."

Prompted by random curiosity while I was browsing one day in a Chicago public library, I took from the open shelves a tiny volume called *Three Lives* and looked at a story in it, entitled *Melanctha*. The style was so insistent and original and sang so quaintly that I took the book home.

As I read it, my ears were opened for the first time to the magic of the spoken word. I began to hear the speech of my grandmother, who spoke a deep, pure Negro dialect and with whom I had lived for many years.

All of my life I had been only half hearing, but Miss Stein's struggling words made the speech of the people around me vivid. From that moment on, in my attempts at writing, I was able to tap at will the vast pool of living words that swirled around me.

But, in the midst of my delight, I was jolted. A left-wing literary critic, whose judgment I had been led to respect, condemned Miss Stein in a sharply-worded newspaper article, implying that she spent her days reclining upon a silken couch in Paris smoking hashish, that she was a hopeless prey to hallu-cinations and that her tortured verbalisms were throttling the Revolution. I was disturbed. Had I duped myself into worshiping decadence?

Believing in direct action, I contrived a method to gauge the degree to which Miss Stein's prose was tainted with the spirit of counter-revolution. I gathered a group of semi-literate Negro stockyard workers—"basic proletarians with the instinct for revolution" (am I quoting right?)—into a Black Belt basement and read *Melanctha* aloud to them. They understood every word. Enthralled, they slapped their thighs, howled, laughed, stomped and interrupted me con-stantly to comment upon the characters.

My fondness for Steinian prose never distressed me after that.

Her latest book, *Wars I Have Seen,* begins in the usual Steinian manner of evoking her on-the-spot consciousness in repetitive rhythms about life and memory and books, about the 19th century as opposed to the 20th. But soon the war intrudes, and her narrative becomes drenched in the horror of Hitler's brutality in France.

With the exception of Jack Belden's *Still Time to Die,* I know of no current war book that conveys a more awful sense of the power of war to kill the soul, of the fear, the rumor, the panic and the uncertainty of war.

Indeed, Miss Stein possesses a great, perhaps even unfair, advantage over other writers about the war, for she exultingly admits that she loves confu-sion, that she finds no real difference between peace and war and life in gen-eral. Boasting cynically, she says: "I do not like to fish in troubled waters but I do like to see the troubled water and the fish and the fishermen . . ."

The long wait for Eisenhower's landing in Normandy is dug up out of the unconscious of the French people and given voice (try reading this and the following quotations with your ear or punctuate with your eyes or read Miss Stein's *Narration* or practice by reading the Old Testament or Hemingway): "To be sure when there is a war the years are longer that is to say the days are longer the months are longer the years are much longer but the weeks are shorter that is what makes a war."

The constant sense of impending death is rendered thus: "the air at night, when the moon is bright is full of them going over to Italy to do their bombing and the mountain makes a reverberation as a woman said to me like being inside a copper cooking utensil well when you keep on thinking how quickly anybody can get killed, just as quickly as just very quickly, more quickly even than in a book . . ."

She explains why statesmen blunder into wars: "they are still believing what they are supposed to believe nobody else believes it, not even all their families believe it but believe it or not, they still do believe it, believe what they are supposed to believe. And so naturally they believing what they are supposed to believe make it possible for the country to think they can win a war . . ."

Miss Stein is much clearer about peace terms than are many of our Senators. She says: "if the winner wins, then the vanquished should give in, and why ask for terms beforehand, if the winner is going to be generous he is going to be generous and if he is not going to be generous he is not going to be generous. . . . Unconditional Surrender and then let them be generous or not."

Miss Stein, whose defiant prose was forged out of her fight against the foggy logic of the 19th century, declares: "In the 19th century, there is the feeling that one is justified in being angry, in being right, in being justified. In the 20th century it is not that it is right but that what happens truly happens." And: "I suppose that is the reason that I so naturally had my part in killing the 19th century and killing it dead, quite like a gangster with . . . a tommy gun."

Her view of civilization is bleak: "Really and truly this time nobody in their hearts really believes that everybody that anybody will be peaceful and happy, not anybody, not even the immense majority believe any such thing . . ."

Commenting upon the complexity of French politics, she describes a doctor who was "anti-Russian he was anti-Anglo-American he was anti-German, he was anti-De Gaulle he was anti-Vichy he was anti-Petain he was anti-Maquis he was anti-persecutions he was anti-collabo, he was anti-bombardments he was anti-militia he was anti-monarchy he was anti-communist he was anti-everything."

Other Steinian propositions are: Only a foreigner like Hitler could be so bent upon destroying Germany. When a German is not winning, he runs like a rabbit. The Maquis were "not too favorably regarded by their own countrymen, it was a kind of Valley Forge with no George Washington." And if you beat the white of an egg in a cup of water, and drink it, diarrhea will stop.

Her description of how she welcomed the American troops sounds like a steal from Father Divine (who is definitely 19th century): "wonderful that is all I can say about it wonderful, and I said you are going to sleep in the beds where German officers slept six weeks ago wonderful my gracious perfectly wonderful."

Wouldn't it be strange if, in 1988, our colleges made the reading of *Wars I Have Seen* mandatory, so that our grandchildren might learn how men felt about war in our time? Wouldn't it be simply strange if Miss Stein's grammarless prose was destined for such a strange destiny? Would it not be strange if anything strange like that did happen?

PM Magazine, 26 July, 1946, pp. m15

Between Laughter and Tears

Waters Edward Turpin, *These Low Grounds* (New York: Harper and Bros.)
Zora Neale Hurston, *Their Eyes Were Watching God* (Philadelphia: J. B. Lippincott Co.)

It is difficult to evaluate Waters Turpin's *These Low Grounds* and Zora Neale Hurston's *Their Eyes Were Watching God*. This is not because there is an esoteric meaning hidden or implied in either of the two novels; but rather because neither of the two novels has a basic idea or theme that lends itself to significant interpretation. Miss Hurston seems to have no desire whatever to move in the direction of serious fiction. With Mr. Turpin the case is different; the desire and motive are present, but his "saga" of four generations of Negro life seems to have been swamped by the subject matter.

These Low Grounds represents, I believe, the first attempt of a Negro writer to encompass in fiction the rise of the Negro from slavery to the present. The greater part of the novel is laid on the eastern shore of Maryland where Carrie, upon the death of her slave mother, is left to grow up in a whore-house. After several fitful efforts to escape her lot, Carrie finally marries a visiting farmer, Prince, with whom she leads a life of house-hold drudgery. Having helped Prince become the leading Negro farmer in the county, Carrie rebels against his infidelities and domination and, taking her two young daughters, runs away. Years later Prince discovers her and persuades her to return home. As she is about to make the journey, she is murdered by Grundy, her drunken and jealous lover. The two daughters return to the farm; Blanche remains with her father, but Martha flees North to escape the shame of pregnancy when her lover is killed in an accident. Martha's subsequent career on the stage enables her to send her son, Jimmy-Lew, to college to become a teacher. The novel closes with a disillusioned Jimmy-Lew comforted by his wife because of his bitterness of the harsh and unfair conditions of southern life.

The first half of the book is interesting, for Turpin deals with a subject which he knows intimately. Those sections depicting post-war Negro life in the North do not ring true or full; in fact, toward the conclusion the book grows embarrassingly sketchy, resolving nothing.

Oddly enough, Turpin seems to have viewed those parts of his novel which deal with the modern Negro through the eyes and consciousness of one emotionally alien to the scene. Many of the characters—Carrie, Prince, Martha, are splendid social types; but rarely do they become human beings. It seems that Turpin drew these types from intellectual conviction, but lacked the artistic strength to make us feel the living quality of their experiences. It seems to me, he should strive to avoid the bane of sheer competency. He deals with great characters and a great subject matter; what is lacking is a great theme and a great passion.

Their Eyes Were Watching God is the story of Zora Neale Hurston's Janie who, at sixteen, married a grubbing farmer at the anxious instigation of her slave-born grand-mother. The romantic Janie, in the highly-charged language of Miss Hurston, longed to be a pear tree in blossom and have a "dust-bearing bee sink into the sanctum of a bloom; the thousand sister-calyxes arch to meet the love embrace." Restless, she fled from her farmer husband and married Jody, an up-and-coming Negro business man who, in the end, proved to be no better than her first husband. After twenty years of clerking for her self-made Jody, Janie found herself a frustrated widow of forty with a small fortune on her hands. Tea Cake, "from in and through Georgia," drifted along and, despite his youth, Janie took him. For more than two years they lived happily; but Tea Cake was bitten by a mad dog and was infected with rabies. One night in a canine rage Tea Cake tried to murder Janie, thereby forcing her to shoot the only man she had ever loved.

Miss Hurston can write; but her prose is cloaked in that facile sensuality that has dogged Negro expression since the days of Phillis Wheatley. Her dialogue manages to catch the psychological movements of the Negro folk-mind in their pure simplicity, but that's as far as it goes.

Miss Hurston *voluntarily* continues in her novel the tradition which was *forced* upon the Negro in the theater, that is, the minstrel technique that makes the "white folks" laugh. Her characters eat and laugh and cry and work and kill; they swing like a pendulum eternally in that safe and narrow orbit in which America likes to see the Negro live: between laughter and tears.

Turpin's faults as a writer are those of an honest man trying desperately to say something; but Zora Neale Hurston lacks even that excuse. The sensory sweep of her novel carries no theme, no message, no thought. In the main, her novel is not addressed to the Negro, but to a white audience whose chauvinistic tastes she knows how to satisfy. She exploits that phase of Negro life which is "quaint," the phase which evokes a piteous smile on the lips of the "superior" race.

New Masses, vol. 25, 5 October 1937, pp. 22, 25

Blurb

Fritz von Unruh, *The End Is Not Yet* (New York: Storm Publishers)

Scorning the vast authoritative constellations of ideology of both Left and Right, and trusting his heart—as all artists should do and as all real artists have always done—for the truth of reality, Fritz von Unruh, in his novel, *The End Is Not Yet,* has thrown up a titanic imaginative drama of life in our times.

The End Is Not Yet is the only novel that I have read since the war that adequately depicts the Gothic madness of Naziism, that reveals the full frenzy of its brutality, the inhumanity and irresponsibility of its leaders, and the great problem which Naziism posed and still poses for all mankind.

The End Is Not Yet contains scenes which I shall never forget: the love scene amidst the gargoyles of Notre Dame; the scene of the girl placed in a cage with a gorilla; of Hitler's capture on the outskirts of Paris; of Hitler's insane attempt to raise a girl from the dead; the underground chamber of death; and the cameos of perversion, sadism, masochism, which read like the pages from a journal of psychoanalysis.

The End Is Not Yet is truly an eruption from the human heart, and, like all such outpourings, it is as ambiguous as life itself. Mysticism and realism, lyricism and drama, sentimentality and cynicism mingle and surge in its pages as in daily life. In the end, the reader's mind is drenched in a sense of reality that is as fantastic as it is overwhelmingly incredible. Not many civilized people will miss reading Unruh's novel. I don't say that they will like it, but I do say that they will be moved, awed, and frightened by it, as well they might be.

A Junker's Epic Novel on Militarism

Fritz von Unruh, *The End Is Not Yet*

It is fitting that the first impressive artistic accounting of the horrors of German-Prussian-Nazi militarism should come from the pen of a refugee who spent seven and a half years of his youth in a school for Prussian princes. It has been claimed that Germans cannot change, cannot assimilate democratic ideals. Well, Fritz von Unruh changed long before Hitler came upon the scene.

A dissenting voice from the Junker class is long overdue, but the reader can be assured that his wait has not been in vain, for *The End Is Not Yet* is a novel in the grand manner, embracing history, politics, love, war, psychology and religion and boasting a cast of characters that stretches from Hitler to Communists, from atheists to rabbis, from terrorists to prostitutes.

This novel is a fantasy, a political nightmare, and in it von Unruh employs every technical device which the novel form has to offer to communicate his vision of reality. The end-product is something compelling and arresting beyond the ordinary.

Superficially, this book is a fantastic representation of the struggle of Hitler, Hess, Ribbentrop and so on as they collide with the monarchists, Communists, terrorists and workers who have sworn to exterminate them. Intrinsically, it is a dramatic and poetic confrontation, in terms of the wildest fantasy, of the forces of fascism with the traditional hopes of men seeking world brotherhood.

There are scenes that you will never forget: the underground chamber of death, the love scene under the gargoyles of Notre Dame, the placing of the Jewish girl in a cage with a sexually stimulated ape, Hitler's insane attempt to raise a girl from the dead and Hitler facing his would-be murderer and overpowering him with words. And there are cameos of sadism and masochism which read like records from a psychoanalyst's case book.

Had this novel appeared a bare two years ago, there would have been an out-cry against it from the center, the left of center and the left, for there existed then a cocksure certainty about the future. But now, for good or ill, that mood is gone, washed away in the resurgence of world reaction and the fight-Russia-now wave. The rebirth of nationalism and the flourishing of tinhorn dictators inevitably have laid easy optimists by the heels.

Von Unruh's nonpolitical wisdom—a wisdom drawn from the heart as artists have always drawn it—makes the yearnings of a Browder no less than those of a Roosevelt seem quaint in a world where Negroes are under daily attack, where the agony of the Jews shames decent men, where trade unionists are being hounded and where the area of freedom shrinks hourly.

Among those who saw into the causes of fascism was Fritz von Unruh, who, even while he was serving in the Imperial Guard, the regiment of German noblemen, had unleashed his pen in a play, *Officers,* against the spirit of dictatorship and war. And more, he chose voluntary exile from his native land before World War I, at a time when the German Empire was at the peak of its power. A man with such a record of intransigence should be listened to when he speaks of war and of peace.

Von Unruh is rash enough to shout what few dare whisper. Fascism, he reminds us, is as strong and as brutal as we indulgently allow it to be. Hitler's strength was partly derived from our identification with many of his aims. Our inability, in the beginning, to resist courageously was partly due to our sharing of his hatred of minorities. In fighting fascism, we are still largely fighting the political projections of our own wishes and desires. Such a thesis is calculated to outrage many Americans who want to have their race hatred and eat it too.

The scope of the novel can be seen from an inadequate statement of its line of action. Kasper Uhle, an ex-Junker soldier and writer living in exile in Paris, is the friend of a Polish dancer, Olenka, who has been daring enough to steal Hitler's last will and testament from Berchtesgaden and smuggle it into Paris. This will, containing scorn for the hope of common men and disfranchisement for the decadent nobility, is naturally the object of frenzied search by every intelligence agent.

In attempting to protect Olenka, Uhle is implicated in a murder, and the Junkers try to blackmail him into killing Hitler when he visits Paris. But Uhle, haunted by the idea of world brotherhood, is seeking a way to cut across the greed, plots, intrigues and rules of society so that he may live free, from the heart, spontaneously. To save his life, Uhle consents to kill Hitler—not for the German nobility, but for himself, for mankind, to rid the world of its greatest murderer.

At the last, however, when he has Hitler unarmed and cornered against a wall, with his gun pointed at Hitler's heart, he finds that he cannot kill him: he feels that he would be but contributing to Hitler's technique of hate and murder. Hitler is rescued by the French police, who spirit him out of France to escape the wrath of the workers.

Uhle, a 20th-century Everyman, obsessed by the image of the pale-faced, bearded soldiers of the trenches—soldiers who remind him of Christ because of the barbed wire wrapped around their helmets—resolves to find another way to help men attain their dream of life and liberty.

Such a summary cheapens *The End Is Not Yet* as much as any summary of similar length would vulgarize *Crime and Punishment*. Von Unruh's theme is much bigger than those which engage our clever, native-born novelists, and he has had to create devices of fantasy to show the disease of fascism as a part of our personalities, as the daytime projection of our fears and hopes.

The result is the biggest novel yet to come out of devastated Europe. Von Unruh's comprehension of the involved and recondite nature of the problem of fascism lifts him, at one stroke, out of the class of fictioneers and onto that plane of writers who, through the prophetic power of their vision, legislate new values for mankind. In the realm of the psycho-political, *The End Is Not Yet* is without a peer in that field of contemporary literature which deals with fascism.

The author does not pretend that the real actions of a Hitler or a Hess were as he depicts them. He takes these gangsters as symbols of the philosophy of hate, and the astounding thing is that he has such a vast array of hate-models to choose from. Our age offers more—and more vivid—examples of destruction than of creation.

One way of describing this book is to say that it is a marvelous nightmare which has the power to shed light upon our waking hours. It depends, for its continuity, not upon the logic of two *plus* two *equals* four, but upon the blooming of opposite images, upon the linking of widely disparate symbols and events, upon the associational magic of passion.

The title reveals the sharp urgency of von Unruh's feeling of our dilemma. Christ used the phrase to indicate that the Kingdom of God had not yet entered history and brought an end to time, and it is with a similar sense of anxiety that von Unruh seeks to enlist the interest of his readers in the contemporary conflict between hope and reaction.

You must read this book because your destiny is being debated in it.

PM Magazine, 4 May 1947, p. m3

A P P E N D I X   B

Bibliography on the Negro in Illinois

While employed by the Chicago WPA, Richard Wright did some original research on the Negro in Illinois, wrote a short piece called "Some Ethnograph-
ical Aspects of Chicago's Black Belt" and compiled a selected bibliography
which the head librarian of the George Cleveland Hall Branch Library found
so useful that she copied it for William E. B. DuBois when he visited the city
in the late 1930s. This bibliography is reprinted here, as it first appeared in
New Letters, vol. 39, no. 11, 1972, with the permission of the Chicago Public
Library.

Bibliography on the Negro in Chicago, 1936

Select Bibliography

Documents

Chicago, Board of Election Commissioners of the City of Chicago, Records
(unpublished).
———, *Council Proceedings.*
———, Police Department, Records (unpublished).
Chicago Crime Commissioners, *Official Record of Proceedings, 1890–1900,*
1903–10, 1929–34.
Democratic National Convention, *Official Report of the Proceedings,* 1920,
1924, 1928, 1932.
Illinois, *Illinois Blue Book,* 1877–1933.
———, *Journal of the House of Representatives.*
———, Laws of Illinois.
Republican Campaign Textbook, 1900, 1920, 1924, 1928, 1932.
United States Bureau of the Census, *Fifteenth Census: Occupation: Statistics:
1930.*
———, *Negroes in the United States.* Washington, Government Printing Of-
fice, 1915.
———, *Negro Population, 1790–1915,* Washington, Government Printing
Office, 1918.

————, *Religious Bodies: 1926.*
————, *Thirteenth Census, 1910: Population.*
United States Bureau of Education Statistics, *Statistics of Education of the Negro Race, 1925–26.* Washington, Government Printing Office, 1928.
United States Congress, *Congressional Record,* 56th, 71st, 72nd, 73rd Congresses.
United States Congress, Senate, *Hearings before a Special Committee Investigating Campaign Expenditures in Senatorial Primary and General Elections, 1926,* 69th Congress, 1st Session, Part II, (Reed Committee).
————, *Positions Not Under the Civil Service,* Document No. 173, 72nd Congress, 2nd Session.
————, *Select Committee on Senatorial Campaign Expenditures,* 71st Congress, 2nd Session, Part 2, Illinois (Nye Committee).
United States Congress, *Senate Subcommittee of the Committee on Post Offices and Post Roads,* 70th Congress, 2nd Session Influencing Appointments to Postmasterships, Hearings. Washington: Government Printing Office, 1929.
United States Department of Labor, *Negro Migration in 1916–1917.* Washington, Government Printing Office, 1919.
United States Women's Bureau, *Negro Women in Industry.* Washington, Government Printing Office, 1922.

Newspapers

Illinois, *Broad Ax,* 1897–1927.
Chicago Bee, 1930–34.
Chicago Daily News, 1905–1934.
Chicago Daily Times, 1929–1934.
Chicago Defender, 1914–1934.
Chicago Evening American, 1922–1934.
Chicago Herald and Examiner, 1920–1934.
Maryland, *Afro-American,* 1929, 1932.
New York, *Amsterdam News,* 1932.
Daily Worker, 1924–1934.
New York Age, 1929–1932.
Ohio, *Cincinnati Union,* 1931–1932.
Oklahoma, *Oklahoma Eagle,* 1932.
Pennsylvania, *Pittsburgh Courier,* 1928–1932.
Tennessee, *Nashville Globe,* 1929.
Washington, D. C., *Washington Tribune,* 1928–1929.

Chicago Journal, 1922–1928.
Chicago Record Herald, 1907.
Chicago Review, 1931–1933.
Chicago Tribune, 1876–1934.
Chicago Whip, 1919–1932.
Chicago World, 1930–1933.

New York Times, 1928–1929.
New York World, 1907, 1928.

Select Bibliography
Books and Publications

Andreas, A. T., *History of Chicago from the Earliest Period to the Present Time.* Chicago: A. T. Andreas, 1884–86.

Annals of the American Academy of Political and Social Science, 1928, "The American Negro" (Donald Young, ed.), Philadelphia, 1928.

Associated Negro Press, *Annual, 1919–20.* Chicago, Associated Negro Press, 1920.

Ayer, N. W. and Sons, *Directory of Newspapers and Periodicals, 1880–1934* (title varies). Philadelphia: Ayer and Sons.

Bancroft, Frederic A., *A Sketch of the Negro in Politics, especially in South Carolina and Mississippi.* New York: J. F. Pearson, printer, 1885.

Binder, Carroll, *Chicago and the New Negro.* Chicago: Chicago Daily News, 1927.

Bogardus, Emory S., *Immigration and Race Attitudes.* Boston and New York: D. C. Heath and Co., 1928.

Bond, Horace M., "An Investigation of the Non-intellectual Traits of a Group of Negro Normal School Students." University of Chicago (A. M. Thesis), 1926.

Bowen, L. de K., *The Colored People of Chicago: An Investigation Made for the Juvenile Protective Association.* Chicago, 1913.

Bowers, Claude G., *The Tragic Era.* Cambridge, Mass.: The Riverside Press, 1929.

Brawley, Benjamin Griffith, *Social History of the American Negro, Being a History of the Negro Problem in the United States.* New York: Macmillan Co., 1921.

Breckinridge, Sophonisba P., "Housing Conditions in Chicago, Illinois. Back of the Yards," *American Journal of Sociology,* 16, p. 433. Chicago, 1911.

Bright, John, *Hizzoner Big Bill Thompson.* New York: Jonathan Cape and Harrison Smith, 1930.

Bunche, R. J., "The Thompson-Negro Alliance," *Opportunity,* VII (March, 1929), 79.

Burgess, Ernest W. and Newcomb, Charles (editors), *Census Data of the City of Chicago: 1930.* Chicago: University of Chicago Press, 1933.

Chesnutt, Charles Waddell, *Frederick Douglass.* Boston: Small, Maynard and Co., 1899.

Chicago Commission on Race Relations, *The Negro in Chicago.* Chicago: The University of Chicago Press, 1922.

Chicago Daily News Almanac and Year Book, 1886–1934.

Chicago Vice Commission, *The Social Evil in Chicago.* Chicago: A report submitted to the Mayor and City Council of Chicago. 4th edition. Republished by Vice Commission of Chicago, Inc., for distribution by American Vigilance Association, 1912.

Counts, George Sylvester, *School and Society in Chicago.* New York: Harcourt, Brace and Co., 1928.

De Saible Association, Chicago, *Souvenir of Negro Progress, Chicago, 1779–1925.* Chicago, 1925.

Detroit Mayor's Committee on Race Relations, *Report,* 1927. Detroit: Detroit Bureau of Governmental Research, 1927.

Detweiler, Frederick German, "The Negro Press in the United States," University of Chicago (Ph.D. Thesis) 1922.

Douglass, Frederick, *Life and Times of Frederick Douglass.* Hartford, Conn.: Park Publishing Co., 1882.

Dowd, Jerome, *The Negro in American Life.* New York: Century Co., 1926.

Drewry, William Sidney, *Slave Insurrections in Virginia (1830–1865).* Washington: The Neale Co., 1900.

DuBois, William Edward Burghardt, *The Philadelphia Negro,* Publications of the University of Pennsylvania. Philadelphia, 1899.

———, *The Souls of Black Folk: Essays and Sketches.* Chicago: A. C. McClurg and Co., 1904.

Duke, Charles S., *The Housing Situation and the Colored People of Chicago.* Chicago, 1919.

Duncan, Hannibal Gerald, "The Changing Race Relationship in the Border and Northern States." University of Penn. (Ph.D. Thesis) Philadelphia, 1922.

Dutcher, Dean, "The Negro in Modern Industrial Society." Columbia University (Ph.D. Thesis). Lancaster, Pennsylvania, 1930.

Embree, Edwin R., *Brown America.* New York: Viking Press, 1931.

Farley, John William, *Statistics and Politics* (2nd ed.). Memphis, Tennessee: Saxland Publishing Co., 1920.

Feldman, Herman, *Racial Factors in American Industry.* New York and London: Harper and Brothers, 1931.

Ferguson, George Oscar, "The Psychology of the Negro; An Experimental Study." Columbia University, (Ph.D. Thesis), New York, 1916.

Fisher, Miles Mark, *The Master's Slave, Elijah John Fisher.* Philadelphia: The Judson Press, 1922.

———, "The History of the Olivet Baptist Church of Chicago." University of Chicago. (A. M. Thesis), 1922.

Frazier, E. Franklin, *The Negro Family in Chicago.* Chicago: University of Chicago Press, 1932.

Gibson, J. W. and Crogman, W. H., *The Colored American.* Atlanta: J. L. Nichols and Co., 1903.

Harris, A. L. and Spero, S., "Negro Problem," *Encyclopaedia of the Social Sciences,* XI, 335–56.

Harris, H. L., Jr., "Negro Mortality Rates in Chicago." *Social Service Review,* I, March, 1927.

Harris, Norman Dwight, *The History of Negro Servitude in Illinois and of the Slavery Agitation in that State, 1719–1864.* Chicago: A. C. McClurg and Co., 1904.

Herrick, Mary Josephine, "Negro Employees of the Chicago Board of Education." Chicago: University of Chicago (Master's Thesis), 1931.

Hershaw, L. M., "The Negro Press in America," *Charities,* XV (1905), No. 1.

Herskovits, Melville J., *The American Negro. A Study in Racial Crossing.* New York: A. A. Knopf, 1928.

Holland, F. M., *Frederick Douglass, the colored orator.* New York, 1891.

Howard, Oliver Otis, *Autobiography of Oliver Otis Howard, Major General, United States Army.* New York: Baker and Taylor Co., 1907.

Johnson, Charles S., *The Economic Status of Negroes.* Nashville: Fisk University Press, 1933.

———, *The Negro in American Civilization.* New York: Henry Holt and Co., 1930.

Johnson, Claudius O., Carter H. Harrison, *I, Chicago.* University of Chicago Press, 1928.

Johnson, James Weldon, *Black Manhattan.* New York: A. A. Knopf, 1930.

Jones, John G., *The Black Laws of Illinois and a Few Reasons Why They Should be Repealed.* Chicago: Tribune Book and Job Office, 1864.

Kingsbury, J. B., "The Merit System in Chicago from 1915 to 1923," *Public Personnel Studies* (November, 1926).

Langston, John Mercer, *From the Virginia Plantation to the National Capitol.* Hartford, Conn.: American Publishing Co., 1894.

Legislative Voters League of Illinois, *Assembly Bulletin,* 1917–1934.

Lewinson, Paul, *Race, Class and Party.* London: Oxford University Press, 1932.

Lewis, Lloyd and Smith, Henry Justin, *Chicago: The History of Its Reputation.* New York: Harcourt, Brace and Co., 1929.

Locke, Alain Leroy, *The New Negro. An Interpretation.* New York: A. and C. Boni, 1925.

Loggins, Vernon, *The Negro Author.* New York: Columbia University Press, 1931.

Lynch, John Roy, *The Facts of Reconstruction.* New York: The Neale Publishing Co., 1913.

Mark, May Louise, *Negroes in Columbus.* Columbus: Ohio State University Press, 1928.

Mason, M. C., "Policy of the Segregation of the Negro in the Public Schools of Ohio, Indiana, and Illinois." Chicago: University of Chicago M. A. Dissertation, 1917.

Mays, Benjamin Elijah and Nicholson, Joseph William, *The Negro's Church.* New York: Institute of Social and Religious Research, 1933.

McLemore, Frances Williams, "The Role of the Negroes in Chicago in the

Senatorial Election 1930." Chicago: University of Chicago M. A. dissertation, 1931.

Mecklin, John Moffatt, *Democracy and Race Friction; a Study in Social Ethics.* New York: Macmillan Co., 1914.

Merriam, Charles E., *Chicago: A More Intimate View of Urban Politics.* New York: The Macmillan Company, 1929.

Merriam, Charles E. and Gosnell, Harold F., *Non-Voting: Causes and Methods of Control.* Chicago: University of Chicago Press, 1924.

Miller, Herbert Adolphus, *Races, Nations and Classes.* Philadelphia: J. B. Lippincott Co., 1924.

Morton, Richard Lee, *The Negro in Virginia Politics, 1865–1902.* University of Virginia, Charlottesville, Virginia, 1919.

Morton, Robert Russa, *What the Negro Thinks.* New York: Doran, Doubleday, Page and Co., 1928.

Municipal Voters' League of Chicago, *Reports,* 1915–1933.

Negro Yearbook and *Annual Encyclopaedia of the Negro.* Nashville, Tenn., Sunday School Union Print., 1912.

Nowlin, William F., *The Negro in American National Politics.* Boston: The Stratford Company, 1931.

Olbrich, Emil, *The Development of Sentiment on Negro Suffrage to 1860.* University of Wisconsin, Madison, Wisconsin, 1912.

Park, Robert E., "Mentality of Racial Hybrids," *American Journal of Sociology, XXXVI* (January, 1931), 534–51.

Park, Robert E., "Negro Race Consciousness as Reflected in Race Literature," *American Review,* I (1923), 505–517.

Park, Robert Exra, "Methods of a Race Survey," *Journal of Applied Sociology.* X, (May, 1925), 410.

Park, Robert E., "Racial Assimilation in Secondary Groups," *Publications of the American Sociological Society,* VIII, 1913, 75–82.

Pendleton, Mrs. Leila (Amos), *A Narrative of the Negro,* Washington, D.C.: Press of R. L. Pendleton, 1912.

Penn, Irvine Garland, *The Afro-American Press and Its Editors.* Springfield, Mass.: Wiley and Co., 1891.

Pennsylvania Department of Public Welfare, *Negro Survey of Pennsylvania.* Harrisburg, 1928.

Pidgeon, Mary Elizabeth, *Negro Women in Industry in 15 States.* Washington: Government Printing Office, 1929.

Quaife, Milo Milton, *Checagou.* Chicago: University of Chicago Press, 1933.

Reckless, Walter, *Vice in Chicago.* Chicago: University of Chicago Press, 1933.

Reuter, Edward Byron, *The American Race Problem: a Study of the Negro.* New York: T. Y. Crowell Co., 1927.

Reuter, Edward Byron, *The Mulatto in the United States.* Boston: R. G. Badger, 1918.

Rhea's New Citizen's Directory of Chicago, Illinois and Suburban Towns. Chicago: Press of W. S. McClelland, 1908.

Robinson, George F., "The Negro in Politics in Chicago." *Journal of Negro History,* XVII (April 1923), 180–229.

Rood, Alice Quan, "Social Conditions among the Negroes on Federal Street between 45th Street and 53rd Street." University of Chicago (A. M. Thesis), 1924.

Sandburg, Carl, *The Chicago Race Riots, July 1919.* New York: Harcourt, Brace and Howe, 1919.

Scott, Emmett Jay, *Negro Migration During the War.* New York: Oxford University Press, 1920.

Simkins, F. B., and Woody, R. H., *South Carolina During Reconstruction.* Chapel Hill: University of North Carolina Press, 1932.

Spero, Sterling D. and Harris, Abram L., *The Black Worker.* New York: Columbia University Press, 1931.

Sutherland, Robert Lee, "An Analysis of Negro Churches in Chicago." University of Chicago (Ph.D. Thesis), 1930.

Taylor, Alrutheus Ambush, *The Negro in the Reconstruction of Virginia.* Washington: Association for the Study of Negro Life and History, 1926.

————, *The Negro in South Carolina During the Reconstruction.* Washington: Association for the Study of Negro Life and History, 1924.

Thomas, William Hannibal, *The American Negro.* New York and London: Macmillan Co., 1901.

Wallace, Jesse Thomas, "How and Why Mississippi Eliminated the Negro from State Politics in 1890." University of Chicago (A. M. Thesis), 1923.

Wallace, John, *Carpetbag Rule in Florida.* Jacksonville, Fla.: Da Costa Printing and Publishing House, 1888.

Washington, Booker Taliaferro, *Frederick Douglass.* Philadelphia and London: G. W. Jacobs and Co., 1907.

————, *My Larger Education; Being Chapters from my Experience.* Garden City, New York: Doubleday, Page and Co., 1911.

————, *The Story of the Negro, the Rise of the Race from Slavery.* New York: Doubleday, Page and Co. 1909.

Washington, Intercollegiate Club of Chicago, *The Negro in Chicago 1779–1927.* Chicago: Washington Intercollegiate Club, Vol. I, 1927; Vol. II, 1929.

Wells-Barnett, Ida, *How Enfranchisement Stops Lynching.* New York: Original Rights Magazine, Charles Lenz, 1910.

————, *Southern Horrors: Lynch Law in All Its Phases.* New York: New York Age Print, 1892.

White, L. D., *Prestige Value of Public Employment.* Chicago: University of Chicago Press, 1929.

Who's Who in Colored America. New York: Who's Who in Colored America Corporation, 1927.

Wilson, Edward E., "The Responsibility for Crime," *Opportunity*, VII (March, 1929), pp. 95–97.
Winston, Sanford, "Studies in Negro Leadership; Age and Occupational Distribution of 1,608 Negro Leaders," *American Journal of Sociology*, 37, p. 595. Chicago, 1931.
Wood, Junius B., *The Negro in Chicago*. Chicago: Chicago Daily News, 1916.
Wooddy, Carroll H., *The Case of Frank L. Smith*. Chicago: University of Chicago Press, 1930.
Woodson, Carter Godwin, *A Century of Negro Migration*. Washington: Association for the Study of Negro Life and History, 1918.
———, *Free Negro Heads of Families in the United States in 1830*. Washington: The Association for the Study of Negro Life and History, 1925.
———, *History of the Negro Church*. Washington: Associated Publishers, 1921.
Woodson, Carter Godwin, *Negro Orators and their Orations*. Washington: Associated Publishers, 1925.
———, *The Negro as a Business Man*. Washington: The Association for the Study of Negro Life and History, 1929.
———, *The Negro in Our History*. Washington: The Association Publishers, 1922.
Woofter, Thomas Jackson (editor), *Negro Problems in Cities*. Garden City: Doubleday, Doran and Co., 1928.
Work, Monroe Nathan, *A Bibliography of the Negro in Africa and America*, New York: The H. W. Wilson, Co., 1928.
———, "Negro Real Estate Holders of Chicago." University of Chicago (A. M. Thesis), 1903.
———, *Negro Year Book*, Eighth Edition, 1931–32. Tuskegee: Negro Year Book Publishing Co., 1932.
Wright, Richard Robert, "The Industrial Condition of Negroes in Chicago." University of Chicago (D. B. Thesis), 1901.
Young, Donald R., *American Minority Peoples*. New York and London: Harper and Bros., 1932.

1. *A Souvenir of Negro Progress*, issued by the De Saible Association, Inc., Chicago, 1925.
2. Bousfield, M. O., "Reaching the Negro Community," *The American Journal of Public Health*. (1934) Vol. 24, No.
3. Chicago Board of Health, Annual Report.
4. Chicago Citizens' Association, Annual Report.
5. DuBois, W. E. B., *The Black Princess, a novel*. (1928) New York: Harcourt, and Brace & Co.
6. Eleazer, Robert B., *America's Tenth Man*. (1935) Atlanta: Commission on Education and Race Relations, p. 10.

7. *Five-Year Report of the Michigan Boulevard Garden Apartments Building Corporation.* (1935) Chicago. Feb.
8. Gosnell, Harold F., *The Negro Politician in Chicago.* (1935) Chicago: The University of Chicago Press.
9. Graham, Irene J., "Family Support and Dependency among Chicago Negroes, a study of unpublished census data," (1929) *The Social Service Review,* Vol. III, No. 4, Dec.
10. Kingsley, Rev. Harold M., *The Negro in Chicago, a Spiritual Interpretation of an Economic Problem,* (1935) Chicago: published by the Chicago Congregational Missionary and Extension Society.
11. Houser, Susie A., "A Community-Serving Church," *The Southern Workman.* (1925) Vol. LIV, No. 2, Feb.
12. Matloch-Simon, Elizabeth and Simon, Hubert, *Chicago's First Citizen— Jean Baptiste De Saible.* (1933)
13. Olcott, Jane, *The Work of Colored Women,* (1919) New York: The Colored Committee War Work Council. 115 p.
14. Sweeney, W. Allison, *History of the Negro in the World War.* (1919) Chicago: Privately printed.
15. *The Negro in Chicago, 1770–1929.* Chicago: published by the Washington Intercollegiate Club. (1929)
16. *The Negro at Work During the World War and during Reconstruction,* (1921) Washington: Washington Printing Office, U.S. Dept. of Labor.
17. *Negroes in Chicago,* Annual Report of the Chicago League on Urban Conditions among Negroes. (1918–1920) Chicago: The Chicago Urban League.
18. Harris Jr., H. L., M.D., "The Health of the Negro Family in Chicago." *Opportunity,* Sept. 1927.
19. *Inter-racial Situation in Chicago,* by the Chicago and Survey Division, Industrial Relations Dept. of the Inter-church World Movement. (1920) Bull. No. 1–2.
20. Harris Jr., H. L., M.D., "Negro Mortality rates in Chicago." *The Social Service Review,* Vol. 1 No. 1 Memorial Fund, Chicago, p. 22. III. maps.
21. *Preliminary Study of Inter-racial Conditions in Chicago.* (1920) Made under the Survey Division, Industrial Relations Dept. of the Inter-church World Movement of North America, Home Missions Council. New York, p. 15.
22. *Chicago Race Riots,* by Carl Sandburg, with an introduction by Walter Lippmann. (1919) New York: Harcourt, Brace and Howe. p. 71.
23. "The Problem of the Negro" by A. P. Comstock. The American Journal of Sociology, Vol. XVIII, No. 2 p. 16.

A P P E N D I X   C

Notes relative to a 1944 project, never completed, for a Negro anthology

Books to be read for anthology, for first chapter entitled "The Abortive Will to Power"

  1. Classic volume on Reformation
  2. DuBois' description of the slave trade
  3. Taussig's book on *Rum, Romance and Rebellion*
  4. *The Condition of Man* by Mumford
  5. Geise's book on Western civilization
  6. Gibbons' *Fall and Decline of the Roman Empire* [sic]
  7. Spengler's *Decline of Western Man*
  8. Nietzsche's *Will to Power*
  9. Freud's *Totem and Taboo*
 10. Eric Williams' book on Capitalism and the Slave Trade
 11. Reik's book on sex economy
 12. Pushkin and Dumas
 13. Max Weber, *Capitalism and the Protestant Ethic*
 14. Marx, *Das Kapital*

In Wright's unpublished notes, p. 3

List of books, probably made in 1946, which Wright took with him on his first French trip or books he recommended to someone in Paris

   I. Nelson Algren *Never Come Morning*
  II. The complete poems of Kenneth Fearing
 III. *Wasteland,* Jo Sinclair
  IV. Anais Nin
   V. *Dark Legend* [by F. Wertham]
  VI. Work on women in America (Ed Aswell)
 VII. Psychiatric documents
VIII. Wright in English

IX. *American Dilemma* [by G. Myrdal]
X. Sylvia Beach, *Memoirs*
XI. French lit. expression of women
XII. Chicago school of sociology

List made by Wright in 1947 of books he wanted to take with him when he moved to France

Books to take:

Dictionary (large one)
Two copies of my own books, each
As If
Kierkegaard's volumes
Nouvelle Pitit Larousse [sic]
Scrap books
Shakespeare
Take complete *Twice a Year*
Take some of Mencken
Science and Sanity
Reik's three volumes on sex
Poems of Eliot, Crane, Auden and
    Fearing
Stein's works
Hemingway's short stories
Greek Drama
Capital
Man in Western World
The Prince
Lay My Burden Down, folklore
    from Library of [Congress], Wash-
    ington
Get a Bible from Bill Targ
Reality and Illusion, Cauldwell
Finnegan's Wake, Joyce
Marginal Man, Stonequist
Linguaphone records
Philosophy of Literary Form
Lessing

List established in 1946 or 1947

List of books

Wright left a list of some sixty titles and authors, indicating in some cases that he had "two copies"; this list is probably one of several he drew up before leaving for Paris in 1947, when he disposed of part of his library he did not want to take to France. The books which do not appear in his library in 1965 are:

Aling. Reveille for Radicals
Austen. Pride and Prejudice
Anand. Coolie
Barnhill. West African Rhymes
Belfrage. A Faith to Free the People
Bowen-Rusby. Economics Simplified
Burgess. Who Walk Alone
Carse. There Go the Ships
Cohen. All God's Children
Davidson. Steeper Cliff
Dehan. Just Steward
Dostoievesky. Brothers Karamazov
John Faulkner. Men Working
Forbes. From Red Sea to Blue Nile
Ginsburg. E Stato cosi (Italian)
Ginsburg. La strada chc va citta
  (Italian)
Halsalle-Jones. German Woman and
  Her Master
Hecht. Guide for the Bedeviled
Hichens. The Parradine Case (2 vol-
  umes)
History of the Communist Party of
  the Soviet Union
Logan. Negro's Faith in America
Maeterlinck. L'autre monde ou Le
  cadran stellaire (French)
Maugham. Posledni Pulsilink (Czech
  language)
Maxwell. Folded Leaf
Mezzrow. Really the Blues
Milne. Red House Mystery
Olsen. Alarm of the Black Cat
Eliot Paul. Last Time I Saw Paris
Plato. Socratic Discourses
Plato. Trial and Death of Socrates
Ripley. Believe It or Not
Schwartz. How to Write Confes-
  sional Stories
Trent. Das in Dead
Swift. North Star Shining

APPENDIX D

Notes taken after reading *How to Write a Play* by Lajos Egri

1. Formulate a basic *premise.*
2. Select a *pivotal character* who will go all the way to achieve an end, avenge an injury, real or fancied, and
3. Line up and *orchestrate* the characters so that
4. The *unity of opposites* will be iron-clad.
5. Begin the play at the *point of attack,* the turning point in the lives of the characters, and arrange that
6. Every *point of attack* will begin with *conflict,* which is always *slowly rising,* and the basis of *conflict* is
7. *Exposition, perpetual exposition,* which provides *transition* from *conflict to conflict,* each ending on a higher plane, each a minor play in itself, all heading toward proving *premise.*
8. *Slowly rising conflict,* the product of *exposition* and *transition,* creates *growth* of characters that go
9. From one *emotional pole to another*—from love to hate, etc.—which creates *crisis,* the point for *decision* to lift play to still higher plane, resulting in
10. *Climax* that follows *crisis,* and *climax* is *proof* of *premise. Proof of premise is obligatory scene.*
11. The aftermath of *climax* is *conclusion.*
12. *Dialogue* is the *articulation* of *exposition.*

Index